The Astrologer,

the Counsellor and the Priest

CPA Seminar Series

The Astrologer,
the Counsellor and the Priest

Two Seminars on
Astrological Counselling

Juliet Sharman-Burke

and

Liz Greene

Centre for Psychological Astrology Press
London

First published 1997 by the CPA Press, BCM Box 1815, London WC1N 3XX, UK, www.cpalondon.com

First paperback edition 2005.

THE ASTROLOGER, THE COUNSELLOR AND THE PRIEST

ISBN 1 900869 30 6

British Library Cataloguing-in-Publication Data. A catalogue record for this book is available from the British Library.

Printed in Great Britain by Antony Rowe Ltd, Chippenham, Wiltshire, SN14 6LH.

Table of Contents

Part One: Astrological Counselling
by Juliet Sharman-Burke

Part Two: The Astrologer, the Counsellor and the Priest
by Liz Greene

Part One: Astrological Counselling

by Juliet Sharman-Burke

This seminar was given on 11 February 1996 at Regents College, London as part of the Winter Term of the seminar programme of the Centre for Psychological Astrology.

Introduction

In today's seminar we will concentrate on the practical and emotional issues involved in setting up an astrological practice. We will look at how to work, the boundaries involved, the place of work, fees, times, and other earthly matters. We will also look at the communication between the astrologer and the client, both conscious and unconscious. That isn't quite so earthly, but it is practical because it can make the difference between a really helpful and insightful reading and an unhelpful, amateurish, or even destructive consultation. It is naturally right and proper that each of you will want to develop your own personal way of interpreting a chart – how each astrologer looks at the planets, aspects and houses is always something very personal. After all, astrology is an art, and the expression and understanding of art is unique to each individual. However, there are some basic guidelines which are important, as they provide the firm framework in which your work can flourish.

In the same way that an artist needs the right kind of light in his or her studio to work really effectively, or a cook needs a certain standard of kitchen and equipment with which to function efficiently, so the astrologer needs an appropriate space and framework in which to work. This may be partly practical with respect to a physical work room, but it is also symbolic in terms of the framework that time provides. These parameters are important. As our focus at the CPA is psychological astrology, we need to consider carefully the impact on the psyche of both the astrologer and the client that a psychological reading may have. The impact is often unconscious, which is all the more reason for the astrologer to be aware of and to look out for things which are not verbalised directly but may be communicated indirectly.

Our first topic will cover the practicalities of setting up an astrological practice. Then we will do a basic communication exercise which might reveal some of the difficulties involved as we attempt to convey our ideas to others. It might also reveal how difficult it can be to listen. We will then look at some of the many different ways of communicating information to a client during an astrological consultation. We will also explore some of the potential difficulties that might emerge in communication, which will include the transference (the feelings the client brings to you) and the counter-transference (your response and feelings about what the client is bringing).

One of the objects of today's seminar is to learn some helpful communication techniques which can be used when practising psychological astrology. After all, there is not much point in knowing all the technicalities of a chart if you can't communicate them to your client in a way that is helpful and therapeutic! So we will start right away with the practicalities.

Boundaries

Clear, firm boundaries are essential for the astrologer. It is very important to get these well in place for yourself and understand how necessary they are, because if you feel clear and confident, then the client will, in turn, feel safe. As the astrologer, the one who is managing the session, it is your job to provide a safe place in which the work can be done. Just as in alchemy the alembic provides a strong and solid container within which transformation can occur, so when reading an astrological chart the setting and the boundaries of time provide a safe container for the work. Poor boundaries are like a leaky alembic, and it becomes very hard to keep the work focused and contained.

These days, it would seem that, at last, astrologers are being taken increasingly seriously – our image is becoming less cranky and folksy, and more professional. We are gradually getting a more respectable public image,. So it is important that we help to promote ourselves as intelligent, responsible professionals rather than a bunch of weirdoes – which is, unfortunately, the way we have often been, and to some extent still are, seen! Astrology deserves to be acknowledged and used by more than just a "New Age" subculture. If we take ourselves seriously as professionals and behave accordingly, we have a much better chance of being taken seriously.

One of the ways we can improve our public image is by behaving like professionals. True professionals ideally should not let their boundaries become blurred. What I have noticed with a great many astrologers is a tendency to lose a firm sense of boundaries and act rather unprofessionally. For example, we may ask those who aren't clients for personal birth data, and then proceed to dazzle the people in question with astrological information about themselves which was actually unsolicited! You know the sort of thing I mean – "When is your birthday?" The innocent person then reveals his or her date and hears, "Oh dear, you must really be going through it just now, with Saturn crossing your Sun and Mars squaring it." In this scenario the imaginary person has not asked for any information, and has no idea at all what kind of information they have revealed by giving their birth date. Understandably they may feel invaded or manipulated, and quite possibly frightened as well.

True professionals tend to wait to be consulted before offering advice. How would you like it if you went to a party, and a doctor whom you had never met before approached you and said, "Do you ever have night sweats?" And when you innocently answer, "Why, yes, sometimes," he then says, "Ah, you are about the right age, clearly you are approaching the menopause. That must be quite upsetting, especially to your sex life!" How would you feel?

The general public are, in the main, unaware of the extent to which they can lay themselves open by giving their data to a psychologically oriented astrologer. They do not realise the extent to which their inner world is mapped out, and therefore people's horoscopes should be treated with great respect. This also applies among astrologers. Just because someone is himself or herself a student or practitioner of astrology, that doesn't mean that their boundaries should be disregarded by other astrologers. In the same way that an analyst or therapist should ask a patient's permission before discussing the person's material in a seminar or in published work, so should astrologers afford their clients the same respect. A chart, when it is being looked at from a psychological point of view, reveals very personal information and gives the astrologer quite an advantage over the client, which should always be used in the client's interest rather than as an unfair advantage.

The room

We can develop a sense of professionalism in the way we create our work space. Of course, not everybody is necessarily going to have access to a separate "consulting room", which would be ideal. Nevertheless, it is important to create a space that feels pleasant, private, and workmanlike. I will never forget someone telling me that, when he had gone to consult an astrologer, he had been taken into a bedroom! Even though he and the astrologer sat on chairs, not on the bed, it was still clearly a bedroom and he experienced it as somewhat off-putting and certainly not very professional.

Audience: Was that because of the possible sexual implication?

Juliet: Yes, I think so, at least partly. Although in the example I am referring to, nothing improper happened – as far as I know – there was still a rather-too-intimate feeling about the room. After all, a bedroom is a very personal, private place and space, and it does feel emotionally intimate as well as lending itself to fantasies of seduction. If you are a woman and you invite a male client into your bedroom, he might start wondering if he might be getting more than an astrological reading! It could offer a possible double meaning, couldn't it?
Maybe we should think more about what we communicate with the various kinds of objects, decoration, and colours in the different

rooms of our homes. The client sees the room before the reading is given, so a communication has already been made non-verbally from the astrologer to the client. A lounge or living room has a slightly impersonal or "staged" quality, because this is where we invite other people into our space. We tell other people about ourselves by choosing a certain curtain pattern or style of sofa or painting on the wall. If you upholster your sofa in a flowery Laura Ashley print and cover the walls with botanical prints, you are telling people something about yourself that you want them to know.

It's a bit like what the MC represents in the chart – it's the face we choose to show to others. But a bedroom reflects our most personal tastes. The only people we invite into our bedrooms are people we know well – our families, our lovers, or maybe a close friend. We aren't trying to show people an image – in our bedrooms we are most relaxed and most ourselves. The bedroom is where we put our fluffy soft toys and pictures of lovers and special souvenirs and the nightdress or pajamas we sleep in. It can overwhelm a client, because it is so personal.

A client also needs to feel that privacy is guaranteed when consulting an astrologer, so conducting a reading in a place where other people may walk in, or where it feels as if someone else in the vicinity can hear what is being said, is obviously distracting. The client should feel "held", both in the physical space provided by the astrologer and by the fact that the astrologer is acting professionally and correctly.

Ideally, the consulting room should be private, clean, and comfortable – in other words, the kind of place that would put a person at ease. If possible, have two chairs which are fairly equal. After all, if the client is perched precariously on the uncomfortable hard-backed upright chair while the astrologer is lounging luxuriously in the easy chair, it will undoubtedly arouse unpleasant feelings of envy. Yet if the astrologer is looking ill at ease on the uncomfortable chair, the client may feel guilty!

A nicely furnished room may put a client at ease, yet if there are lots of very personal things around it can be distracting. For example, if your room is filled to the brim with hundreds of Christmas cards and photos of friends, family, and children, it might give the impression that your life is incredibly fulfilled and busy, which may evoke envy or feelings of inadequacy in the client. If a client is consulting an astrologer because they are lonely and can't make relationships, and they then walk into your room only to be confronted with a pinboard full of children's drawings and cards from friends, it may make them feel that you would not understand them, as you obviously have so many people in your life. This may not necessarily be true in reality, but it may be perceived as such by the client, and that can already set up an edge without anything even being said. If possible, the space should be pleasant and "easy-on-the-eye" without being too intrusive. If the astrologer's life and family dominate the room in terms of photos or other personal paraphernalia, the client may feel overwhelmed or unimportant.

Let me give you an example. I had a phone message which my daughter took, asking me to ring a prospective client. When I returned the woman's call I announced myself, and she said very conversationally, "Oh, thank you for you calling me back. Was that your daughter I spoke to on the phone?" I said, "Yes," without even thinking, and she said, "Well, in that case there is no point in our continuing this conversation. I can't possibly see anyone who has children, because I am on an IVF programme and it is far too upsetting for me. I know I would feel too envious." That was unusually honest of the client and she was very clear about what she was prepared to tolerate. But not all clients are quite so in touch with their feelings or able to articulate them so freely, and they may suffer in silence.

I'll give you another example. Once, when I was seeing a client out at the end of a session, the postman happened to have just visited, and there were a lot of letters on the mat. The client said, "Look how many people write to you. No one ever writes to me." The fact that most of the letters were bills did not occur to her. She imagined that they were all from adoring friends and family members. She had Venus square Saturn in her birth chart and had a tendency to feel unloved, and my mat full of letters seemed to confirm how unwanted and neglected she believed she was by other people.

Naturally, if you get it right for some clients you will get it wrong for others, and, after all, you have to feel comfortable in your own space. It is no good turning your home into a hospital waiting room so as not to offend a sensitive and lonely client. A certain amount of personal memorabilia can also reassure some clients that you are a member of the human race, and not some kind of space creature who can foresee the future. And of course it is not possible to avoid all outside intrusions, like a child answering the telephone or a postman delivering mail. Nor should we seek to try. The opposite problem may happen – a client coming into a consulting-room which is totally silent, visually cold, and completely devoid of personal objects may wonder why the astrologer has no family or friends. But we can avoid extremes and minimise things which are obvious and controllable.

Audience: I have a funny story I would like to tell. I used to have a small parrot, a cockatiel – you know the sort, grey with a yellow head – and I kept his cage in the room in which I saw clients. I used to let this bird out to sit on my shoulder when I gave chart readings. He was always very good and sat very quietly, although once he climbed down off my shoulder and left a little gift on the chart I was doing, sort of like an additional planet! But anyway, one day a client came in, a man, and when he saw the bird he reacted very violently, and shrank into a corner and began shouting, "Get it out of here! Get it out of here!" It turned out he had a phobia about birds. I then found out he was a child psychologist. Although I thought it was very funny – this client looked after the psyches of children but he couldn't deal with his own! – I realised that the parrot was something I really didn't have the right to impose on clients.

Juliet: Well, I believe that is true – pets can be very distracting and not every client will feel comfortable with your cat or dog or parrot or guinea pig. But maybe something important came out of that reading – your client couldn't very well deny that he needed to look at some of his own issues!

Privacy

Another thing that can be very distracting is the telephone. The obvious solution to this is an answering machine, as there is nothing worse for a client than being in a session in which you keep interrupting your own or their flow to answer the phone. And of course it is also useful to have an answering machine to take messages from clients wanting to book appointments.

Audience: I remember going to an astrologer who had the telephone in the same room, so we could hear it ringing loudly during the consultation. There was an answering machine, and it was on, so the astrologer did not pick it up, but I could faintly hear messages being left, and it was quite unnerving. It really cut across the space. I do remember feeling very uncomfortable, as if something very private was being constantly invaded.

Juliet: That's interesting: you didn't like it. I think that is one of the best check-points that you can use for your own style of astrological practice. It is always a good exercise to put yourself into your client's shoes. If you were going to see an astrologer, what would make you feel confident and comfortable? What would make you feel that this person knew what they were doing and that they were professional? If you would feel comfortable in that space, then the chances are that it will feel all right for your client too.

Time

The length of a session is a really crucial boundary, and it is something which should be decided by the practitioner in advance of a session. From my own experience I feel that one and a half hours is about the right amount of time. After that, a person's capacity to listen and take information in begins to diminish, and the alertness of the astrologer may also decrease. Each person must, of course, find his or her own comfortable level. However, having found the right amount of time for yourself, it is important to stick to it. It is best to be clear about time from the very beginning, so that when a person first asks for an appointment you are able to state, "My sessions are X hours long," which then gives the client a time-frame to work from so that they know where they are from the outset. It is often helpful to restate it at the beginning of the session, so that when your client comes in you can say, "We have got an hour and a half together today," or "We have got two hours," or however long you feel is appropriate. This maps out the boundaries for your work together.

Some clients really need more than an hour and a half. What can work well in that case is to set up two appointments, the first appointment for an hour and a half and the second appointment for an hour. This gives enough time to work through the chart quite thoroughly. You can also adjust your fee accordingly, stating that the first session costs X, because it includes all the work of preparing the chart beforehand, while the second session, which is to continue what has been started in the first, costs Y. If you offer that as your package, the client can take it or leave it. Of course, many people offer just one session and then decide at the time whether they are going to offer another one, which is another way, equally valid of doing it. But between an hour and a half and an hour and three quarters is as much time as either you or the client can usefully work.

Audience: What happens when the client doesn't seem satisfied and wants to go on longer?

Juliet: Some clients are very "hungry" and just keep on asking for more, even when they are actually not able to listen or take any more in. Often it is because they are enjoying the attention and don't want it to stop. After all, many people never get to enjoy the luxury of a couple of hours where everything that is said is focused just on them! And there might be much deeper things going on, too, related to feeling unfed by mother and wanting the astrologer to supply what was missing. That is what we mean by transference, which we will talk about more later. It is important to remember that just because the client *wants* more, it does not necessarily mean they *need* more. There is a difference!

Audience: I had an experience of going on for three hours with one client because she seemed to need so much. Afterwards I was completely exhausted, and she still went away unhappy. It did not seem to matter how much I gave in the way of time – it still wasn't enough.

Juliet: That's right – lots of something doesn't necessarily mean it is good! It seems to me that what your client really wanted was something very different from astrological information, and probably no amount of time given to a chart reading could ever have provided it. I do think that three hours is too much. Both of you get exhausted, and nothing is accomplished. As I said before, an hour and a half is about the right length of time. If you state the length of the session clearly at the time you make the appointment, your client knows in advance what to expect in terms of duration, and how much time they will get for their money. If you offer the possibility of a two-session appointment, then neither you nor your client need to feel anxious about whether you are going to have enough time.

The important thing is that, having set a time, you stick to it. Of course it can be hard. You may have a difficult client, perhaps one who says that what you are giving them isn't good enough, which often results in the tendency to give more time to try to make up for their dissatisfaction. The astrologer then feels he or she has failed. That is what we call counter-transference. But the truth is that if they are that dissatisfied, another ten minutes isn't going to make it any better, because the dissatisfaction is coming from an unconscious source that has nothing to do with what you are telling them.

Audience: I had a client who spent most of the session arguing with me about the validity of astrology, and by the time we actually got around to looking at the chart properly it was almost time to stop! I felt in that instance that I needed to give my client more time.

Juliet: Well, I am not so sure. I feel strongly that boundaries are boundaries, and if your client knows clearly that he or she has got an hour and a half and chooses to spend that hour and a half arguing the toss about the validity of astrology, that is up to them! Of course, it may be that you as the astrologer need to state, at some point, that if they continue to argue about theoretical issues there will be no time to look at their individual chart. Then you are making sure they are aware of the choice they are making.

It is certainly not uncommon for clients to want to delay the ending of a session. Quite often a person will burst into tears in the last ten minutes of the session. Or they start coming up with something really startling or very dramatic, like recovering a lost memory or a story of abuse or rape, which attracts your attention just as you are about to send them out of the door. Or they may suddenly start asking you personal questions in a friendly and conversational way, making you feel as if it would be rude to stop. Some clients do this because unconsciously they need to feel in control, especially if what the astrologer says has really got under their skin and they feel somehow they have lost control. So they try to show that they can control the session, themselves, and the astrologer, by deciding themselves how long the session will last – even if it means apparently going out of control in order to achieve it!

Audience: That happened to me, actually. Just before the end of a session, the client started to blurt out a horrible story of a rape incident which she had never told anyone about before. I didn't dare say, "Time is over."

Juliet: That's where having good, clear boundaries becomes so important. In such instances it might be more helpful and containing to say something like, "That sounds awful/very painful/very distressing, and it sounds like it might help to talk about it some more. We are running out of time and can't possibly do this justice now. Can we make another appointment?" You can offer them an appointment time then and there, to come back and discuss it more deeply. I think that is ultimately more satisfactory than allowing yourself to be seduced into giving extra time because there is a "crisis".

Audience: So it's not okay to say, "Time is up, but it sounds very interesting, let's go on."

Juliet: I don't think so. What can be important for the astrologer to recognise is that there may be something in the client that is, albeit quite unconsciously, trying to stop the separation. The client is getting attention and concern which feels good, and he or she wants it to go on. If this is the case, it really means that the client is not going to be able to take in anything you are saying anyway. So it might actually be more helpful if you say something along the lines of, "I think what you have to say is really important, and we would probably do it more justice by talking about it in the next session." If they then say, "I don't want to do that, I can't come back," then it can't be that important.

Audience: Sometimes it could be genuine, though. There may be very special circumstances when someone gets really upset or hysterical, and you can't just stop the session and throw them out.

Juliet: I am not suggesting that the distress is not genuine. I am saying that boundaries are important, and although they may feel punitive at the time, they do actually have the effect of making a client feel safe. To maintain boundaries you do need to keep a beady eye on the time, and it is useful to have a clock in the room so that you and your client can both see the time and you can both be aware of it. If somebody looks as though they are beginning to get upset and you see that time is running out, you can glance at the clock and say, "We have got ten more minutes left," and if the client starts falling apart, that's the time to say, "I don't think we have enough time to get into this now, but let's arrange another appointment." The last ten minutes can then be used to ground the client and organise another meeting.

Audience: What do you do, though, if a person is very emotional, crying and sobbing and so on, and it is time to stop? You can't throw someone out if they are really in a state, can you?

Juliet: Of course you have to use your instincts and act sensitively, but you do have to end the session. You can say something like, "We do have to stop now, but clearly you are very upset, so I will get you a glass of water while you have a few minutes to get yourself together." This way you can leave the room to get the water, which breaks the intensity of the session, and it gives your client a little time and space alone to compose himself or herself. If you have someone else coming straight afterwards, you could offer the distressed client an opportunity to sit somewhere else for a little while, or you could offer them the option of sitting in the room until they feel calm.

Audience: In therapy, time is very important, and clients expect a strict time structure. In astrology, when you don't have that setup, isn't it more loosely based and easy-going?

Juliet: We are still professionals and should respect time as do other professionals. Also, our line of work is psychological astrology, which is more likely to work on people's deeper feelings. Therefore, as in therapy, the boundaries are very important. When doing psychologically oriented astrology it is likely that the work will have an emotive effect on the client, and this needs to be contained in a safe structure within a boundary of time and place. Knowing your limits about time, and treating your time professionally, are ways of keeping the relationship clear and safe.

Audience: I have had my horoscope done by many different astrologers. I like to compare different styles and approaches, and I must say that I agree with what you are saying. One astrologer was rather lax about time. I wasn't told how long the session would be, and it lasted well over two hours, but I do know I kept wondering how long I would have, and it did make me slightly nervous. Another astrologer gave me a clear message about how long the session would be and stuck to the time, and I felt much more comfortable. Because I knew in advance how long I had, I thought carefully about what things I really wanted to discuss, and that meant that we didn't just meander on talking about things that weren't really important.

Audience: I always buy a 90-minute tape, so that when the tape stops, so does the session.

Juliet: Well, that is one way of handling the time! It does rather put the onus on the tape machine to contain the session, though, and what if the battery runs out without your noticing? I do think it is wise if you keep an eye on the time yourself, and be aware of how the session is going. If you feel that your client is getting upset, you can warn them, "We are going to have to stop soon." That way you can use the last part of the session to round things up – a bit like calling time in pubs, when the barman gives you a chance to buy one more drink or warns you it is time to finish up the one you are on! Some clients need a little time to "earth" themselves before ending, and as always these are things you cannot predict but have to act on by intuition at the time.

We might also think about why it is so hard for some of us to make firm boundaries with regard to time. Some of you seem to be describing situations where you have felt very guilty about ending the session, because someone was upset and crying. Think about this. Is it that you don't want the client to think you are hard and unfeeling? If this is the case, then you are more concerned with how the client sees you than with what might be good for the client. Are you afraid the client will go off and kill themselves if you end the session when they are in a state? That is taking a lot of responsibility for someone else's choices. Or maybe you find it hard to cope with someone's upset, and feel you have to make them "better". That might say something about whether you are able to handle strong emotions in other people, which is something we will be talking about later today.

Audience: I have noticed that children are pretty good at trying to squeeze out a little more time. My son always waits until I am just about to turn out the lights at bedtime, before telling me some tale of tragedy or woe which captures my interest and prolongs bedtime for another half hour!

Juliet: That is a good example, and in the case of both children and clients, they will often try to push the boundaries to see how far they can go. And curiously enough, although they may indicate that they want you to keep giving them more, the reality is that, once they know you are in charge, they feel safer. The feeling of power they have if they can talk you into giving them something extra may feel heady, but it can also evoke a feeling of being unsafe. In the case of an astrological client, they have got their hour and a half and you should give them your all during that time and do everything you possibly can to enlighten, inform, and instruct in whatever way you can. But there has to be a limit. In therapeutic settings, clients do feel safer when the therapist doesn't run over, even though they might not like it.

Audience: I had an experience of running over when doing a reading, which left me feeling very vulnerable. I felt I allowed myself to be set up. I had a client who was very distressed, and the longer we went on, the worse she got. I felt totally torn between feeling we needed to stop and feeling mean because she was in such a state.

Juliet: That is what I meant – you were worried about feeling "mean", which means you were worried about your own image. Equating boundaries with being "mean" is something which is probably worth your looking at more closely. The astrologer-client relationship does conjure up the parent-child archetype – the all-knowing, all-powerful one versus the ignorant, powerless seeker. As this archetype springs into action both unconsciously and frequently in both astrological and therapeutic work, it has to be handled very sensitively. In the case of parenting, it is a difficult task and a sensitive balance for a parent to create a situation in which a child can develop his or her own individuality but also feel contained within firm boundaries. The old saying goes, "Spare the rod and spoil the child" – suggesting that letting a person have just what they want when they want it may have a detrimental effect. It is very similar when working astrologically. If you can really believe within yourself that it is not actually helpful for a client to be able to get away with steam-rolling you, the astrologer, into having more time, it makes it much easier to keep to the boundaries.

Audience: Certainly I would agree – feeling truly convinced inside that what you are doing is right is the key. I remember having trouble with my daughter when she was very little. She woke up in the middle of the night, and unless I took her into our bed she wouldn't go back to sleep. She would just cry pitifully, and I would always give in to her, but it did start to seriously disrupt my and my partner's sleeping patterns. Also, there was the issue about her always being between us. I got so worried about it that I talked to friend of mine who is a child psychotherapist, who told me that actually it was terrifying for a child to feel that much power. Although my daughter seemed to be getting what she wanted, it wasn't doing anything for her feeling of being securely contained and boundaried.

Once I had got firmly set in my mind that it wasn't good for her, it all came together. That same night I went into her room when she started up, and told her (even though she was only fourteen months old and couldn't really hold a conversation!) that I wasn't coming back. Then I walked out of her room. She carried on crying for a bit – I stood outside and listened – and then I heard a huge sigh of defeat, and she went to sleep and didn't do it again. But I know that it was only possible for me to do because I knew inside that I was not being helpful to her by being "nice". I think you can translate this into the astrology session as you being "the mother who knows where the limits are."

Juliet: Thank you for that. That is a lovely example. I quite agree that you have to feel right inside, and only then can you be firm. If you are dithering you can be swayed. And you might need to explore the reasons why you are dithering.

Another thing that it is important to be clear about is situations when the client rings up five minutes before the session and says, "I'm running late, can I come at 10:30 instead of 10:00?". You can say, "Well, yes, you can, but you'll only have an hour, or we can reschedule." This issue has arisen in the CPA supervision groups, and I have often heard students report that they have been expecting somebody who has rung up saying they are running late. In the cases where the astrologer has moved the starting time and run on over the normal finishing time, there has been a sense of the session being disrupted and messy. It started messy and feels messy all the way through.

There is a feeling of the boundaries being pushed about in this kind of situation, which often ends up with resentment on the part of the astrologer, and it is difficult to conduct a session well when you are feeling resentful. Sometimes, even if there is a "good" reason for the lateness, such as a traffic jam, there is often a kind of unconscious assumption on the part of the client that we will sit about waiting for them – they are supposed to be the focus of our lives. The astrologer may pick up this unconscious assumption, which is actually the way a child thinks ("Whatever time I come home from school, Mummy will be there waiting"), and that can lead to a lot of resentment if nothing is said or done to affirm our own boundaries.

Sometimes the reasons for being late are perfectly legitimate, and rescheduling the appointment takes account of this and doesn't penalise the client. However, if you allow the session to run over you are really penalising yourself, and you are saying to the client, "My time isn't really important, I don't mind it being pushed around." This is not the kind of message which makes the client value and feel confidence in the astrologer, because the astrologer doesn't seem to value and have confidence in himself or herself.

Fees

Fees are a delicate subject for many astrologers. There is still some disagreement about whether we should be charging for astrological charts at all, and if so, how much. And because it is difficult to work out how good we are, it is difficult to set a fee for ourselves. Obviously nobody can tell you what to charge, but when you are setting your fee it is worth taking into consideration how much it cost you to train as an astrologer – the investment of time, courses, books, therapy and supervision, and so on. It is helpful to look at your fee as a reflection of where you are professionally, how much training you have done, how much experience you have had, how far you've come, how many years you have been at it, and how much work you have done on yourself.

An astrological reading is so personal and unique to both parties involved that there is no sense in trying to evaluate how "good" you are and setting your fee accordingly. You will probably suit some clients, and will therefore be "good" for them, and you will not suit others so well, which might make them feel you were "no good" for them.

Obviously, if you are just starting to read charts professionally and are charging a fee for the first time, you might not feel very confident or experienced, and you can let your fee reflect that. Nevertheless, you have to remember that you are charging for your time. This not only includes the time spent with the client, but also the time spent working on the chart beforehand – which, after all, should be included in the fee. So think about that quite carefully, and once you have worked it out you should arrive at a fee you feel good about. It is worth talking to fellow astrologers to find out what they are charging, and then you can consider whether or not your fee is too high or too low in comparison. Once you have set your fee, be clear about it when setting up your appointment.

Audience: What about "sliding" fees? Some people might find it very hard to pay what I feel I am worth, and other people can pay it easily. Is it acceptable to set different fees according to the client's situation?

Juliet: That is a question you must answer for yourself in the end. In therapeutic work, many therapists use "sliding" fees, because going twice or even three times a week to a therapist can very quickly use up whatever money a person has got! The clients with more money are, in effect, subsidising the ones with less money. But therapy is ongoing work, with plenty of time to negotiate fees and discuss any emotional issues that might come up around payment. With an astrological reading, it is a one-off, and it is very hard to make any assessment of a person's financial situation. After all, the client could arrive in rags and tell you they were terribly poor, and then turn out in the end to be Howard Hughes!

I personally feel that with one-off readings a set fee is best, and if a person doesn't have that much money, they can save up over a period of time. If you know someone's circumstances are very hard, or have a special reason to want to help them, that is your choice, but it should be an exception rather than the rule. Also, because most of us work by referral, clients tend to talk among themselves, and if one client has paid £X and told his or her friend, then the friend may be very angry if you suddenly turn around and say, "I charge £Y." Quite rightly, they will want to know why they are being charged more, and then what are you going to tell them? "I am charging you £Y because I heard from someone that you have a lot of money!"? Or if you charge them less, they will go back to the first client and tell them, and then you will have that person on the phone asking why you charged *them* more.

Audience: I must say I still have problems about accepting a fee for astrological readings. There is a part of me that feels it should be a service to humanity, something spiritual, and it is not really okay to charge for it. I do feel quite uncomfortable if I ask for a fee. I find myself justifying what I do and why I do it, and I know I can feel quite defensive about it. I really don't quite know why – I spend my time, I spend my energy, I give as much as I can to my clients, yet I still feel uncomfortable about what I have offer if I have to ask for money.

Juliet: It sounds as if, among other things, you are dogged by the charge that is so often levelled at therapists – how can you care about someone and charge them money for your care? You have to separate in your mind what you are charging for and what you cannot charge for and are giving freely. What you charge for is your time, your experience, your knowledge, and your skills – everything you have had to learn about astrology in order to be able to read a chart. What you give freely to your client is your attention, interest, empathy, and feelings. These things are not for sale. If you are genuinely "with" somebody, it is something that cannot be bought. Clients pay for your time and experience and expertise, not your emotions. Your feelings aren't for sale. And if you don't especially like a client, but still feel some empathy and can give them a positive and helpful chart reading, you have earned your fee.

Payment represents a boundary between you and the client which is healthy. It gives the client dignity and the sense of being a customer. If you don't charge, but give all the goodies out freely, you can either become a figure to whom the client must feel endlessly grateful, like a parent, or someone who is totally taken for granted, again like a parent! That does not make for a good, equal relationship. Also, the client who pays a fee feels he or she has the right to complain if you have given a poor reading. But if you haven't asked for a fee, or only a very low one, then the client might feel obligated, and feels too guilty to make a valid complaint. Sometimes offering things out of charity can make people very angry, because if what is offered isn't up to scratch, or isn't at all what they asked for, they feel they have no right to complain. Asking for a fee also puts the astrologer in the position of having to take his or her work seriously and do the best job possible.

Some people do not really want things to be given to them out of charity, even if they say they do, because it implies that they are to be pitied or that the astrologer perceives them as incompetent and helpless, which can be very hurtful and insulting. Stating your fee tells them that you value your own work, and it also tells them that you see them as an adult who is capable of recognising the value of the work as well.

It is a good idea to get a client to contribute something financially, even if you are asking for a low fee, because it makes them take the transaction more seriously. Once money is involved, the dynamic becomes more serious and there are fewer parent-child projections stirred up. It can get messy if you do charts in exchange for another service – like, for example, "I will cut your hair if you read my chart." This can sometimes work, but it can also get blurred, and then it is amazing how quickly resentment sets in. You might start thinking, "I spent far longer on her chart than she did cutting my hair..." or, "I did a really good chart reading, but she didn't do my hair well at all." A clear boundary on payment does eliminate that kind of problem.

When you are bridging the gap between student and professional you can offer your services at a reduced fee, a bit like apprentice hairdressers or beauticians. This can alleviate your guilt about feeling you are not yet worth a full fee, yet it also acknowledges the degree of study and knowledge you have gained thus far. It also prepares you for the point at which you can start charging a market fee.

The question about fees, and how one goes about asking for them, is obviously a sensitive area, and it is therefore worth spending some time getting your orientation right to make sure you feel good about whatever you decide to do. As with the boundaries of time, money can stir up unconscious issues in both the astrologer and the client, and it is also worth asking yourself what deeper reasons there might be for not valuing the work you do. So much of our communication with our clients is nonverbal, and a lot of it doesn't even concern what is actually in the chart. When you tell the client you charge £X, and you feel confident that you are worth that, you are saying something about the value you place on astrology. The client hears this unspoken statement and is more inclined to be open to what you are saying.

Audience: I always feel more in charge in situations when I know I am going to have to pay. I agree with you – it gives me the right to complain or feel dissatisfied if I want. It sets up a boundary which I think is very helpful. What you have just said really helps me not to feel uncomfortable with the whole issue about money.

Telephone contact

Juliet: When a client rings for an appointment, it is useful for you to gather as much information as you can on the telephone, or in person if it is a personal request. Some things to ask are: What are you are hoping to get from a reading, and is there a specific focus? Sometimes a person will say, "Just general interest," in which case you could prompt a little with, "What has sparked your general interest right now? What has made you ring at this particular time?" The client's response can often give you some information about how to approach the chart.

Another thing that is useful to know is who referred the client to you. This, too, will give an idea of their expectations and a sense of where they are coming from. For instance, it might be a recommendation from one of your other clients, who benefited from the experience and spread the word. This means the client will already know something about the sort of work you do, so you know that you are likely to be what they are expecting. However, if the referral is more impersonal – through an advertisement in a magazine, or a card in a shop – it is a good idea to get a bit more information from the client as to what kind of reading they are wanting. After all, a psychological view on astrology is not what everybody wants or expects from a reading. A bit of time to talk on the telephone also gives you an opportunity to get an idea of the client.

After all, if you are inviting a complete stranger into your home, you need to feel comfortable that they are the sort of person you feel you could work with. It is also helpful to remember that your own needs and limits are as important as the client's. You don't have to make an appointment for every person who asks. If someone makes you feel uncomfortable or anxious, it might be better if you referred that person on to someone else, or recommended that they write for a list of practising astrologers from someplace like the Faculty of Astrological Studies. You could say something like, "I am afraid I am very booked up at this time, but it sounds as though you are urgent, so I would suggest you ring X," or, "I have the feeling I would not be the right astrologer for you to consult, as I specialise in a different area." There is no point in setting up an appointment with someone whom you have already conceived a dislike for, or whom you know will be very difficult or unpleasant, because this will come out in the session and you will feel resentful while the client will feel rejected.

It is a good idea to give a prospective client a brief but concise description of what sort of service you offer. This should include the time, the fee, and the kind of orientation you use, as well as what you can and can't do. It not uncommon for astrologers to get confused with psychics or clairvoyants, so it is worth finding out about the sort of expectation the client has got.

Audience: I had a very unpleasant experience which confirms what you are saying. When I first started doing charts I advertised in my local paper, and a man rang up saying he wanted a chart done. I asked what he was interested in finding out through astrology, and he was very quiet for a minute or two, and then he said that he was a shoe fetishist, and wanted to know what sort of shoes I wore! I felt quite frightened at first, although then I started feeling rather sad and sorry for him. Of course I didn't offer him an appointment. But if I hadn't asked and had just offered an appointment, and he had turned up, it might have got very uncomfortable.

Audience: I always send my clients a written confirmation of our telephone conversation, which restates time and fees and a brief description of the way I work.

Juliet: That's a good idea. Obviously you will all have to work out what suits you personally, but whether you send written information or make it clear on the telephone what you offer, the client should be given enough information to be able to decide if you are the sort of astrologer he or she is looking for. And whether you are wearing the right sort of shoes! Having set up the appointment, it is a good idea to ask for a deposit. You can spend a lot of time and energy on a chart and then feel very angry indeed when the client doesn't show up.

Audience: Do you charge for missed appointments?

Juliet: Well, it does rather depend on how it is missed. If someone has to postpone or rearrange for a legitimate reason like illness, I would not charge, but if someone simply did not turn up and did not call to explain, then I would feel it appropriate to keep the deposit. And again, I would state that at the time of booking, so that the client knows he or she has a choice.

Most professional practitioners, such as private dentists and doctors, will charge for a missed appointment if it is cancelled within twenty-four hours of the appointment. Basically, if somebody rings you the night before and says he or she can't make it, then you reschedule. But if the person rings you up at the time of the session, or simply doesn't show up and then rings and says, "I didn't make it because..." then it seems reasonable to charge for your wasted time. You could have used that time to see another client, or done some other form of paid work.

However, if you are going to do that, it is also only right that you make it clear at the time of setting up the appointment. If people know that they have to pay for missed sessions, they are inclined to take the whole thing more seriously. If they know they will lose their deposit if they don't show up or give notice of cancellation, they tend to think, "I'll jolly well make the effort," and that again is fair enough. They have a choice to come to you, and they have a choice of whether or not to pay your fee, as long as you let them know what it is! They can make those sorts of decisions for themselves, in just the same way that you say to yourself, "I am not working for less than £X a session." It is right to treat clients as adults, because this helps them to feel adult and equal, and they can listen better and take in what you are saying. You will be surprised how much more seriously you are taken if you take yourself and your work seriously enough to set up clear and careful boundaries.

Audience: What if there are really exceptional circumstances, like if someone is involved in a car crash or something?

Juliet: Obviously there are always exceptions to any rule, aren't there? Again, it comes down to boundaries, to clarity, and ultimately to deciding for yourself what you feel is acceptable or not acceptable. All of you will have different limits and different things you are prepared to tolerate. That is, of course, a reflection of personal values, but you should all remember that you are professionals. You have all invested a lot to become astrologers, and you really can't afford to be sitting around waiting for people who have changed their minds about coming and can't be bothered to let you know!

How to get referrals

Another issue we need to look at is the question of getting an astrological practice started. Are any of you beginning to work professionally and finding referrals difficult?

Audience: I have been trying to get going seriously for the past few months. What I notice is that clients seem to come in waves. What has happened to me is that a few clients I have seen have been really positive about their readings, and then I get their entire circle of friends. And then that runs out, and nothing happens! I've been thinking of advertising, but am a little concerned about it.

Juliet: It is a question of building up a network, and as you rightly say, once you have done some people's charts you do tend to get referrals through them. If you advertise, you are well advised to be particular about the clients you see, and try to find out what they are like over the telephone. You can get a reasonable idea on the phone about whether or not people sound a bit peculiar. You also need to be very vigilant about telling them explicitly on the telephone what you have got to offer – the time, fees, deposits, length of session, and so on. And you should make sure you have their telephone number and address as well. If someone is reluctant to give this to you, then you might need to think twice about making the appointment.

If you get referrals through past clients, and the person says, "My friend Jack, who was recommended by his friend Jill, came to see you and thought you were good..." then at least you know the line of reference. But if you get somebody cold off the street, you have no way of knowing anything about them. You must be aware that astrology advertisements can sometimes attract rather strange people, as the shoe fetishist example demonstrates! Astrologers might also be rather strange people, but mostly, I think, we are pretty harmless! This means you might also need to think carefully about your personal working circumstances. For example, if you are a woman working alone from home in the evening, and you get an unknown male client, you do need to give some thought to safety.

Audience: I have some experience of that! I put a couple of leaflets around the place, and one of the responses I got was from a man who said he was generally interested in having his chart done. But when he turned up he was actually writing for a sadomasochist magazine, and he wanted me to write a column for it. Luckily I had a sense of humour. I burst out laughing and said, "I am sorry, but I don't write monthly astrology columns." He was okay. He wasn't a nasty man, and he went away with dignity and no harm was done, but it was a great big waste of my time! And if I had been unlucky and he hadn't been okay, it wouldn't have been a very pleasant experience.

Juliet: That is one of the reasons why it is a good idea to make sure that you and your client have the same expectations of what is on offer! If you do advertise, it is a good idea to choose your words very carefully, so that there is no doubt about what sort of service you are offering. Advertising in "New Age" magazines, sending round flyers at astrology groups, or putting your card up in health food shops or alternative healing centres is a good way to get started. With ordinary magazine and newspaper advertising, you do need to be quite careful about the magazines you choose, because you can end up spending quite a lot of money and not getting much in return.

Perhaps one of the best ways of getting clients who want the kind of work you have to offer is to make yourself known as an astrologer by writing or teaching. There is certainly no better way of learning a subject than to teach it or write about it!

Reading friends' charts

Audience: I have a problem about whether I should do charts for my friends for free.

Juliet: That can be a difficult issue which is fraught with potential problems. Firstly, you need to think about whether you would ask one of your friends to do a job for you for free which is normally part of their paid work. For instance, if you have a friend who is a decorator, would you ask him or her to paint your living room for free? Or a friend who makes curtains – would you ask him or her to run you up a couple of pairs for nothing? If you would not feel all right about asking them, then you should consider why you feel bad about charging them for a chart reading.

Of course I am talking about when you are working professionally, and not at the stage of study when you are practising and looking for "guinea pigs". Even when you are using your friends as "guinea pigs", many hot issues can inadvertently get highlighted, and you may become a very good astrologer but lose all your friends in the process! You may touch on sensitive areas such as family stuff, which can feel too exposing, or you can use your prior knowledge of the person to "fit" your astrological perceptions into. That can feel quite intrusive. And of course there are other questions around about whether one can truly be objective enough to do a friend's chart.

Audience: If I ever do a good friend's chart I always have problems about when to stop and how to stop. We often end up drifting into general conversation at the end. How can you prevent that with someone you know well?

Juliet: You have to be very clear about the boundaries beforehand, and say something like, "If you want me to do a reading for you, we have to set it up properly, as if you were a client, not a friend. That means you should pay the going rate of £X and make a proper appointment with me and stick to the time. If we want to extend the visit we can have a coffee afterwards, but we will go into a different room and we will stop talking about astrology. We'll talk about the weather or whatever! This way I will feel my professional boundaries are intact."

Audience: What if you don't have anywhere else to go? I live in a studio flat.

Juliet: It is still important that the session is finished properly, which may involve the client-friend going out, walking around the block, and coming back in as a friend, not a client. Although this sounds a little formal, it changes the feeling atmosphere entirely. I do realise that not everybody has got the space to have a special room that can be set aside for consultations. That is obviously ideal but is by no means essential.

Audience: Nowadays I try to avoid doing charts for friends, because the last time I did, the session got quite highly charged and I felt it rather changed the nature of our relationship afterwards. There is something about doing the charts of friends and family which is easier because you can see how the aspects may work, but in another way it is limiting because you are so aware of trying not to be intrusive.

Juliet: There is always difficulty in reading for people that you know well. It is often better to refer them to another astrologer if you feel that your friendship is more important to you than the reading, or, indeed, if you think it may compromise the relationship. It obviously depends a lot on the type of friendship and the quality of relationship, so it is not possible to be absolutely black-and-white about it. Generally speaking, as you get more professional and your boundaries get more set, your friends tend to stop asking in the way that they do when you first begin. When you are starting out you are usually very enthusiastic, keen to talk astrology at any opportunity, and ready to do anyone's chart to get experience and practise. But as you start to work more professionally, you gradually become less inclined to go on about it to everybody. It's a bit like being a doctor, who doesn't especially want to go to a party and hear about somebody's aunt's arthritis. As you do astrology more and you do it more professionally, you don't necessarily want to do it everywhere for everyone, and that is something that develops as your own inner boundary.

There are no hard and fast rules about anything. The most important thing is for you to work with each individual individually, given your own personal approach and your own starting parameters. Obviously every rule has exceptions, and there is room for flexibility. But you have got to have something firm set up within which you can then be flexible.

Audience: I think it is very much an evolutionary process that goes on as you get more experience.

Juliet: Yes, I agree. With experience you begin to become more and more aware of what you can and can't manage, and what you should and shouldn't be doing. If, for example, you have a client who is extremely distressed in the session, you might need to think about whether what you have to offer is enough in the astrological framework, or whether this person would not be better off considering some therapy. It is useful to have some referral networks to hand, where you have a list of therapists you know and trust – or perhaps a list of different schools of therapy, or some knowledge of the various organisations designed to help with particular problems, like Alcoholics Anonymous, Narcotics Anonymous, and so on. You don't know what sort of problems your clients may have, and nine times out of ten, nothing much will be needed. But when something does happen and you suggest the client might benefit from some sort of therapy, it is nice to have something to offer rather than vaguely saying, "There are plenty of people out there who could help you," without being very specific.

An astrological session may be the first point at which a person might become open to accepting that they may have something to work on. Quite often people will consult an astrologer rather than a psychotherapist or counsellor when they have a problem, as they may think a person has to be crazy or in really bad shape to seek therapeutic help. They can rationalise going to an astrologer by saying to themselves, "I'm just curious. I don't have to take it seriously." There is also sometimes the secret fear that a therapist will declare them clinically mad, and then they will have to accept this diagnosis, and maybe even get taken off in an ambulance! However, if the astrological reading is sympathetic and constructive, the client might be inclined to use it as a starting point for a deeper inner journey.

Audience: I guess there are lots of other things you might be able to recommend, from refuges to different classes. I can recommend the magazine *Holistic London*, which has information on masses of alternative options from yoga to pottery classes.

Juliet: It feels positive to be able to offer a client something encouraging and affirming, although obviously what they do with that information is up to them. An astrological reading is very different from a therapy session. After all, the astrologer is being active and interpretive and trying to give the client things that they can easily digest and take away – "one-liners" that can stick in their mind and prove to be very useful.

Audience: What I hate is not getting feedback. I often wonder what some clients do with the information they gain (or don't gain!) in the session.

Juliet: It can be very frustrating when you have worked hard with someone for a couple of sessions and then you don't hear from them again. But I am afraid that it does rather go with the territory. It boils down to having the faith that the input you offer during a particular session will actually benefit the client, even if you don't see the results right there and then in the session. You are left hoping and believing that something will come to fruition out of it. Sometimes a client will get in touch after a long period of time, maybe even a few years, to say that things finally began to make sense and that they found the reading very helpful. Don't forget, also, that some people take longer to register the impact of something that touches them emotionally. They may not feel what they are really feeling until some time afterward.

Just because you never hear again from a client doesn't necessarily mean it was unhelpful. Remember the Bible story, when Jesus healed loads of lepers? Out of all those who were healed, only one came back to say, "Thank you!" and acknowledge his help! People can behave very strangely when they feel gratitude. Sometimes a client may feel you have done a lot for them, but they are quite unable to say this, out of pride or embarrassment. Some clients even go away feeling a little angry *because* you have helped them, because they hate to admit that astrology really works, or that a complete stranger has been able to offer them insights which they didn't think of themselves. You may also reflect on your own lives, and remember that there might have been people who have helped you immensely, but you may never have been in a position to acknowledge that to them directly.

For instance, I had a well-known writer as a client, whose 3rd house Saturn conjuncts her Sun in Gemini. She felt a huge sense of gratitude to her English teacher for the sound foundation he had given her. As you can imagine, her 3rd house Saturn in Gemini had given her a strong sense of inadequacy in her attempts at communication in her childhood. But she found that, by using her Sun creatively and her Saturn as a taskmaster, she could write very well. However, she never forgot the impact this particular teacher's commitment and style of teaching had had on her. Long after she had left school and started writing successfully, she wanted to trace him to say thank you. But she could not, and she had to be content with treasuring him silently in her heart. I tell you that story because our work can have the same profound effect, although we do not always have the satisfaction of hearing it from our clients.

Exercise one: listening and hearing

Now we can do our first exercise. What I want to do is to pair you off into twos. Two people should spend five minutes each talking to the other person. It doesn't have to be about anything in particular – it doesn't even have to be astrological. It can just be a description of who you are, where you live, or what you do. It doesn't have to be personal or heavy – just something that you want to say. Then it's the other person's turn. After that we will come back to the group to discuss how easy or difficult it is to simply listen. This exercise can be carried out in peer groups as a way of experimenting with the art of listening.

[Time out to do the exercise]

Can we have some feedback now on how you felt in your pair?

Audience: I found it was difficult not to interrupt my partner's conversation. I kept wanting to ask questions and get more information. I also found myself wanting to put some of my own ideas in.

Juliet: It is an exercise in which you can experience what it is like to listen, and you might realise that sometimes it is easier to speak than to sit with someone who is trying to get something out but can't find the words. Your instant response is to put words into the other person's mouth. Also, you may not pay attention to what the other person is saying because you are busy thinking of what you want to say when he or she is finished. We do like the sound of our own voices. We have all got things to say, and sometimes it is difficult not to thrust those things on somebody else. So it is a very delicate balance. That's the point of the exercise – how to listen without interruption, without helpful comments, and without bringing one's own needs along. I saw a dedication on a record album once which said, "There are those who listen, and those who wait to speak. This album is dedicated to the listeners."

Audience: I suppose I assume that anyone can listen, and there is nothing very special about it. But perhaps you do need to be trained in it to do this kind of work.

Audience: I had just the opposite experience. I had no problem listening, but when it came to be my turn to talk, I found that I didn't really want to say anything. I felt slightly uncomfortable, as though whatever I said couldn't possibly be as interesting as what the other person just said. I know I have this problem, which I can see happening in social situations. I am always listening to other people, and then sometimes I feel very angry because no one wants to know anything about me. But I learned something from this exercise. I think I use listening partly as a way of hiding my own shyness. I am interested in what other people have to say, but it isn't just that.

Juliet: This is also a very important issue. Many people are attracted to the helping professions for exactly the reason you have just given! We may become listeners because we don't feel we have anything valuable to offer in our own right. This can be a very useful skill if you are an astrologer or a therapist, but it isn't a good recipe for feeling happy and fulfilled when you are not working! That might be something you could take away from the seminar and work with.

Communication skills

Now we are going to look at some basic communication skills which you might like to incorporate into sessions. After all, while we are reading a chart there may a number of things going on which need attention. We need to find words to convey to our clients what the complexities of their charts show us.

Confirmation and verification

During the course of a session it is important that you and your client are speaking the same language. Because astrology is like a language, it is especially important that you translate it clearly and don't leave your client to guess or intuit what you mean. Astrologers talk to each other in short-hand: "He has Sun-Saturn in Pisces...She has Moon- Pluto in Scorpio..." This will give another astrologer a clue about the person being thus described, but it will make no sense at all to a client who is not familiar with astrology.

Using astrology in such ways can be as alienating as a psychiatrist talking of a patient with "a narcissistic personality disorder with paranoid-schizoid tendencies." Another psychiatrist may get a sense of what is being discussed, but the patient will not understand the label, and unless the whole thing is put in context there is a danger of the person being stripped of his or her humanity. And people do come with misconceptions about certain astrological symbols. They read things in the astrology columns in the papers, or hear things from their friends, and they say, "Oh, no, is my Moon really in Scorpio? I read that this means I am untrustworthy and violent!" If we use astrological language during a chart reading, we should always explain what we mean in ordinary language. Psychotherapists and psychiatrists are accused of talking in "psycho-babble". We need to be careful of talking in "astro-babble".

At this point it is worth considering how shameful it can be if we are being spoken to in a language that we imagine we are supposed to understand, yet don't. To cover our shame we pretend we do understand, when actually we haven't a clue. It is like the story, "The Emperor's New Clothes" - do you all know that story? No? It is about a vain Emperor who loved beautiful clothes.

A couple of bogus tailors came to court to sell the Emperor a wonderful cloth, so magical that "only clever and intelligent people can see it". The cloth needed vast quantities of pure gold thread which the emperor readily supplied, and the tailors set to work at their looms busily weaving fresh air. When the Emperor sent his lieutenant to see how the cloth was coming along, the lieutenant had heard that only clever people could see the cloth and, not wishing to look a fool, he said it was beautiful, although in truth he could not see anything! When the Prime Minister heard that the lieutenant thought the cloth a marvel, he too did not wish to look a fool, so he agreed that it was beautiful, and so did all the others who trailed in to see the tailors hard at work sewing nothing! Eventually the Emperor walked stark naked through the streets at a huge parade, and all the people of the town agreed with each other that his coat was the finest they had ever seen – until a small boy who had not heard what he was supposed to see asked, "Why has the Emperor got nothing on?" and they all realised they had been fools!

Translating a language often involves asking for more information to ensure that there is an accurate understanding of what is being communicated. For example, if a client says, "I'm hot!" you might need to find out if they are saying that the room is hot, or they are hot because they have got too many sweaters on, or they are hot with embarrassment or shame, or they are hot because you have made them really angry. What are they saying? You can say something like, "I'm trying to make sure I understand what you're saying. Are you saying you are feeling hot because the room is too warm, or are you saying that you are hot with embarrassment?" This way you are making sure that you and your client are in agreement and understand each other.

In other words, you may need to get more information on something before making assumptions. Sometimes a client might be very straightforward and is able to articulate his or her feelings in a clear way. At other times there may be undercurrents that you need to explore. It is rather like the story of a mother who was determined to give her daughter "the correct facts of life", and had long been waiting for her daughter to ask a question about sex so that she could do her motherly duty properly. One day her little girl burst into the kitchen asking, "Mummy, where do I come from?" The mother instantly took her cue and began the detailed explanation of reproduction, whereupon the little girl interrupted, " No, I want to know where I come from – Manchester or Leeds? Quick! my friend is outside and she wants to know!" We can get so caught up in looking for what we want to look at that we may ignore the person sitting in front of us, and fail to notice or address their issues. This, of course, echoes our previous discussion about listening carefully to what is being said – the difference between being a "listener" or one who "waits to speak". Astrologers need to be both.

Paraphrasing

Paraphrasing is a combination of restating and confirming at the same time. In other words, you can pull what the client has been saying into a sentence and run it by them for confirmation that you are both on the same wavelength. You assume that you have understood correctly what has been said, but you paraphrase to make sure. For instance, you might say, "You are feeling hot and uncomfortable when talking about intimate relationships, is that right?" and the client has an opportunity to say, "Yes, I do feel like that," or "No, not at all, you've got it wrong." At least you are clear that you both understand and agree. Paraphrasing is also a useful technique for giving the client an opportunity to hear what he or she is actually saying. Sometimes we chatter away without paying much attention to our own words, but if we can hear what we have just said it can have quite an impact.

Audience: I think my failing is that I never give the client much time to talk. I am so busy trying to give them as much information as possible that I don't allow much time for discussion. After all, there is so much to convey to a client about their chart, and I like to give them their money's worth.

Juliet: What you are saying reminds of a time when I was in the Danish Centre for lunch. They have a wonderful smorgasbord, where you pay a set amount and eat what you like. I was fascinated to watch a woman take a plate and cram it full with heaps of salads and savoury dishes as well as meringues and cream and chocolate cake, all jammed together on the one plate. It looked as if she was afraid she could only have one visit to the serve-yourself bar, and was absolutely determined to make the most of it, possibly in an attempt to get her money's worth! I couldn't help thinking, though, that the tastes must have been blurred and spoiled by being lumped together like that. Certainly the visual impact was!

Perhaps we, as astrologers, are so afraid of not giving our clients their "money's worth" in the alotted time that we end up thrusting all the information that we can possibly think of upon them. It ends up being like that plate, with the prawn cocktail and the chocolate cake all piled together. I get an impression of physical or psychic indigestion following in hot pursuit! I would suggest you take your time, and if it means that less gets done, more may very well be achieved. A client can always return for a second helping!

Audience: I always prepare great sheafs of notes and try to come up with a really clear idea of the person behind the chart, but I am often thrown when the person turns up and doesn't seem at all as I had imagined. This really floors me.

Juliet: It really isn't possible to work out in advance what you are going to say. You must obviously look at the chart placements, the transits, the progressions, and so on, and you can get an idea of the aspects of tension and flow. But I don't think you can ever say, "I'm going to interpret this as that," until you have met the person. It is only when you meet the person "cold" and together start the process of understanding how each individual lives his or her chart that the exciting part of the work really begins. It is usually only by gentle probing and gathering of information that the chart begins to mean something. For instance, a 4th house Neptune might mean a missing or alcoholic father, or perhaps a deeply loved and idealised father, or even a father who is a priest or an artist, but you won't know which, if any, of these possibilities it might be until you talk to the client about his or her father.

The preparation of the chart is an important ritual. Most of us now use computers, which means you only have to press a button and bang! it's all there. Even though I use a computer for calculation, I still like to hand-draw the horoscope myself, as it gives me time to reflect and connect with the positions and aspects on the chart. In the bad old days before computers did all the calculations, I used to find it a mysterious and exciting process to watch a chart unfold as you gradually find the signs and houses and then fill in the planets and then the aspects. I enjoy the process of seeing the chart emerge. It certainly helps to get to know it and begin the process of working with it imaginatively

Audience: I do all of that, too. I find myself sitting and drawing up the chart, and then setting myself an hour where I just sit and meditate quietly on it, because I can't seem to work it out just using my intellect.

Audience: I feel that unless I've done a huge amount of work beforehand, I might be guilty of letting the person down because I haven't really grasped the chart or done enough preparation on it.

Juliet: We all know that the proof of the pudding is in the tasting. It doesn't matter how many good ingredients have gone into the pudding if it doesn't taste nice and it is not enjoyable. The important thing in a chart reading is how well you actually relate to the person sitting in front of you in the here-and-now. This is the point at which you must put your knowledge into words and convey something to your client that he or she is able to understand and use. This is where you are listening and being aware and paraphrasing and restating, and such communication can be very affirming to the client. The whole point of doing any reading is to give a positive, educative and enlightening experience to the person who comes, rather than a chance for you to show off your knowledge. It is not a power trip.

Body language

It can be useful to describe some particular behaviour or body language of the client in order to draw their attention to it. You can see from the way a person is sitting how tense and nervous, or how at ease, they are. You might be able to use some of their body language to say, "Did you realise how tense your fist was while you were talking about your mother/father/child...?" Or, "I couldn't help noticing that you were gripping the chair when you were talking about the situation at home. I wonder what that tells us?" You can also get a sense of when something you are saying has "struck home" because the client may react physically although not verbally. Very controlled people often do not want you to know that you have said something which has moved them, but their physical gestures and movements may tell you that you are on the right track. Of course, you may not feel it is appropriate to interpret the body language, perhaps because it might be too intrusive at that moment or with that particular client, in which case you will still be able to use the information privately. You can observe all sorts of things about the way a person is sitting, wringing their hands, blushing, avoiding eye contact, and so on, which are all worth noting – either to the client, if it is at all useful, or to yourself as an indication of how far to go and whether you are going in the right direction.

Clients vary enormously, and you can never make a hard-and-fast rule as to what to interpret and what to simply be aware of yourself. Very often it is kinder to notice something than to ignore it. For instance, if someone's eyes fill up with tears but they are not actually crying, you might notice it but say nothing out of embarrassment. I think it is often more helpful to stop at that point and say something like, " I see that what I said then, or what we were talking about just now, has moved you..." This gives the client permission to feel sad, angry, or whatever, and lets them know that it is all right to voice it, rather than ignoring the misty eyes. Ignoring this kind of thing may give the client the notion that you are not able to hold their pain, which, in turn, can feel dismissive or rejecting. It is true that many people do feel embarrassed or ashamed of crying in front of a stranger, but as long as you, the astrologer, feel all right about it and treat it something normal and permissible, your client will be free to express his or her feelings honestly.

Using your own feelings to communicate to the client

If it is not possible to interpret behaviour or body language, you can use your own feelings to check out how your client might really be feeling. You can say something like, "Have I upset you by saying that?" or "I feel what I just said has hurt your feelings," or "I feel I have made you angry. Is that true?" In other words, you are feeling something and then checking it out with your client to find out if your feelings make sense to them. After all, just because we are astrologers, this does not mean we can't occasionally add 2 + 2 and get 5! It also gives your client a chance to disagree with you if necessary.

In the same way, if you have somebody sitting in front of you looking very tense, sitting bolt upright, gripping the chair, perhaps even trembling, you might want to clarify what the tension is about. You might gently question to ascertain whether they are tense with fear, nerves, or anger. I once had a client who was moving about in the chair and looking distinctly uneasy. I said I couldn't help noticing she seemed uncomfortable and she said, "You are right. I am dying to use the bathroom, but I didn't like to ask!" You might assume that a client is fearful when he or she might actually be furious, or you may think the client is furious when they are really feeling hurt. Assumptions can be dangerous as they are not necessarily accurate. We assume that other people are going to show their emotions in exactly the same way we do ourselves, but of course people are very individual in the way they exhibit tension, anger, and fear. Many people take on an angry grimace when they are in pain, or react with a compulsive laugh when they feel hurt. You have probably heard the joke about the word "assume" – making an "ass" out of "u" and "me"!

You will obviously need to use these techniques with some discretion, trying to check things out gently without being punitive or intrusive. After all, an astrological consultation is supposed to be constructive and helpful, not a psychological assault course. Your aim is to affirm your client's process, not to go at him or her with a sledgehammer!

How to phrase things and ask questions

When questioning a client on how events unfolded in their life, it is gentler to use "when", "where", and "how", rather than "why". Asking a client why tends to put them on the defensive. If you say,

"Why did your relationship start to deteriorate?" it sounds rather punitive, as if it was the client's fault. But if you say, "When did you notice that the relationship first started to change?" or "How did it feel when things started to change in the relationship?" it leaves more scope for the client to open up. "Why did you do that?" or "Why are you angry?" or "Why are you hurt?" are all likely to elicit a defensive response.

We sometimes forget that thinking psychologically is not something everybody does. We are used to it because we have studied and trained to understand that things often happen in people's lives because of unconscious motives and feelings. We ask ourselves, "Why?" and sometimes get an answer because we are trained to listen to ourselves. We take it for granted that if a relationship breaks up, both people were contributing to making that happen. But the client may feel it broke up because of money pressures, or the interference of their mother-in-law. Asking "Why?" implies personal responsibility, and suggests that the client should immediately know the answer. Many people aren't prepared to face that yet. You can use language in a way that will either encourage a client to open up or push him or her into shutting down.

Try to find ways of saying things which will be helpful and facilitating, and try to avoid putting your client on the defensive. You can check this out for yourselves. For instance, how you would feel if someone said, "Why are you clenching your fists?" You might not know you were doing it, and you could feel very embarrassed. You might think, "Why shouldn't I clench my fists? And what's it to do with you anyway?" Or you might think, "I really don't know why. Isn't that stupid of me?" But if somebody says, "I notice you are looking rather tense – your fists are quite tight, and I wonder if it has something to do with what I am saying?" then you might still not like it, but it is less accusatory than "Why?"

It is important to avoid accusing or shaming your client, which, as an "authority figure", you could easily find yourself in the position of being able to do. After all, the dynamic of the session puts you, the astrologer, into the position of being seen as the "authority", and puts the client into the position of being "the one who doesn't know". This can very quickly turn into a power struggle between the "all-knowing, powerful parent" and the "ignorant, impotent child".

Audience: I am sometimes quite surprised at how scared of me my clients seem to be. I tend to think I am easily approachable and ready to listen and understand, but they seem quite guarded. With some clients you can really feel they are on their "best behaviour". I find it rather strange.

Juliet: I don't think we should overlook the power struggles that go on unconsciously with "authority figures". The astrologer's position of the "authority figure" can make some clients feel very angry and aggressive, because that is how they felt about their parents. It can make other clients feel very frightened, as if they think we are going to pronounce their doom. One woman who came for a chart sat with her hands shaking when I started the reading. I told her that I had noticed this, and did she feel uncomfortable about coming to an astrologer? She told me that she was terrified I would tell her something terrible, like she was going to die soon, or that her husband would leave her. We may not like the idea that we are "in authority", but like it or not, that is often how our clients will see us, even if we are as nice as pie. And many people are also inclined to see "authority" as something bad or negative. Authority is, in itself, neutral – it is only how it is used which makes it positive or negative. The same goes for power.

Language techniques

Let's carry on with more language techniques. For instance, how do we convey things we see in a chart without becoming accusatory or intrusive?

Audience: I would like to know how to get talking about difficult parental aspects. Supposing you have got client with a badly aspected Moon opposing Saturn. How would you say that they might have had a difficult relationship with their mother?

Juliet: You could start by opening up the stage for discussion with something like, "I wonder what sort of relationship you had with your mother?" Wondering leaves a lot of scope for discussion. The client might say, "It was all right," which would not get you very far! So you could then try, "It would seem that, from the combination of the Moon, the planet which describes feelings and emotional needs, with Saturn, the planet of discipline and restriction, that things may not always have felt very free and easy between you and your mother. Would that be right?" Or you could say, "I have sometimes seen this combination when there was a feeling of some restriction connected with the mother. Would this apply to you?" And then you open up the space for your client to comment, to agree and expand, or to disagree.

Phrases like "It seems as if..." or "When I have seen this before, it sometimes meant..." provide a way of suggesting something without making it into a hard and fast statement. "It seems as if you might have experienced your mother as rather aloof or cold and distant" sounds less accusatory than "Your mother was aloof, cold and distant." This statement does not open up easily into discussion. Such a statement might provoke a defensive or protective response: "She couldn't help it, she had six children to feed and no money..." However bad a parent might have been, children usually feel fierce loyalty to their parents, and this can happen even if they have been beaten and abused. By sounding as if you are accusing the parent, you push your client into polarising.

Also, many people feel guilty about having negative feelings about their parents. They may have very good reasons for the angry or negative feelings, but they still feel guilty because we are all supposed to love and honour our parents. So if you force someone to own the bad feelings by being too definite, they may fight back by denying them, whereas if you give them space they might feel they have permission to feel negative things. Using phrases like "It seems..." gives space. It could yield, "Well I did feel her to be distant, but then she did have six children to feed and no money...But I suppose I was frightened of her coldness." In other words, if you leave things open for discussion, your client is more likely to discuss things with you.

Parental images in the chart can also mean a lot of different things. Moon-Saturn isn't always an aloof or restrictive mother. She might just have been terribly tired and worked too hard, or money was tight. In other words, her *circumstances* might have been restrictive, rather than her *character*. The client might feel very sympathetic and responsible toward his or her mother, and not at all resentful. We don't know this unless we ask the client. We should never assume that Moon-Saturn or any other difficult Moon aspect means the mother's personality is negative. Also, Saturn can mean a strong mother. Using words which aren't negatively charged, like "strong" or "hard-working", is sometimes better than saying "restrictive" or "repressive". "Strong" can be a good quality. The client can then say, "Yes, she was really strong, but I found her very repressive," or, "Yes, she was very strong, and I really admire and respect the way she looked after six children without having any money." You are giving the client the choice of recognising how they feel about the mother's Saturn qualities.

In the session

I would now like to go more deeply into what goes on in a session. As we touched on earlier, it is obviously very important to try to ascertain from a client what he or she expects from the session. It is a good idea to be clear about their expectations and wishes and clear about what you are offering, so that you can avoid disappointment when what you and they have in mind are not the same. It is also important to remember the ultimate aim of any session, which is primarily to be constructive, enlightening, revealing, and helpful. This can sometimes involve referring the client on, as well as giving insights yourself. As I said earlier, I believe in having a referral network of therapeutic organisations or therapists that you know to be good readily to hand, so that if it is appropriate you can recommend that your client does further work. A chart reading, particularly a psychologically orientated one, can often provide the opening for a person to get into deeper work.

Unconscious communication

Psychological terms such as transference, counter-transference and projective identification describe the feelings which flow from your client to you and you to your client. The communication between astrologer and client is often unconscious. Freud said, "It is a very remarkable thing that the unconscious of one human being can react upon that of another, without passing through consciousness." Transference describes the feelings that a client, often unconsciously, transfers onto you during a session. Counter-transference is what you experience in response to those feelings, also often unconsciously. The transference-counter-transference is what goes on between you and the client on a feeling level during a session. The essence of transference is that the feeling content is subjectively real to the client, no matter how far it may be from your reality. The client may be transferring onto you, albeit unconsciously, feelings of you being the powerful authority, perhaps like mother or father. If that client's experience of mother or father was a negative one, for example, they may already have negative feelings toward you without having met you, simply because you represent some sort of authority.

As we discussed earlier, feeling ambivalent towards authority is not at all uncommon. After all, we all started out as children, both needing and resenting parental authority. We wanted our parents to be wise, in control, and powerful. We turned to them to sort out difficulties and provide food, clothes, and shelter, and we often expected unlimited supplies of pocket money and chauffeuring. Yet at the same time we felt powerless and at their mercy! There may also have been a fear that "goodies" would only be given in reward for good behaviour.

In other words, if we are not good we will not be loved. There is a constant tension in most children between wanting to bite the hand that feeds and being terrified to, in case there is no more food! Now, if you translate those often very unconscious feelings into an astrological setting, you can get a client who wants nothing less than everything from you, and yet resents you for the perceived power you have in being able to "see" or "know" things about them.

The counter-transference is what you feel in response to the client's transference. It is your response to what they bring to you. I will give you an example of this from a book by Patrick Casement, called *On Learning from the Patient*.[1] Patrick Casement, a Freudian analyst, wrote this very good book largely based on how much he learned from his mistakes rather than his great successes, which makes it very human and readable. An example he gives of a counter-transference response is of a client who constantly complained about her parents not having done enough for her. They didn't help with her education, they didn't give her enough affection, they didn't encourage her, and so on. The therapist felt the client was ungrateful and that her complaints were unjustified. He found himself feeling infuriated with the client. It turned out the therapist felt his own children were ungrateful, and it became clear that this client was representing an unresolved conflict in the therapist's own life. Of course, there were other issues which belonged in the therapy, but it was important for the therapist to own his own conflict and not project it onto his client.

Another example from this book deals with what is known as projective identification. This means that a client will do more than project feelings onto you – the client unconsciously makes you feel the same as they do, and indeed may even make you feel the feelings they cannot bear to feel. In other words, you may suddenly find yourself feeling quite frightened in a session, but not know why because you may not have any personal reason to feel especially frightened. However, you could be picking up your client's fear.

Casement uses this example to describe projective identification. A couple who had been married for ten years were referred to him because the wife was experiencing a great deal of pain during intercourse, for which there were no medical grounds. During the first session it was revealed that the couple had had two children, both of whom had died from the same congenital disease. The eldest child first became ill at about eighteen months, when the woman was already pregnant with the second child, and died at the age of two.

It transpired that both babies had a congenital disease which was incurable and fatal. The second child also died at the age of two. It was an absolutely horrendous story, but the woman had not been able

---

[1]Patrick Casement, *On Learning from the Patient*, Tavistock Publications, London, 1985.

to express any grief at all. She had not cried when either child had died, she had not cried at either child's funeral, and she told Casement that when she talked to her friends about it, the friends all begged her to stop, because they couldn't bear listening to the story. It caused them such pain and anguish that they simply couldn't bear to hear any more.

Casement said that while he was hearing this story, he became so distressed inside that he felt as though he was screaming and crying and howling. While he was well aware that this was a terrible, tragic story, and that he would naturally have felt moved and saddened at hearing it, the way that he was feeling in the session was inappropriate because it wasn't his grief. He realised that what he was feeling was actually his client's grief. She could not bear to feel it herself, so she unconsciously communicated it to others, who then felt it for her.

Casement then knew that she had to find a way to own that grief herself, and that once she could, through the therapy, begin to acknowledge those losses and feel the pain, she could begin to grieve herself. She needed to release some of her pain through crying and mourning. The clue for Casement was the degree of emotion he felt, which he knew was out of proportion as it was not his personal pain. Of course he would have felt empathy, but he felt positively torn to shreds inside, as, of course, she would have felt had she allowed herself to feel.

This can sometimes happen in astrological sessions. Sometimes you can get overwhelmed by feelings that the client is unconscious of or unable to express. Of course, how much can actually be done in an astrological reading for something as severe as Casement's client is debatable, and you have to able to make at least some assessment of the level of integration of your client. There are clients who are quite psychologically sophisticated. They may already have done work on themselves in therapy, for instance, and are well connected with what they are feeling. With this kind of client it is possible to do deeper work than with those who have never acknowledged that they have an inner world and might be very frightened by it. What you need to work out inside yourself is whether you are feeling your own feelings, or whether you are feeling them on behalf of the client. If they are on behalf of the client, you need to work out how you can feed them back to the client in a way that is acceptable to him or her.

For instance, you might feel very angry when you have a client who tells you about being very ill-treated but seems very calm about it. This client might say, "My husband beats me up regularly but it is not really his fault because..." The client is seemingly accepting of the situation, but you suddenly start feeling quite angry. The anger you feel is on behalf of your client. It is not yours, unless, of course, your husband happens to be beating you, or your father beat you up when you were a child. To hand the anger back to the client, you might say something like, "It makes me feel really quite upset to hear that," or "I feel quite angry to hear that," which gives your client a chance to own their anger or upset, or perhaps to wonder why they have not felt anger themselves.

There are other times when you might feel very opposite to the client. They might be busy blaming somebody – husband, wife, boss, child, parent – saying how awful this person is, yet you find yourself feeling quite the opposite. You may be feeling sympathy for the client's partner or boss or parent or child, and inside you are hearing a different side to the story. You may be picking up the thing that the client is not feeling – the ambivalence in their feelings – or you may be picking up the fact that the client is projecting something aggressive in himself or herself onto the other person. If you are aware of this, you can gently feed it back to them.

After all, part of the purpose of looking at a horoscope psychologically is to try to empower your client, to help him or her become a bit more conscious. If you have knowledge of something, you have some degree of choice. If you don't know, then you can't choose, and you remain driven by unconscious forces. Freud said, "Where there is *id*, let there *ego* be," meaning roughly, "Make unconscious desires and wishes *(id)* conscious, so that the ego (the conscious, managing part of the psyche) can do its best to negotiate fulfillment of those wishes." Also, knowledge sometimes has the effect of changing a deep-rooted problem. Just being aware of it changes the way the client feels about himself or herself, as well as making them aware that they have other choices. It can also change the way the client interacts with the outside world, because there is not so much projection.

Pointing out patterns

If you are able to work more deeply with a client, you can sometimes point out to them what sort of familiar patterns they are repeating. For example, there may have been a difficult childhood situation, and a person who has felt very unloved in childhood may keep being drawn into relationships in which they are and/or feel unloved because it is what they know best. This is what Freud called "repetition compulsion".

Suppose you had a very unloving mother, and throughout your childhood you felt deeply hurt and wished that your mother had loved you. There might be a signature for this in your chart, like Saturn in the 10th house square the Moon and Venus. But you aren't really aware of how hurtful all this was, so you only remember that everything was fine and nice between you and your mother. When you are an adult, maybe you are aware of your Moon-Venus, but the 10th house Saturn doesn't mean very much to you, except that you are always worried that people in authority will think you aren't good enough. But you keep getting involved with people who don't seem to want you.

Freud would say that your constant liaisons with people who don't love you, liaisons in which you are constantly trying to make them love you, would be a repetition compulsion. You are unconsciously trying to heal the earlier wound. Alternatively, you could begin to accept that there was a wound, and acknowledge that something awful did happen which hurt badly, and you can slowly start to mourn the loss and allow it to be the way it really was. You don't necessarily have to go through the hoop of getting into impossible relationships if you disentangle yourself from the past, which includes accepting that it cannot be rectified in the past, only let go of in the present.

I have heard many clients say that it is their families or friends or partners who should be in therapy, not them. Sometimes this may be the case, but it is also their problem. To this sort of statement I might say something like, "It is your choice to continue battling with such impossible people, isn't it?" A client said to me that it finally occurred to her that she had to remove the hook from herself rather than trying to wrench it out of others.

Audience: With respect to illness, there seems to be a lot of talk about people having made themselves ill by their own negativity. I personally feel that if somebody is ill, it is extremely difficult to start dealing with issues like self-victimisation and how you have brought it on yourself and the psychological dynamic that is operating. Once somebody has got something like cancer, I somehow feel that it is irrelevant trying to apportion blame.

Juliet: I definitely think that when people are ill, it is extremely destructive to say, "It's your fault you are ill." I do know that there is this kind of "speak" around – that if you have got an illness it has something to do with what you have drawn down on yourself. This is rather a punitive way to look at it. It is sometimes more constructive to think of illness as the expression of something, rather than the result of something. The "something" might be something positive trying to get out, which can't get out any other way because there is a conflict. Illness aside, if you get a client who says to you that they are constantly getting involved with men who beat them up, or are attracting destructive relationships of any sort, you have to start saying, "What's the pattern here, where is this coming from?" If the client can start to make some of those patterns conscious, then he or she can start to work with what might become possible. Of course you will be able to identify the various aspects of the chart where some of those issues might lie.

Audience: When I am trying to interpret a parental aspect, I usually try to consider the negative side of the aspect as well as the positive side. I think it's necessary to emphasise both. For example, suppose someone has a Moon-Saturn aspect. I might interpret this as a cool or distant mother. But I would also emphasise the positive effect of discipline and reliability, because that would be associated with mother too.

Audience: It is only since I had a child myself that I have been able to approach the parental patterns in people's charts, not so much from the point of view of the parent's character and archetypal image, but from the point of view of, "How did this person's parent deal with the configuration in their child's chart – a child who sees mother with a

Moon-Pluto edge, or a Uranian edge?" I have started to wonder how effective the actual mother was in being able to deal with the child's expectations, rather than seeing the mother as the "bad guy", which I used to feel. If you have a very Plutonian child (like I do! – my daughter has Moon conjunct Pluto) then you have to deal with a lot of dark energy coming out of that little person, which you know she is projecting on you. I will never forget the relief on my daughter's face when my boyfriend said, "Yes, sometimes I feel like eating mud," and she burst out laughing and said, "Thank God for that. Somebody else feels like that around here." When I approach someone's chart, those are the questions I am ask myself – not so much, "Oh, this person had a very detached, difficult mother," but rather, "this person is likely to have experienced their mother in a very cool, detached way. How did their mother respond to that?"

Projection

Juliet: Indeed, it is certainly important to remember that, when you see an aspect which describes a parent – let's say, for example, Moon opposition Uranus – it describes the client's experience of mother, which does not mean that the mother is necessarily like that. But it is the way that the client is likely to perceive her. Our earliest projections of our own qualities are always on our parents. The parents may have just enough of those qualities to be good hooks, but our interpretation of them comes from within us.

I have noticed a tendency in some astrologers to look at an aspect like Moon-Uranus and say, "Your mother was unpredictable and aloof," or, "She was ambivalent about having children." That gives mother all the responsibility for being unpredictable and ambivalent. It might be more helpful to say, "You may have difficulty in owning both your free spirit and your need for security, so you may own one half and project the other. This may manifest in you seeing your mother as being cold or aloof, and yourself as loving and wanting closeness. Or you may experience your mother as being clingy when you want her to let you be free." Whatever the scenario, you do have to let the client know that the aspect belongs to him or her and, as such, needs to be appropriately owned. It is quite common for one part of a chart to be acceptable to a person, while conflicting factors are not acceptable and therefore get projected.

As an example of this, I had a client with Moon in Libra opposite Mars in Aries. When we began to talk about her family background, she said, "My mother never gave me any space to be myself. It was as if I didn't exist. She was always pushing her own emotions at me, and never listened to anything I said." She was very angry when she said this. As the session went on, this client did exactly the same thing to me. She kept talking and pushing her emotions at me, and whenever I tried to say something or give an interpretation she would interrupt and contradict and just go on talking. I started feeling just like what she said she felt like when she was a child. She was not owning the Mars side of her.

Audience: So you are saying that, in order to help the client make the best out of their chart, you have to help them own it, in this case both the Moon in Libra and Mars in Aries?

Juliet: I think so. You see, you can only change something if it is yours to change. You can only make the best out of something if it is yours to make the best out of, and if you don't realise it is yours then you can do nothing with it. After all, you can't change anyone else, only yourself.

One way of helping a client to own the two or more planets involved in a difficult aspect is to encourage him or her to imagine the planet – say, Uranus – locked in a room forever with the other planet – say, the Moon – and to imagine what the two of them would have to do in order to get along. Ask the client to imagine the dialogue between these gods, describing the airy, visionary Uranus confronting the ever-changing Moon moving from a sliver of light to bright and full and back to dark again. Then see if he or she can identify it as an inner dialogue. Try to encourage the client to visualise the conversation. You could say something like, "You have got opposing energies connected within you for life, and it is up to you to make the best of them or the worst of them. You need to acknowledge that you are both security-loving and freedom-loving at the same time. That may feel uneasy at times, but both sides are part of you."

Audience: I guess most charts will have areas of conflict, and most people want to avoid conflict, don't they?

Juliet: It is true that we seek to avoid anything that hurts. According to Freud, that is how the psyche is programmed. He postulated that the unconscious thrust of the psyche, the *id*, is basically pleasure-orientated – that is, it moves toward and seeks out that which is comfortable, easy, sensuous, and enjoyable, and it seeks to avoid pain and discomfort. So if we follow this line we can say that we wish to avoid anything difficult. We now encounter a Moon-Uranus aspect – two planets made of very different stuff – which presents a conflict, and conflict is difficult. One way of coping with conflict is to ignore it. It is often easier to ignore or project one planet and own the other, the one that we feel more at home with for whatever reason. This could translate into, "I am a free spirit, I hate to be tied down, but my mother was so clingy and possessive." Or, "I am a home-loving body and was perfectly happy to stay put, but my mother was always moving and travelling."

The trouble is that when you project something, it can end up with throwing the baby out with the bath water. Everything goes out – not just the bad qualities, the bits that you don't want, but all the good bits as well. So alongside the disagreeable stuff, a lot of valuable stuff goes as well.

Audience: Would you say that, in general, personal planets are more easily owned than the outer planets? What I mean to say is, how do you know what will be projected and what the client will own?

Juliet: You won't know until you have talked to them. I don't think it is possible to say definitely how any chart will work for a person until you have discussed it with them. We can make educated guesses, one of which is that generally personal planets are more easily owned than the outer ones. Another good guess is that in a woman's chart the Moon and Venus are more likely to be owned, while the Sun and Mars may be projected, and *vice versa* in a man's chart – certainly, that is, until around mid-life, when there is often a change around. And another good guess is that if there is only one planet in a particular element, it may be hard to own and express. But they are guesses.

Audience: So you can't be sure beforehand what a client will project?

Juliet: It is very difficult to look at a chart and work out what they will habitually project. Once the person is there, you can begin to see whether they are able to own something or whether it is always "mother's fault" or " father's fault" or "the family's fault" or "the teacher's fault" or "the government's fault" or "the boss's fault". You might hear about a whole line of people who have treated the client badly, and you start smelling a rat and wondering what part the client might be playing in this setup. By the same token, if someone comes along and says, "Everything is awful and it is all my fault," I might say, "Oh, really? It's interesting that you are that powerful."

Audience: I had a client who blamed herself for her terrible childhood. Both her parents drank heavily – they were both alcoholics. My client had Neptune in Virgo opposition Sun and Moon in Pisces, and her family life was pretty dire. She always believed it was her responsibility, that she was not only responsible for being part of that family but was also responsible for making it so bad.

Juliet: That is a common pattern of children of dysfunctional parents. Children who have got parents who are in some way inadequate often feel that they have to first look after the parent before the parent can be in good enough shape to look after them. When that fails, they blame themselves. Of course, in an ideal family setup, parents "ought" to be healthy enough in mind and body to be able to look after their offspring physically and emotionally. But if the parent is dysfunctional, it doesn't matter what the child does. He or she will not be able to make mother or father better. That is one of the other things that you have to allow for when you are doing charts: you won't be able to fix people, often because the past is unfixable.

Coping with the client's pain

Audience: So what do you do with an unfixable past?

Juliet: You ask yourself what can be done with the unfixable pain, and if your answer is, "Nothing," it can at least be acknowledged and allowed. It can be allowed to remain unfixed, and mourned and acknowledged. It is like being with somebody who is ill – it is quite difficult just to *be* there, isn't it? We often seek out something we can *do* - a cold flannel or a hot flannel or a hot water bottle or a pill or a potion. We ask, "Is there anything I can *do* to make you feel better?" What we really mean is, "It is really horrible for *me* to sit here watching *you* so ill." Sometimes all the patient wants is for somebody to be able to bear to sit with them while they feel terrible, not try to change them, nor try to do anything except possibly acknowledge their pain, accept it, and bear it with them. Sometimes that is our role in an astrological reading – to listen to a client's pain without trying to change anything, particularly that which can't be changed.

Audience: I think that's true. After all, being a human being involves accepting pain, doesn't it?

Juliet: The wounded healer, Chiron, is a useful image for this experience, because he is half-animal, half-god, and he is wounded in his animal part. The pain can't be healed, it can't be taken away, and it can't be made better – it is ongoing. Through the pain, or because of the pain, if you like, a great deal happens – in his attempt to cure his own wound, Chiron found cures for many others. He also gained insights, understanding and compassion, all of which he used in the healing of other people. But Chiron's own pain could not be healed, and he simply had to bear it. We all have pain that we have to bear. We all have disappointments and sorrows, some great, some small. Reading a chart may involve trying to make some of the client's grief at least bearable, if not fixable, because the grief is named and acknowledged.

Another reason that Chiron is a good image to describe humanity in general is that he is not clear – he is neither one thing nor another. In other words, he is a messy image. He is not mortal and he is not divine – he is both and neither. One of the things that we find most difficult to cope with in ourselves is the fact that our insides are messy and ambivalent. We are full of conflicts – our emotions and logic do not agree very often. We are sometimes divinely inspired and sometimes we behave like animals. We can think one thing and feel another, and we can even feel different ways about the same person or thing! It is very confusing. How can we have nice tidy insides if there are so many opposites and conflicting forces within?

Myths and fairy tales often describe this messy and ambivalent mixture. Myths give us images of semi-divine creatures, many of whom are highly ambivalent. Fairy tales, many of which appeal to children, present opposites in the more digestible form of the good princess and the bad princess, the nice sister and the nasty sister, the bad stepmother and the good real mother, and they are very clearly defined. There is a sense of clarity and safety in knowing who is good and who isn't, yet the child, on an unconscious level, is dimly aware that the good mother and the wicked step-mother are the two sides of one person, and that we are, in fact, both Cinderella and the ugly sisters all rolled into one. We have to come to accept that ambivalence in ourselves, which is represented by all the various conflicts in the chart, and that is quite difficult. We prefer to split it and project one part out onto someone else! However, if we can tolerate our own ambivalence it makes it possible for us to tolerate other people's. We become less irate and righteous, and more compassionate.

When we look at a chart we could describe it to our client using the image of a stage with a cast of actors and a set of roles or characters the actors will be playing. They are all vital to the success of the play and have all got to be paid full attention to. You can't honour one actor over all the others – otherwise the rest of the actors in this particular play are going to be unhappy, and they might creep out and disrupt the audience and ruin the performance. Inequality leads to resentment. This is what often goes on in our own psyches, and the planets, signs, aspects and houses reveal the plot and characters. If we give our Sun-Venus the best roles and stick Pluto in the chorus, sooner or later there will be trouble!

Audience: I like the use of the word "honour". It has a connotation of respectfulness

Juliet: It is important, I believe, to give all aspects of ourselves dignity, and to try to help our clients do the same for themselves.

Working with couples

Working with couples is quite different from working one to one, and there are some points which I would now like to mention with regard to communicating the information in the charts. As a great many people consult the astrologer about their relationships, we will all get clients who want to ask about their own chart in relation to somebody else's. I prefer to do a synastry or chart comparison with both parties present because, in my experience, when one half of a couple brings the partner's chart or asks that it be set up, it is, more often than not, a means of finding out something which will in some way give them power over their partner. Of course, there are situations where the partner just refuses to consult an astrologer, or doesn't want to do any real work on the relationship, and the person who has come is left having to do all the work themselves. But a good deal of the time, there are power issues involved, and the person wants ammunition in order to blame the partner for whatever is going wrong. It can be important to recognise when this is happening.

If a person brings the partner's chart without the partner, and I feel it is appropriate to discuss the relationship without the partner being present, I will mainly try to work with that individual's chart, to see where they may be projecting their own stuff onto their partner. Very often the problem issues that arise in relationships are fairly classic examples of element-type projection. For example, a fiery man is in a relationship with an earthy woman. He complains that she is not spontaneous and fun. He says, "All she thinks about is whether the electricity bill has been paid." She complains that he is impractical and that what he calls spontaneity makes it impossible to have an orderly life. She says, "Things don't just happen, you have to plan them." Both partners have a point, and neither one is right or wrong, good or bad. It is like comparing an apple and an orange. How can you say an apple is better than an orange? They are both fruit and they both have their vitamin content. They are both healthy, and they are quite different – no better and no worse, but just different.

That is how I work with this kind of situation. If both people are present, I try to show the couple that, first of all, the thing they most like and are most attracted to in each other is also the same thing that is driving them crazy. The fiery man likes the practicality of the earthy woman, but he will complain of her being boring and lacking in spontaneity. The earthy woman likes the excitement and risk-taking of the fiery man, but hates being expected to change at a moment's notice. The same sort of polarising happens with air and water. If only one half the couple is present, I try to emphasise that person's attitudes and responses to the situation, but with the same goal in mind.

Very often, presenting the astrological information in this very basic way helps both people to begin to look at the relationship as a meeting of two different but equally worthwhile people. Then talking about particularly difficult synastry aspects, like one person's Saturn opposite the other one's Moon, is less threatening, because initially there is a validation of the separate identities of both people. That makes it clear that I am not on either person's side. This is very important in working with couples. Also, it is important to mention the "good" contacts between the two charts – even if there are very few of them! – as a balance every time you talk about something difficult. I try to give both parties space to say their bits, and try to keep the time I spend on each one equal. It can also be important to speak first to one partner individually, calling them by name, and then turn to the other, calling them by name as well, and describing how that same astrological situation looks from *their* point of view. This can sometimes feel a little clumsy, but it is worth the effort because both people feel noticed and heard.

There is often a tendency with couples for one person to try to do all the talking. He or she is usually the one who pushed to have the chart reading, and is also the one who has the most questions about the relationship – and the most comments about why their partner is doing everything wrong! It is very common, and maybe even inevitable, for both people to try to "win" the astrologer to their point of view, although they might do it in very different ways. If a relationship is in trouble, it is natural for both parties to want backup for their feelings of being hurt or angry. So, of course, each one will try to get you to feel very sorry for their plight, and very annoyed at the partner who has done this to them. The astrologer needs to make sure that he or she is able to take the middle ground and not get manipulated into making judgments or taking sides. The same thing applies when one person arrives with their partner's chart. They may work very hard to get you to feel sympathy for them, and they want you to make negative statements about the partner who is making them unhappy.

Audience: I also feel it is important to be neutral, but sometimes the client gets very angry about it! I did a chart for a woman who brought in her husband's chart and asked me to look at it. She felt he was making her very miserable. I stayed mainly with her chart and tried to stress her contribution to the trouble, and although I mentioned basic astrological interpretations of things in his chart, none of them were negative statements – just general things like, "He has the Sun in Taurus and security is important to him." I also said, "I am sure he may be projecting things onto you, too, but as he is not here to discuss this with me, I cannot be sure what those might be." My client got very angry, and then she said, "You're saying it's all my fault. I don't want to hear any more of this." She could not understand neutrality. To her it was either one person's fault or the other's.

Juliet: Sadly, sometimes this happens. Not everyone can accept the idea that they might be seeing things in a distorted way because they are projecting, or that they might be helping to make things difficult. You might have to say something like, "Your husband is probably also contributing something to this trouble, and I am sure he has issues he needs to look at. But right now it is important for us to discuss ways in which you can help yourself and understand your own feelings." It is important not to be seduced into siding with the client. This is what I meant when I said that sometimes people want information to get power over their partner, or to be able to quote the astrologer as an authority when accusing the partner of being a terrible person.

Sometimes when a couple come for a synastry, one partner will sit very silent and a bit sullen, because he or she was steam-rolled into coming by the other partner and isn't really open to hearing what the astrologer might say. One of the means by which one partner often manipulates the other is by hinting, before and even during the session, that the astrologer already knows all about the situation and is on their "side". This can understandably create sullenness and defensiveness in the other person. It is important to ask each partner individually what they hope to get from the synastry reading, which means that the silent, sullen one has to say something, even if it is "I'm only here because he/she insisted that I come."

You can often get through this kind of hostility by letting this person know that you are neutral and not about to pass judgment. You might say something like, "I am sorry you have been pushed into coming – it is really much more helpful if both people want to understand something about the relationship. A chart comparison is never about whose fault it is, but it can reveal a lot about where two people misunderstand each other. If it will make you feel more comfortable, I would be happy to set up separate sessions and do both your charts individually." This usually does the trick of communicating to the person that you are not secretly in alliance with the other partner, and that you are genuinely concerned for both people.

Difficult aspects like Saturn in one chart making a square or opposition to Mars or Pluto in the other chart are never easy to talk about with a couple, because they often have different levels of awareness. The language you use is really critical, and it should never communicate blame to either partner, or imply some kind of horrible pathology. Bruno Bettelheim said in his last television interview that, in order to understand the destructive behaviour of a very disturbed child, you had to understand how much terror that child felt inside, and if you understood that, you would realise that the child was acting from that place of terror. Most of the time, people do not mean to be destructive to each other. Something inside is driving them. No relationship problem is ever solely and entirely the fault of one person, and if you really understand this then it is not so difficult to remain at the centre and try to help each person understand a little more about how the other one is feeling.

Let's say that you see something like the man's Saturn opposite the woman's Sun, and she is insisting that he always restricts her or criticises her. You might first ask both people to limit their comments to a description of what they feel, rather than what they think the other person is doing to them. This subtle difference can have a powerful effect on how they think and talk about what is happening between them, and opens the possibility that neither person is acting from malice or nastiness, but from some other motive which is misunderstood, such as insecurity. The astrologer can then act as the mouthpiece for each planet, describing its needs and way of expression.

Audience: But what if you really feel it is one person's fault? There are relationships where, for example, the man goes out and gets drunk and comes back and beats up his wife. You can't say she is as much to blame for that as he is.

Juliet: Although we cannot condone violence, I don't think that either person is "to blame". The reasons why people behave compulsively like that are usually very complicated, and generally speaking, the family background of both people is involved, as well as pressures like money or the demands of children which bring both people to breaking point. And it is the woman's choice to stay in the relationship. When patterns of persecution and victimisation happen in a relationship, there is something in both people which has drawn them into that situation and makes them choose to stay there.

We can never know the full story of any couple in a session of an hour and a half, and unless you have Charles Manson sitting there, it is safe to assume that neither person actively and consciously wants to be destructive and harmful. They are driven into behaving destructively by something inside, and that is what the astrologer can help them to find out. I always prefer to err on the side of caution, and I would try to understand why a particular man might behave violently, rather than just thinking, "Oh, all violent men are the same, and she ought to leave him immediately, poor thing." Also, I would try to understand what factors in a woman might have attracted her to this kind of man, and whether she is doing anything unconsciously to stir up his angry feelings. That isn't blaming anybody.

Clients will often come with questions about whether they should get involved in a certain relationship, or whether their relationship is about to end, or whether they should leave their partner. They may do this individually, but sometimes couples want to know these kinds of answers as well in a synastry reading. Naturally, the astrologer cannot answer such questions, because no chart comparison can tell us what someone should do or what will happen. It is our job to help both people understand the kind of energy that is at work in the relationship, and what it is bringing out of both of them, and what each of them needs from the other. Then they can make their own decisions. Sometimes, no matter how carefully we phrase things, a couple who are really into a dog-fight will go away interpreting what the astrologer has said entirely differently, and they will use the reading to justify breaking up. There isn't anything we can do about this when it happens, other than to ensure that there is a tape of the session and that we have been careful, clear, and neutral in what we have said.

Questions about death

Another area which clients often want to discuss is death. This can be distressing for the astrologer as well as the client. I'll give you an example. A woman phoned up for a chart reading. She said on the phone that she was familiar with astrology, but the reason she wanted a chart done by a professional astrologer was because she had "recently lost a baby". Those were her words on the phone.

I prepared her chart and looked at the transits and progressions. When she turned up, she brought with her a chart of her son, who had died at two months from a cot death. I was completely thrown, because from the way she had described the "loss of a baby" on the phone, I had understood that it was a miscarriage, and I was unprepared for the fact that it was a two-month-old boy that had died. It turned out that she did not want a reading for herself, but she wanted me to look at the baby's chart and tell her why he had died.

This was a really difficult session. I looked at the child's chart, but I realised that no matter what clever stuff I could come up with in terms of transits and progressions, it would not help this woman. She wanted to know why, and neither I nor anyone else could tell her. It transpired that she had not really allowed herself to grieve. She didn't cry, nor did she talk about her feelings – her way of trying to deal with it was intellectually, and she thought that if I could give her a "reason" it would make her feel better. However, I felt it was somehow wrong to be looking at the chart of the little dead baby and trying to find out something from his planetary placements that would justify his death. So instead we talked about how difficult – impossible, even – it is to bear the dreadful pain of the death of a child.

There are times when it can be helpful to talk with a client about a particular transit or birth chart placement in the client's chart in relation to a loved person's death. This is not to find a justification for the death, but to communicate some sense of what the death might mean to the person who has been left behind. But I think, to do this well, we need to make sure we are not colluding with the client's attempts to avoid grief. When questions about death come up and the client wants to know why, we should never be ashamed of saying, "I don't know."

There is, of course, a lot of discussion among astrologers about which transits and progressions point to death. People may say, "When am I am going to die?" My answer is, "I haven't the foggiest!" I personally don't believe we should ever try to predict death. It is interesting with hindsight to see the aspects around at the time of a death, and probably many of you have looked at the chart of a parent or friend or client who has died to see what you could find. I have done this as well. But I personally stop short at trying to predict or "guess" when a death is likely to occur. For one thing, I can't see the point. And for another, if you are wrong, you may have upset a person unnecessarily.

I heard the story of a woman who was told by a "seer" of some sort that she would die in her thirtieth year. She refused to marry or have children, so as to avoid the pain it might cause, and she lived through her thirtieth year in trepidation. At the end of the year she was still alive, and only then did she decide to marry and "get a life". As far as I know, she is still alive. She could equally have made the prophecy a self-fulfilling one. Another woman I knew of had been told she would die around a certain time, and she went into hospital for a routine operation. The operation was successful, but for no real reason she started to bleed, and never regained consciousness. Now, we can speculate that either the "seer" was right, or the woman decided she was going to die and did. Who knows? But I certainly would not want to have on my conscience the notion that I might have encouraged someone to give up on life.

The Greeks had many myths about mortals who, after consulting an oracle which gives warning of death, do their best to avoid the oracle and change their fate. Oedipus' father was told his son would kill him, so he tried to kill Oedipus, failed, and Oedipus ending up killing him inadvertently. Perseus' grandfather was told his grandson would kill him, so tried to kill both his daughter and grandson. In the end, when he was a very old man, having presumably lived a sorry life empty of the joy of a family, grown-up Perseus, at an Olympic games, threw a discus which accidentally hit and killed an old man – his grandfather!

"You can run but you can't hide!" seems to be the message. So why run? We spend so much time trying to avoid death that in doing so we overlook life. When we get clients who want to know about their death, maybe it is a useful thing to try to get them to look at life, which as astrologers we can do, even if it involves pain and disappointment. That is better than trying to predict or explain death, which as astrologers we can't do.

The severely disturbed client

Sometimes the astrologer has to cope with a severely disturbed client. We may also get clients who have drinking or drugs problems. I once had a client who turned up drunk, and so I sent him away. I once had a client who asked if he could light a joint in the session. I said,

"No!" I make a point of never working with anyone under the influence of drugs or alcohol. If the client wants to have the reading, he or she needs to turn up sober, and then we can discuss the drink or drug problem. But when someone is tight or high they are not going to be in any position to take in what you are saying, and even if you record the session, it can be distressing for the astrologer because the emotional contact and communication with the client are so disturbed.

An elderly woman once came along to see me at the recommendation of her parish priest. I never found out how this recommendation came about, or how this priest had heard of me. This woman seemed all right, a bit odd, perhaps, but all right, until I mentioned that her Sun in Leo was "royal". I can't remember the exact words I used, but the minute I mentioned "royal", she slipped into a long and involved story about how she was really the Queen, or rather, how she should have been Queen but was cheated out of her birthright by wicked ministers. She was very knowledgeable about the royal family, mentioning names and dates in a very convincing way. She spoke very good upper class English, too, with all the affectations of the aristocracy! In spite of myself I was finding myself almost believing that she had been cheated out of her rightful place.

This is a very difficult one, because really mad people can get under your antennae and you can find yourself getting caught up in the madness. This is because, in a person who is in a psychotic state, the unconscious has swamped the ego, and this can also trigger the unconscious of the therapist or astrologer. Luckily I did not jump right in with her, but obviously the chart reading was mostly impossible, because once she got going on her hobbyhorse it was difficult to get a word in edgewise. Before I mentioned the word "royal" she had been quite subdued, very meek and mild. When she left she promised to invite me to Windsor as soon as the situation was resolved. I haven't had my invite yet!

We often get clients in severely disturbed states. Sometimes this is because they are afraid of going to see a psychiatrist, and feel that somehow an astrologer is likely to be more sympathetic – perhaps because they imagine we are a little mad as well! Also, psychiatric labels can be very rigid and imprisoning, and an astrological chart can offer a different perspective. But I do believe this kind of situation needs to be handled very sensitively. There is usually a lot of fear in someone who is in a near-breakdown state, and you need to be able to contain the client's fear and not react with fear of your own.

Audience: Would you tell someone you thought they were mad? Or that they were going into a breakdown?

Juliet: I would not say to someone, "I think you are mad." After all, what does the word really mean? With respect to the elderly lady who should have been Queen, I didn't say to her, "You are quite mad, of course you aren't meant to be Queen." What would have been the point? She would have become very defensive and upset and would have left, and there wouldn't have been any chance to communicate any further. As it was, there wasn't much chance anyway, but sometimes there is, if you show some willingness to accept the client's state of mind without passing judgment on the truth of what they are saying. Statements of that kind are usually symbolic, anyway, and on that level they are true, and need to be listened to.

I had an elderly client who had been in the concentration camps. She and her husband had survived and afterward had a family, but she had never really got over the experience. I wonder if anyone really can. Anyway, she had suddenly developed a terrible pain in her right leg. She had gone to the doctor and he hadn't found anything at all wrong with her – she was very healthy for her age. But the pain wouldn't go away. She had no knowledge of astrology before she came to see me. She said, "I know what this pain is. The doctors are stupid and don't know what they are doing. I was shopping at Sainsbury's, and a black scorpion crawled up my leg and bit me. The poison is still in my body. Thank God it didn't reach my heart, or I would have died." I didn't say, "You silly woman, you are quite mad, there are no scorpions in England, and certainly not at Sainsbury's!" In fact she was telling the truth, except that it was a symbolic truth. The scorpion was not a real scorpion, but was her image of the dark forces which nearly destroyed her earlier in her life, and the poison was, indeed, still in her body. It hadn't reached her heart, which I believe meant she had not lost her ability to love.

Sometimes a client will tell you on the phone when they make the appointment that they are at breaking point, or that they have just been in psychiatric hospital. Here I think it is important for the astrologer to feel safe and confident in dealing with severely disturbed states. If you feel you cannot handle a client in this kind of state, it might be better to suggest that the client sees a therapist, or an astrologer with therapeutic training. You will not help the client if you are frightened and unable to discuss things which you feel are too irrational.

But if you have some therapeutic training, and feel you can cope, it can be very helpful to a frightened and disturbed person to have a perspective which is not strictly clinical. This is especially true if the client is also willing to work with a therapist. I have had clients like this get in touch after many years, who told me that they were very grateful because they felt contained and could talk without worrying about being given a diagnosis. One client said she had remembered certain things I had said about the chart and had held on to these statements like a sort of "magic talisman" during the really bad times.

Personal relationships with clients

It is a very knotty issue when you have a client you fancy, or one who fancies you. If you meet them for the first time in the astrologer-client role, it is worth remembering that a fair amount of projection will be going on. The client may be seeing you as the perfect person, the one who "knows" and "understands", and you may well get all sorts of wonderful things projected on you which won't last long if you pursue the relationship outside the session. Also, you may project a lot of wonderful things on the client, especially if you are going through a lonely time in your life, and playing the role of the astrological counsellor might feel especially good because you feel needed and are "the one who really understands". Do you remember the Rolling Stones song about the fortune-teller? It ends with the lines,

"Now I'm married to the fortune-teller,
And I get my fortune told for free!"

After all, there are going to be power issues on both sides involved in this sort of attraction, and even if your Venus is conjunct his Mars that does not necessarily mean it is a match destined in the stars! Of course, the astrologer-client relationship is not the same as the therapist-client relationship, in the sense that the astrologer sees the person once or maybe twice. The deep dependency and regressive or childlike feelings which develop in psychotherapy do not occur in an astrological session. So in theory there is no reason why, if there is a genuine mutual attraction between astrologer and client, there should not be the possibility of a relationship. But there are usually powerful projections even in only one session, and this creates an inequality and imbalance of power.

There is a lot of concern around at the moment about the abuse of professional power – some therapists, doctors, and priests have all been caught "with their pants down", abusing their position of power and trust with vulnerable clients. When we read about these cases, we feel angry because there is so much of the parent-child archetype involved in this kind of relationship, and it is a little like child abuse. Even though we don't have the same kind of relationship with our clients as an analyst does, we still have a lot of power because the client sees us as knowing so much more. And this can be abused. Often people come for chart readings when they are going through a very vulnerable and confusing time, and this brings out a childlike desire to find someone who "knows" and can guide them.

I don't think there is any hard and fast rule about astrologers making personal relationships with their clients, as there is (or is supposed to be) with therapists and their clients. But it is a good idea to remember the issue of power, and to ask yourself, "Am I attracted to this client because he/she needs me and thinks I am wonderful? Am I in love with the good feelings created by the client's fantasy of me?" If the answer to either of these questions is "Yes", then maybe it is not a good idea to pursue a relationship with the client until some time has passed and there is a chance to meet the client socially on equal ground. Also, you could ask yourself, "Is the client attracted to me because of me, or because he/she sees the chance to get a free ongoing supply of wisdom and answers?" If the answer to that one is yes, then you may be setting yourself up for a lot of hurt later, because after a while you will start feeling used.

I have heard several stories about astrologers abusing their position with clients, who looked up to them as a combination of parent and source of wisdom. Instead of thinking, "I must never get involved with my clients", or thinking the opposite – "I am free to do what I like because I am not a therapist" – we should ask ourselves what the basis is for the attraction to that individual client. As usual, it is better to err on the side of caution. I also know of some very good relationships which have begun with a chart reading. So it can sometimes work.

Splitting

Audience: Can I go back to what you said earlier about fairy tales and learning to accept ambivalence? I believe that children need to have firm definitions of right and wrong in order to make sense of the world. That was always the function of religion. But that makes me think that it is not possible to avoid the problem of integrating the more difficult things in the chart. You have to give your children the opportunity to ground themselves in some kind of structure so they can feel safe. But that means they can't live all the aspects of themselves. It is impossible for that to happen during childhood.

Juliet: Well, it can during childhood. It is true that very small children need, first of all, to have clarity. After all, think of where they are coming from – a place of complete chaos, a place where everything is experienced through feeling. Then they have to work out concepts and cause-and-effect. It is such a complicated process of transition that, to start off with and in order to make some sort of sense of things, they have to be allowed to split good from bad. Then, gradually, the splitting starts to come together. That begins in childhood. They begin to learn that the mother who is sweet and good and kind is the same person who denies them what they want and is therefore nasty and bad and cruel. Very often they will say, "My mother's an alien," or "When she's nasty she's a witch."

Helping a child to understand where the line is drawn doesn't mean you have to tell the child that things inside him or her are bad. No planet or aspect or sign in the chart is "bad" in itself. What is important is how it is used. For example, if your child has a very strong Mars, lots of Aries and so on, it is important to teach the child that they live in a world with other people and can't always have their own way. But you don't do that by telling the child, "You are selfish and bad."

Children are surprisingly realistic, maybe more than many adults, and if the reality is made clear to them, then they can adapt. If you constantly tell a Mars child they are selfish, then the child may grow up split off from Mars, and then Mars will get projected and it will come back into the child's life anyway, but sometimes in a destructive way. Instead, you might say something like, "I know you want to watch television all the time, and you don't like it when other people have programmes they want to watch, but the rules in this family are that everyone gets their turn. That is fair, because everyone in this family is important. When you grow up and can buy your own television set, then you can do what you like with it!"

Audience: I've noticed what you are calling "splitting" in my own child. She hasn't actually decided for herself what things are, so one minute something is good and then the next minute it is bad. It is as if she is in confusion about it. I have wondered whether a parent's job is to help the split and say, "That's bad," and "That's good." Then she would feel secure and safe and comfortable. But I see what you mean about distinguishing between character and behaviour.

Audience: Wasn't that always the function of fairy tales? To show good and bad as part of one thing?

Juliet: Yes, that was the function of fairy tales, although I am not sure they were created with a "function" so much as arising spontaneously and containing deep truths about life.

Audience: I don't think it is such a good thing for modern children's stories to have only good characters and endings. There isn't any ambivalence, and people are always ambivalent.

Juliet: Well, you see, parents got in and psychologised life in a very black-and-white way. They said, "This is all terrible, all these stories are very destructive, children shouldn't be allowed to think this way." In fact it is very useful and necessary for children to be allowed a safe vehicle for their violent feelings. They have got violent feelings whether we like it or not, and if they are completely sanitised and all cleaned up and made beautiful, then they have to push those feelings underground. Then they feel very ashamed of them, and think to themselves, "There is something wrong with me because I have got these feelings." A lot of these intense, violent feelings are connected with Pluto, so you can see why sometimes many adults find it so hard to work with their Pluto.

Take politically correct nursery rhymes, for example. Children aren't nearly as worried about political correctness as adults are. In fact it is likely that they find it completely unnatural. It is when adults project onto children, which of course they do like mad, that you see all this cleaning up and romanticising. In a sense, these adults are projecting their own splits on children and wanting to create ideal children who are free of the kind of ambivalence the adults themselves feel and can't cope with. Children see things in a very different way. So I wouldn't worry about whether you should do anything for your daughter or not. I think she will go back and forth and feel confused until she doesn't need to do it any more. That is part of the process of integrating.

Of course, a person may stay split, and that's where a defence mechanism which is healthy in very early childhood becomes counterproductive in adulthood. Ideally you should use a defence mechanism appropriately, and when you are little, certain things are genuinely very dangerous. All grownups are potentially huge sources of danger. If you think about it, a little child is completely dependent on the grownups who are in charge of them, and any of these adults might at any moment do away with them. Think about how small and vulnerable they feel, and how easy it would be for an adult to annihilate them – snap! just like that. That's what children feel. That's their reality. And it can be a healthy defence, because if a child senses something not quite trustworthy about a particular adult, then the child will run away or go very quiet and not share important secrets. But a lot of people don't get through that very black-and-white fear which is meant to protect helplessness, and then they grow up still believing that the world, the boss, the partner, are all capable of wiping them out in the way they felt that their parents might if they displeased them.

To a parent, this fear and suspicion on the part of their child is a terrible thing, and a blow to the parent's image of being a good parent. How could my child possibly think that I might abandon him/her on a railway station, that I would actually go away and leave him/her? But that isn't how a child perceives things. How many times, when you were little, did you get left behind, and you thought that your parents had gone forever and left you? Maybe you said something to them about this fear, and your parents said, "How could you possibly think I would do something like that? Of course I wouldn't leave you in a hotel room on your own!" Sometimes they do, but most of the time parents don't. Of course it happens, but generally speaking, most parents don't deliberately set out to abandon their children. To a child it is possible that, when their mother turns up five minutes late to pick them up from school, the mother is not going to come at all, or that when the mother leaves them alone in a shop for a minute or two, she has gone home and abandoned them.

Audience: But aren't children very adaptable and able to recognise the changing needs of a situation? Also, regularity of care on the part of the parent could help a child learn to trust more, so there would be a more realistic response to the actual situation.

Juliet: Adaptability of defences is something which is very much present in the small child. But if this adaptability doesn't get reinforced in childhood through gradual integration of good and bad, and you never learn how to change your defences to suit the environment, what will happen is that you will end up as an adult with the defences of a five-year-old when it is not actually necessary. Everybody needs defences, but you should have appropriate defences depending on where you are. If you are in the city you might need burglar alarms, but if you are in the country you might need bear traps or wolf pits if you are in that sort of environment. You have got to think of the kind of environment that you are in, and the kinds of defences that you will need, and how they will have to change. As you get older things change, but if your personality is very entrenched in being terrified because you think that anybody in power is going to kill you, then you can become very rigid and frightened of life.

This is one of the theories of a woman called Dorothy Bloch. She wrote a wonderful book called *So the Witch Won't Eat Me*,[2] which is all about children's fear of infanticide, of being killed by their parents. She discovered that this was a very common, worldwide fantasy, although often very unconscious. She likens it to Freud's Oedipal complex. Freud got hold of the idea that Oedipus killed his father and married his mother. But the reason that he got into that position in the first place was that his parents had had an oracle that the son would grow up and kill the father and marry the mother. So they tried to kill him first, by abandoning him on a mountain. Freud conveniently eliminated that preliminary episode from his theory. Block reckons that, because he didn't have his own analysis, he couldn't face his own very primitive fears of potentially being wiped out by his parents. She is saying that the fear of being annihilated is something which is very much present in the small child. If somebody treats you badly, you will be annihilated. If somebody gets angry with you, they will kill you. That is the bottom line.

You see, that's where you've got to try to work out where the client is in terms of splitting and projection. Are the client's defences those of a five-year-old? Or can they accept their ambivalence and adapt to situations as required? In other words, one of the things that you're trying to find out while you are doing the chart is how conscious or unconscious the client is, and what are they able to acknowledge in their own birth chart. And you try to pitch your interpretations

---

[2]Dorothy Bloch, *So the Witch Won't Eat Me: Fantasy and the Child's Fear of Infanticide*, Grove Press, New York, 1984.

according to that. The more of the chart the person owns and is conscious of, the more resources they have to adapt to life. The more a person splits, the more rigid they become in their reactions.

The age of the client

Audience: I think you also have to take into account the age of the person, and whether the outer planets are strong in the birth chart. I think it is easier to work with the outer planets when you are older.

Juliet: Age is certainly another thing that one obviously has to take into account. When you are working with younger people, you have got to have a lighter touch and a lighter tongue than when you have got somebody who is a bit older and who has got more resilience and, hopefully, more awareness.

Audience: I think that's very true. Pre-Saturn return people aren't so well connected to the outer planets, unless there are a lot of personal planets making connections to the outer planets. I find that it is sometimes very hard for a younger person to think of themselves as being depressed, or as having a problem from childhood. The personality hasn't developed enough structure to be able to hold the sense of responsibility that goes along with that sort of knowledge.

Audience: That is a pretty sweeping statement. Surely it varies from one person to another, and also it depends on whether the parents have encouraged the person in childhood to be aware and honest. If the parents keep telling a child with a strong Pluto, for example, "You are bad because you have these strong feelings," then the child might grow up repressing Pluto, but if the parents accept the child's Pluto, then even before the Saturn return, surely it is easier for the person to recognise Pluto feelings.

Juliet: The outer planets have to do with unconscious collective attitudes and feelings, and I think you are right that the early environment affects how we handle these. If the parents are very conventional and structured, then the child may grow up feeling that any unconventional Uranian ideas and strong Neptunian and Plutonian emotions are "bad", and this means the outer planets will not be very well connected to the conscious personality. Some children have strong mystical or transpersonal experiences when they are quite young – for example, I know of someone whose three-year-old son announced one day that in his other life he had been his father's father, and he claimed he could remember it clearly. If this kind of pronouncement is ridiculed by the parents, then the child may not trust other Neptunian experiences and will have a hard time with Neptune later.

The individual chart makes a difference, of course, because if an outer planet is strong it will show in the person's life very obviously. But of course we do change as we go through the Saturn return, and we are usually more solid and defined as personalities afterward. So this does make a difference in how we see ourselves, although it does not mean that a person is not able to be introspective or responsible before the Saturn return. It has something to do with a sense of continuity. The passage of time does make us have more of a sense of a past, and many younger people live much more in the present and don't think of childhood in the same way as someone who has been through the Saturn return.

Audience: This is where the astrologer can throw light into a dark place for the client. I learned a very hard lesson a few years ago. It was actually before my Saturn return, so I can relate to what you are saying. I did a reading for a woman with Moon in Sagittarius square Pluto in Virgo. I have a Virgo Ascendant, and her Pluto fell exactly on my Ascendant, with her Moon in square, in the same degrees. I stupidly didn't pay any attention to that, and proceeded to start talking about all the dark things I could think of about Pluto. I talked about power, rage, feelings of revenge...It was as if I had become her judge, or maybe her parent, and I was telling her this Pluto square was a bad thing to have in the chart. These very judgmental feelings kept coming up and I couldn't stop it. I was feeling very angry without understanding why. The anger went on and on and got worse and worse. Finally I said to myself, "You are digging yourself into a hole and hurting this woman.

You must stop." Eventually I said, "Let's stop this. I'm really sorry. I think I'm speaking from my own problem." It was a really hard lesson.

Audience: What happened then?

Audience: She was fine about it. She said, "You were beginning to remind me of my mother."

Juliet: That is the experience of counter-transference. You were unconsciously responding to your client's feeling about herself, and also her expectation that you, like her mother, would judge her and call her "bad". This is why it is so important for us to understand ourselves before we try to work with clients.

Difficulties, dangers, and risks

We will now look at some of the common danger points or difficulties that can crop up in astrological readings.

Premature solutions and the offering of advice

It is tempting to try to "fix" people's difficulties and dilemmas. When a client comes with a burning issue about whether to change jobs or move house, or whether to change partners, we may fall into the trap of trying to help with the decision. We might feel inclined to offer a solution: "Move house, emigrate, leave your home or partner, train in something..." The anxiety and pain in the client may make us feel quite desperate to help.

This is partly the result of the counter-transference response I was talking about earlier – we feel the client's upset as if it were our own upset and we try to alleviate our own stress by solving the client's problem. If the client is having a very difficult transit or progression, this may be reflected in great indecision and anxiety, and the astrologer picks this up and reacts to it. It is why it is a good idea to look at the transits and progressions beforehand, not only in relation to what the client is going through, but also what kinds of feelings might be coming out in the session.

There is another strand here. We are astrologers, and people ask us for help. We may identify ourselves with a "wise person", someone who "knows". The projection the client may put onto us of the "all-knowing and all-problem-solving parent" may be flattering, and we may want to be that special person. However, the bald truth is that we are not. We honestly do not know what a particular person should or should not do in any situation.

Offering solutions, especially prematurely when the client has not come to that solution yet inside, may not only be unhelpful but even downright destructive. The client may be in pain and we may feel compelled to respond to that pain with a well-intentioned desire to ease it with solutions. However, the danger is that we get so caught up in wanting to find an answer that we might not listen carefully or fully enough to what the client is saying. They are, after all, finding it difficult to stay with their own dilemma because it feels so uncomfortable – that is perhaps why they came in the first place. We, in turn, pick that desperation up from them and fall into the desire to fix it.

So, although it may not be what the client might urge us to do, we are probably better advised to turn to the client's inner world. What has brought them to the dilemma they are in today? What is their part in it? How does their chart influence their decisions? This is a more useful line to take, rather than getting caught up in the external world of making decisions and offering advice. You cannot help with that – that is the client's own business – but you can help them get to know their inner world better, which will, in turn, help give them more freedom of choice and power to help themselves.

No matter how much pressure a client puts you under to tell them what to do, it seems to me to be a mistake to offer "advice". You can make suggestions, and you can make observations, but to give advice can, at best, be patronising and at worst, destructive.

Audience: Don't I know that one! I had a client who was trying to get me to tell him which job to take, and even though I didn't tell him in so many words, he nevertheless took what I did say and turned it into my having advised him on a particular course. When it turned out badly, he blamed me! It was really unbelievable and I felt it was most unfair, yet it happened!

Audience: It happened to me as well. A woman came to see me who was in a very difficult marriage, and I think the only reason she stayed with her husband was because she was financially dependent on him and wanted to enjoy his money. She asked me to do his chart and compare it with hers. Even though I did set up his chart I was very careful to talk only about her responses to his chart placements, not about his, because he wasn't there to discuss it. I don't think she liked this, and also didn't like the fact that I wouldn't tell her whether to leave her husband or not. Then she wanted to know his financial prospects for the next year. She said he was interested in a financial deal with someone and could I advise whether he should go ahead or not. That really felt like a terrible trap to me, so I said that I could not give such advice, even if he had been there to ask, and that if he made a decision to go ahead, then that was his decision.

It turned out that the husband went ahead with the deal and then lost all his money. This woman started ringing me up, telling me that I had encouraged him to make the deal and that it was my fault that they were now poor. When I explained that I had never given any advice of that kind, and that it was all on the tape recording of the reading, she turned it around and said, "But you could have warned him *not* to make the deal, and you didn't say anything. You should have seen what would happen in his chart." Then she began telling me what a bad astrologer I was because I had not foreseen this disaster. It was horrible. For a long time she kept sending me letters blaming me for her bad situation. When her husband left her she blamed me for that too. Eventually she stopped writing. But I felt as if something very dark and slimy had been thrown at me. And even though I was being so careful about not giving advice, it happened anyway!

Juliet: I am afraid it does sometimes, which is why you have to be so careful and so clear, and why it is a good idea to always tape the session! I know some psychotherapists and astrologers who take out legal insurance just because of such people, because there is a type of person who loves threatening legal action, and even if you are proven right in court it can still cost a lot of money and be very stressful. In an ideal world we shouldn't need things like insurance against lawsuits, but the climate being what it is right now, it isn't a bad idea to think about it. Even when you *are* being absolutely clear, there are people who just have to have somebody to blame, and the astrologer is the obvious candidate. This sounds like a terrible situation, because you did all the right things and still got blamed. Fortunately most clients are pretty decent, and don't behave like that. If you have the feeling that you are being set up like this by a client, it is best not to discuss the partner's chart at all.

Clients will often try to manipulate you into giving advice, and then hate you for it afterwards. They want to get rid of that awful feeling of indecision or confusion inside them, and they think that by passing it to you it will feel better. If you get caught up in that and try to advise them, they will fight you every inch of the way and will probably resent you for it. On the other hand, if you refuse to give advice, they won't like that either. Somewhere in the middle, you, the astrologer, have to acknowledge to them how difficult it is to face such dilemmas and how uncomfortable it is to feel such confusion. Yet if they are prepared to accept that, the confusion can be creative, and if they are able to stay with it, the likelihood is that something will eventually emerge.

As with any kind of gestation period, one can get impatient with the waiting involved in making the right decision, but to try to rush or hurry up the process is liable to end in disaster. We all know the dangers of premature births, and the process is not dissimilar psychically. It is flattering to be seen as wise and wonderful, but it is my belief that it is better to be honest with the client and let them know that, even if they may wish to project "The Great Wise One" onto you, you are not prepared to play the part! It is better to say honestly, "I can't possibly tell you what to do. For one thing, I haven't a clue, and also it would be very wrong of me to even try," That is better than colluding with them by offering all sorts of solutions.

Usually there will be an important transit or progression when someone is in this sort of state of indecision and worry, and we know that big transits can take a long time building up and moving off. Sometimes the best thing is to tell the client something like, "There is an important transit of Pluto over your Sun, and this will be going on for many months more. It might not be a good idea to try to push for a decision too quickly, because things inside you are changing and you may not know clearly what you want to do for quite some time." This lets the client know that their state of indecision is appropriate for the time and that waiting and reflecting would be more productive. Then you can talk about what is happening within the client, to help them with that process of reflection.

Audience: The thing that worries me about not giving people advice is that they'll leave. I have heard people say, "I'll go somewhere where I *will* get some advice," and the advice they subsequently get is a lot worse than I might have been able to offer. Isn't it better to give them a little bit of something, so they don't go off and find something worse?

Juliet: That reminds me of the last lines in a poem by Hillaire Belloc, called "Jim - who ran away from his Nurse and was eaten by a Lion":

> "Always keep a hold of Nurse,
> For fear of finding something Worse!"

I am not suggesting that you give your client nothing! What I am suggesting is that it might be better to help your client clarify his or her options, but without saying, "...And if I were you I'd plump for option A." Also, if you don't give them what they are looking for and they go off in a huff and get something somewhere else, that really is their choice and responsibility, not yours.

Audience: What I tend to say in situations when someone is in a serious dilemma and can't make up their minds is the old cliché, "When in doubt, don't." My advice would be geared towards helping someone deal with the confusing process of making the decision, rather than trying to make the decision for them.

Audience: The problem is that you might really be able to see what is best for the person in the long term, and it is difficult to let them go out of your door ready to make the worst decision possible and knowing they will have to deal with the consequences. I have seen this a lot with personal relationship problems. Someone says, "I have just met someone and I am going to leave my wife," and there is Neptune transiting square their Venus, and you know they are going to get into a mess but you can't tell them not to do it.

Juliet: No, you can't. It is their choice and their decision. But you can talk about what Neptune square Venus means, and suggest that the client looks very carefully at their expectations and fantasies. You can help them think about what they are doing without saying, "If I were you I would dump your lover and stick with your wife," or "If I were you I would make sure you get the best divorce solicitor in town." In other words, you don't make the decision for them, but you do offer them a number of possibilities based on whatever is in the chart. You could say something like, "Looking at the chart, I would say that you have the potential for this and that, and there are opportunities for this and that," while avoiding saying, "You should do this and you shouldn't do that."

Audience: What about if Mercury is retrograde and a person says to you, "I'm about to sign a contract next week. Is this a good idea ?"

Juliet: You might say something like, "According to the planetary configurations, it might be helpful if you could wait another week, because things might get a bit clearer." This is better than saying, "Whatever you do, don't sign it."

Audience: Is there that much of a difference? It sounds like a diplomatic way of saying, "Mercury is retrograde, so don't sign!"

Juliet: I feel you do need to be careful how you put things, because there is a danger of scare-mongering too. So if you say, "Whatever you do, don't sign a contract while Mercury is retrograde – it will be disastrous!" you have already made the disaster a reality for the person.

Audience: A lot of astrologers would say, "If you sign a contract now, under a retrograde Mercury, there is the possibility of difficulties, setbacks, or delays." But then you are then implanting in the person's head that the contract is going to cause problems, because when you say "possibility" a lot of clients hear "certainty". How far do you go with issuing any kind of warning? Also, if you believe inside that signing will be a disaster, and you don't say it, how much does the client pick up unconsciously? So when you say "possibility" they hear "certainty" because you really mean "certainty" and haven't said it.

Juliet: I would question whether any astrologer can know with certainty that Mercury retrograde will cause disaster if a client signs a contract. Many people have a story about how they signed a contract under a retrograde Mercury and then got cheated of their money or the contract got lost in the post or the dog ate it or whatever. But all over the world people sign contracts during those periods and many of them come out perfectly all right. It may depend on what the retrograde Mercury is doing in that particular client's chart. If you believe that it always means disaster, maybe you need to think about your interpretation. But this is a very serious ethical question which you will all have to all sort out for yourselves. I personally would always err on the side of caution. I would prefer to say too little than too much.

Audience: Then you get people saying, "Why didn't you tell me?" like the client someone mentioned earlier.

Audience: I can give you an extreme example of this. I had a client who rang up a year after I did her chart, who said, "Why didn't you tell me my husband was going to die?"

Juliet: The answer to that is quite simple: "I didn't tell you because I didn't know." Just because you are an astrologer, it doesn't mean that you are clairvoyant. We can look at events with hindsight (which does, after all, grace us with 20/20 vision), and see exactly what a certain transit or progression meant, because, of course, we can see clearly when we look back. But you don't know what that transit or progression will actually mean for each individual at the time. For some people a Venus-Saturn transit can bring a divorce, and for somebody else it can bring a marriage, but how do you know for sure and certain which it is going to be?

That is why you must be careful with predictions. You can point out trends and rhythms, but you must be very circumspect about the way in which you pronounce forthcoming events. After all, we all have choices about the way we handle things, and part of astrology's strength is to encourage self-knowledge to promote the power of choice. By telling people categorically what a particular transit or progression may mean, we effectively rob them of their choices. This brings us to the next of our dangers in the session – pre-judging situations.

Pre-judging situations

Pre-judging, by which I mean putting our own ideas or moral standpoint onto a situation, gets us into rather deep water. As astrologers we should be impartial interpreters of another's horoscope, rather than promoters of our own personal beliefs. It is not our job to trumpet our own views, even though it may be difficult not to. There may be some very delicate situations which crop up during readings. For example, a client once came to me to ask whether or not she should have an abortion. This is obviously a very emotive subject, and one about which people have very strong feelings. Naturally I was not able to advise her, but we were able to explore her hugely ambivalent feelings around the subject. We discussed it at length, using the chart as a basis, but I never knew the end result.

We may well have strong views about things. For instance, we may feel strongly that people "should never have abortions", or that they "should never bring unwanted children into the world," yet we should resist our inclination to impose our views on our clients "for their own good". If we do allow our personal viewpoints to get in the way we lose our impartiality and will, almost inevitably, fall into the trap of pre-judging. The client is not there to be judged by us. However certain we may feel about the rightness of something for ourselves, we cannot be sure it will be right for the client. Maybe we can be open about certain of our beliefs and attitudes, but equally there are certain things we can't be open about. Above all, we must be aware that there are things which might crop up during our deep encounters with our clients which will present us personally with difficulties, because our own ideas and beliefs are challenged.

When we work with people on deep levels, a broad spectrum of emotional and spiritual issues will emerge, as well as practical ones, and we must be aware that our position is not to judge but to try to interpret the situation. We must wrestle with these knotty problems inside ourselves, not *via* our clients, and we need to understand ourselves pretty well in order to be equipped for the task. This is one of the reasons why the CPA insists on its Diploma Students having their own psychotherapy as part of their training, so that these issues can be fully addressed internally.

Audience: I agree with you in principle. But sometimes I find this kind of detachment very, very hard. It is all right when the issue is simply a different spiritual approach, or a different attitude toward marriage. I don't feel I need to judge people that way. But I had a client once who admitted that he travelled to Bangkok frequently because he liked young boys and he could make use of the pedophile network there without running foul of the law. I felt disgust and anger at this client, and I couldn't control my anger. I asked him to leave, and refused any money for the work I had already done on the chart.

Juliet: That is an honest statement, and I think you did the right thing for yourself and the client because you were honest about where your limits were. If you feel you can't remain impartial and can't avoid judging the client, then you are acknowledging that you cannot really help the client, and it is better not to continue with the reading. Of course, it might be better if you could convey this without unloading strong emotions on the client.

If the client wants to know why you don't wish to continue the session, there is nothing wrong with making a personal statement, saying something like, "I find what you are saying very difficult to discuss impartially, because personally I can't condone what you are doing. It might be better if you saw an astrologer who was able to be more objective, or maybe you could discuss the issue with a therapist, if you are in conflict about it." But you could also look at the reasons for your revulsion, and if in the end it is really an honest inner response and not something which is being exaggerated by your own childhood experiences or even your own projections, then you know your conscience is clear and you have done the best you could.

Facing the client's strong emotions

Another potential hazard that can occur when we interpret a horoscope psychologically is that we may evoke strong emotional reactions in our clients, and we need to be able to handle the power of strong feelings. How do you handle it if a client bursts into tears or gets really angry? Does it frighten you, repulse you, upset you? What do you feel you have to do? Do you feel you have to do anything?

Audience: If someone bursts into tears, I always feel that I have to go over and touch the person, hold their hand, try to comfort or console them.

Audience: I get embarrassed.

Juliet: That is good and honest! Of course that could also be your counter-transference response to their embarrassment. A lot of people do think that tears or emotional outbursts are shameful, and if you think that too, then you may easily feel embarrassed if someone cries. However, if we are working on a psychological level we need to be able to cope with the client's emotions and allow their expression. It is possible to let your client know that tears are all right with you by commenting on them. If a client's eyes start to fill with tears, you can let them know that it is all right to cry by saying something like, "It seems as though what I have said has moved you," or, "I see you feel touched by what I have just said," which effectively gives them permission to be vulnerable with you. That is very different from demanding, "Why are you crying?" or "Are you going to cry?" or something crude or crass like that. It is possible to gently acknowledge that there are feelings around which you are prepared to explore with the client should they so choose. If you feel uncomfortable in the face of such emotions, you might ignore the brimming eyes and briskly change the subject, which gives your client the message, "Not in here, thanks."

Audience: Do you think it is a good idea to encourage a client to cry by saying, "It's good to cry!"?

Juliet: Sometimes by saying anything at all, even it is, "It's okay," or "It's good to cry," you can stop the flow. It is often enough to say nothing but simply be present. Being comforting – like holding their hand or putting an arm around them – can sometimes give the message, "Try to stop crying!" rather than accepting the tears as an expression of their feelings which needs neither to be stopped nor started. And physical gestures meant to comfort can also feel very invasive to some clients. Different people have different tolerance levels when it comes to physical contact, especially with someone whom they have never met before.

Audience: But clients can feel very silly crying can't they?

Juliet: Indeed, they may say, "I feel so stupid crying!" and you can say, "Yes, it may feel embarrassing crying in front of a stranger, but it is also helpful because there are feelings inside which need expression." In other words, you can acknowledge that, yes, it is embarrassing when you find yourself crying in front of someone you have never met before, but it is quite all right. If the astrologer is not flustered or disconcerted by it, but treats it as something quite normal, it becomes more acceptable to the client.

Audience: I know I quite liked it when I was in that situation and I knew that there were tissues at hand.

Juliet: I always have a box of tissues available in the consulting room. They give the message: "I can stand tears." In fact, a number of people have said things like, "Oh, you have got tissues! Does that mean I am going to cry at what you are going to tell me?" or, "Oh, dear, I hope I won't need those!" This kind of statement already gives clues about how the client may be feeling inside.

Audience: I had a frightening experience once with a client's anger. It wasn't really directed at me, but I was saying something about this man feeling unappreciated by other people. I remember he had the Sun opposition Saturn and Mars, and he had said it himself, about feeling unappreciated, so I was working on this theme, and mentioned his father and that maybe he hadn't been appreciated when he was young. His face turned quite red, and he became very angry, and said, "The bastards! They never understand what I'm trying to do. I'm fed up with it!" He got up and began pacing around the room, really angry. I was afraid he would get violent. I was so frightened I didn't say a word. He paced around and went on and on about how nobody understood him, and then he calmed down by himself and sat down again and we carried on. Should I have done something, or said something to quiet him down?

Juliet: It sounds as if staying quiet and calm was the right thing to do. It isn't possible to know for certain if someone has a violent tendency, and we talked earlier about being sensible if you are a woman living alone seeing clients, but if you have got a client through a known referral network and you feel reasonably comfortable, then this kind of anger might be important for the client to express. He needed to know that his anger didn't frighten you. I know it did, because you just said so, but you behaved as if it didn't, and often healthy angry feelings get choked back because of the worry that if the anger is expressed other people will run away. Sometimes just nodding, or saying, "Mmm," can be sufficient – you are letting them know you understand and are listening, but you aren't being patronising. Saying, "Now, calm down," can be very patronising, and it also tells the client you can't handle their anger and upset.

Some clients actually need to frighten others because they feel frightened themselves. Life frightens them, and so does the astrologer, so they get angry because it makes them feel more in control. Anger is sometimes easier to feel than fear, because fear can be interpreted as weakness. Many people get very angry because they feel very small and frightened inside. But you can usually tell when somebody is trying it on this way. If you get the feeling the client is trying to wind you up by making threatening remarks, or showing a theatrical kind of anger, you might say something like, "I get the feeling you are wanting to frighten me. I wonder why you feel you need to do that?"

Audience: I work as a psychotherapist, and I had an amazing example of this. I was seeing a client for therapy, and I think it was in the third or fourth session that he took a wicked-looking little knife out of his pocket. He began talking angrily in exactly the way you describe – a bit theatrical. He kept pointing the knife at me and waving it in the air, and saying things like, "Sometimes I feel so angry I would like to slice people up." At first I felt very frightened. Then I had a sudden intuition. I took a big gamble, and said, "I think maybe you really want to show me your penis, so I can see how big it is. That's why you are waving that little knife at me and trying to frighten me. Is that true?" He went as flat as a balloon. All the anger went out of him. He began to laugh and then said, "Maybe it's true. Why would I want to do that?" and then we could start talking about his feelings of impotence, and so on.

Juliet: It just goes to show that intuition has a big place in our work, and sometimes being too polite and circumspect with a client doesn't do the trick at all. We can all learn from this. You were right on the mark. But hopefully it will not happen to most of us!

Expecting the client to unburden prematurely

There is another potential problem which is the opposite of being afraid of a client getting too emotional. This is the danger of wanting or encouraging the client to unburden themselves too quickly. After all, we are studying psychological astrology, and we have, through the chart, a lot of personal information about the client's parental images and emotional and sexual life. There may be a temptation to be a little over-enthusiastic about getting into deep areas, perhaps before the client is ready, which then becomes counter-productive. Poking around in sensitive areas of the chart must always be done with the client's best interests in mind. Ask yourself silently, "Will my client be helped by what I am about to say, or am I trying to get information for myself and my own interests?" Or, "Is this really going to be helpful, or am I trying to be clever here?" Ask yourself, "If I were in the client's shoes and somebody asked me that question, would I find it helpful or unnecessary?" Use yourself as a sounding board.

I think it is very natural when we are undergoing therapy or training as therapists to spend a lot of time thinking about problems and conflicts. Depth psychology is something it's hard to study without dwelling on all the things that can damage people, and all the complexes and difficulties they have. Also, if we are spending a lot of time painfully exploring our own unconscious issues, we may feel it is only right that everyone else does so as well.

There may be a temptation to start right away with, "There is a very difficult issue here between you and your father, and this has probably made you feel sexually inadequate. That is why you try to overcompensate by having several women in your life." Now, that may be perfectly true, but it might not be the best thing to open the chart reading with. If we do talk about these kinds of problems, it is important to also stress the positive and creative side of a conflict, and not just its destructive side. Most people can take difficult statements as long as they feel they have something left they can feel good about. So we might need to mention the good bit first, like, "Your chart suggests that you have a lot of energy and vitality, and you probably have no difficulty in attracting the opposite sex. But I wonder if there might also be a bit of self-doubt at work here?"

Using too much astrological or technical jargon

Another potential problem when communicating a chart to a client is the use of astrological jargon. I will never forget going to my first astrology lecture and overhearing some "experienced" astrologers talking. One asked the other how old someone was, and the reply was, "He just had his first Saturn return." I remember feeling baffled and also quite alienated, wondering if it meant that astrologers did not mention people's ages in an ordinary way! Of course, when you learn the jargon it obviously becomes second nature, but at first it can be very excluding. I have noticed a tendency in astrologers to talk about people by mentioning a couple of their aspects, which can actually be quite patronising or demeaning. "He has got Sun conjunct Mars conjunct Pluto in Scorpio, so what do you expect?" is a quite de-humanising statement, because it lists a number of planets and assumes that others will come to the same conclusion as the speaker. "Look at all this Pluto, or all this Scorpio!" is something else I hear often, without any attempt at actually explaining what "all this Pluto" means.

When talking amongst ourselves, we use expressions as a kind of short-cut, which can be somewhat risky. After all, how can you be sure that two astrologers will absolutely agree on the meaning of a Venus-Saturn conjunction, or a Jupiter-Mars square? Clarification and elucidation are always necessary, because astrology is an art rather than a science. Astrology, like beauty, is partly in the eye of the beholder, and depending on your own personal outlook and chart you will see a Venus-Saturn conjunction (or any other aspect) somewhat differently from another astrologer who is coming from his or her naturally different perspective. And if we can't even agree with each other about what a certain aspect means, what do you think the client will feel if we say things like, "Well, you are behaving this way because there is an awful lot of Pluto in this chart!"

There are two possible extremes here. There is the danger of talking too astrologically, but the other extreme is using the chart too little, and getting into a counselling-type session where you are communicating to your client well but without astrologically backing up what you are saying. You ought to be able to back up everything that you say to a person with sound astrological definitions, so that the client can see where you are getting your information. After all, you are being consulted as an astrologer, and the client has come for astrological insights, not psychic intuitions! Whatever you are saying to the client should be coming from somewhere in the chart. So if anybody says to you at any point during the reading, "Where did you get that from?" you can say, "Here. This is the part I am looking at...This is the element balance...This is the aspect pattern I am looking at...This is the house placement," to explain where you are getting your information. This also ensures that you are being as objective as you can be, and not just pulling things out of the air because you feel they are true about the client.

Another thing to watch for is how you communicate things. For instance, a woman who came to me for counselling said she had been to an astrologer who had upset her terribly by saying she had no water in her chart and therefore she had no feelings.

Audience: What rubbish!

Juliet: Of course it is. It is also quite possible that the astrologer may not have said it quite like that, but it was what the woman picked up. She felt very hurt and upset about it for a long time. She had strong feelings about having no feelings! So we have to be very careful how we phrase things. For instance, you might say, "Feelings are connected with the element of water, and you don't have any water in your chart," which, put like that, might possibly be interpreted as, "The astrologer is saying I don't have any feelings." We need to be very careful what we say and how we say it, to ensure that our clients are able to take in what we say usefully. And we shouldn't forget that people who are strongly influenced by parental issues may hear the same tune whatever other people say to them, unless it is stated very, very clearly and unequivocally.

Audience: I once got into trouble with a friend whose boyfriend came to me for a reading. He had a lot of Saturn transits at the time. I said it was a time when he might be feeling quite solitary, and he might feel the need for space. He told his girlfriend I had said it was all right for him to be as selfish as he liked! So I see what you mean by people not hearing what you say, but hearing instead what they want to hear!

Juliet: This is one of the advantages of taping sessions – you have a record of what you said and in what context. It means that any unfortunate discrepancies between what you think you said and what a client heard can be ironed out if necessary. Taping is useful for many other reasons too. It makes us more careful about what we say if we know every word is being recorded. And it is a great help to a client to be able to listen to the tape again later, because so much information can be given in a session that it is very difficult to take it all in at one time. Sometimes clients have reported getting a lot out of a tape many years after the session, when something becomes more relevant as they have changed and developed. A chart can never tell us whether a person has worked on becoming more conscious, and when we say things the client may understand intellectually but simply hasn't yet reached the point where they can really grasp it.

Of course, for your own personal growth it is very useful to hear yourself giving a consultation on tape, as it helps you to sharpen your technique and learn from any mistakes. You may be pleasantly surprised at how good you are, and if not, listening to yourself in action can really alert you to your shortcomings, such as a tendency to waffle or fudge or go off the point. The general tone and attitude you show to the client can also be a revelation, because we often don't realise the effect our manner has on other people. A tape can provide you with a lot of material to learn from, with or without the help of an experienced supervisor.

Being more interested in the client's story than in the client

Yet another possible hazard is the vicarious pleasure that we might get when listening to a client's story. For example, we may have famous or unusual clients who are, for that reason, particularly interesting and fascinating. They may be famous or royal in their own right, or they may know lots of famous people. It can be quite tempting to want to hear all the scandal and gossip the client may be telling you about – hearing the inside scoop on the lives of the rich and famous is very seductive.

However, it is important to remember that it is the inner world of the client that our work is about, not their outside circumstances. In order to keep yourself on track, it can help to ask yourself questions like, "Why is this person trying to entertain me? Why are they telling me all these fascinating stories? Do they not feel good enough about themselves without the trappings?" This can help you pull yourself back from being seduced into wanting to hear about Prince This or Princess That or movie star X or pop star Y. Or if they are the famous person themselves, they may need you to relate to them as a person, and not just to their famous image. It is easy to be dazzled and seduced by glamour, but it ends up being for your benefit, not that of the client.

Audience: I had a client once who was the son of a very famous pop star from the 1960's. All I could think during the session about was this man's famous father, who was one of my childhood idols! I kept wanting to ask about my childhood pin-up, and found it difficult to concentrate on my client!

Audience: I had a client who was very "in" with the royal family and kept name-dropping, which was very tantalising. It certainly can make you want to hear all the little secret snippets.

Juliet: So you have some experience of how seductive glamour can be!

The power of predictions

The last point that I want to touch on is the power of predictions. I think we have probably said enough about that already, and have looked at just how careful you have to be when you are predicting, and how aware you have to be that predictions can be self-fulfilling. People can make them self-fulfilling prophecies. They can make things happen, consciously or unconsciously. So you have got to be very, very careful how you phrase things. We forget how powerful we are as astrologers, and how people will come and invest something quite magical in us. Often after a reading we wonder if we have done anything at all, but we could be doing an awful lot of harm. It is always better to err on the side of caution than to go rushing in being too overt and destructive.

I think the main thing is to try to be as aware as possible of all the things that are going on in a session and can potentially go wrong. And you can learn from your experiences. There will be many, and you will learn the most from the difficult ones. Obviously, having some idea of what might be happening inside you will stand you in good stead.

Exercise two: practice at interpretation

Now I would like to try a final exercise. I would like you to break up into groups of four. If there is one person left over, you could join one of the groups, but if there are two or three of you left over, then form your own smaller group. If you are uncomfortable in group exercises, don't worry. It isn't compulsory and you can read a book or something until we have finished. If you haven't brought your chart with you, then you will undoubtedly remember what is in it.

Think about where your Moon is, and what aspects it makes. Each of you should turn to the person on your left, and once they let you know where their Moon is placed and what aspects it makes, try to give a five-minute interpretation. Then the person whose Moon you have just analysed should give you two or three minutes of feedback. After that, they should do a Moon interpretation for the person on *their* left, and so on, so that by the time we have finished, in around thirty minutes, each member of each group should have had their Moon interpreted and should have given feedback to the interpreter.

[Time out for the exercise]

I do realise that it is frustrating to have only a short time to do this exercise.

Audience: I could have done this all day. This was really useful.

Juliet: You learn quite a bit from having your own chart done as well as from doing it for somebody else. Both ways are very helpful. You know how it feels when you are the client at the receiving end, and you know how difficult it is to be the astrologer. It is not a bad idea for students to get together in small groups sometimes to do this sort of practice work on a regular basis. Doing it with one planet is also very useful because it really makes you focus on a certain theme. Although we do some of this in the CPA supervision groups, setting up your own independent study groups is also a good idea.

What I would like to find out from all of you now is whether there is anything particularly interesting or problematic that came out of your group. Is there anything that any of you would like to offer to the rest of us?

Audience: One thing I noticed was that when I started talking about my "client's" Moon, I suddenly felt overwhelmed. I wasn't conscious of myself. I couldn't make any sense out of it. Then I think I gave a very bad feeling to her. She said she thought I felt sorry for her, because of the way I described the aspects, which I now realise is my pattern with clients where I see difficult Moon aspects. It was a great revelation to me. Of course it has something to do with my own badly aspected Moon.

Juliet: How do you think you could change that? Can you say something more about it?

Audience: I suppose I have felt very sorry for myself sometimes, without realising it. Usually I am very rational about my problems. This is what you mean by transference and counter-transference, isn't it? I feel sorry for the client, who might not really deserve my pity, because I secretly feel sorry for myself.

Audience: As the client in that situation, I didn't feel it was necessarily a bad thing. What I mean is, there might be a time when it would be the right thing to show that kind of sympathy to the client. This kind of thing very much depends on where the client is, doesn't it? A few years ago, if an astrologer had spoken to me in that way, I would have felt she was really concerned, although it would also have been a good justification for me to indulge in lots of self-pity. But at this moment in my life I don't feel sorry for myself, so I didn't really feel happy about the interpretation.

Juliet: Were you able to communicate that?

Audience: Yes, I told her that at this point in my life I don't feel sorry for myself any more, and that although I appreciated her concern it wasn't necessary.

Juliet: Good. Did you actually feel sorry for her, or did you just feel overwhelmed by where to start?

Audience: I do feel for people. I don't feel sorry for people. I think I reserve that for myself. But I do feel for them. Whomever I meet, my first reaction is to feel a great empathy for the person's difficulties.

Juliet: How about the observers in the group? Did you notice anything while the interpretation was being given?

Audience: Not really. Only afterward, when the feedback was given.

Audience: I picked it up before it was acknowledged. I felt uncomfortable. I kept thinking, "Can't you say anything really positive about that aspect?"

Juliet: All right, what about the next group?

Audience: As the person giving the interpretation, I experienced a lot of anxiety. When I get anxious, I talk too much. I was also aware of the fact that my "client" was affecting me on the emotional level. Even when I am talking about something more detached – the Moon is pretty emotional to talk about, isn't it? – I have a tendency to just blab. And I couldn't forget that this was a setup. The setup itself was difficult for me to engage in. So I had just another example of how I want to fill in all the gaps and try to ask too many questions.

Juliet: So there is a bit of reluctance to allow any space or quiet. Did that feel uncomfortable for you as the client?

Audience: Yes. I felt a bit overwhelmed. I got difficult and wouldn't give any feedback.

Juliet: Good, you gave her a real-life experience of a client being difficult.

Audience: I was very aware of all these people around in the room, all talking. This kind of exercise is such an artificial situation.

Juliet: Of course it is an artificial situation. But that doesn't mean we can't learn from it. What we are really looking for at the moment is some tips on technique, and perhaps on how things can be done. Unless they go around constantly having their charts done, astrologers don't always get a lot of practice in feeling what it's like to be the client.

Audience: For me it was a really helpful experience, because I learned something about a technique I have been trying out but have never had straight feedback on. Sometimes when I have to say something about a difficult aspect, I try to express it by introducing an imaginary third person into the room. I was talking about my "client's" Moon-Pluto aspect. I said, "Imagine Pluto is sitting over there. She is very intense, and very strong, but she can't really communicate what she needs because she isn't very good at words."

Audience: I found it very comforting to somehow think about Pluto "over there". It seemed less frightening. It made me realise I don't always pay attention to my emotions because I expect to know what they are straight away.

Audience: What I found helpful, when my Moon was interpreted, was for me to actually experience the focus and then the loss of somebody's interest. One minute I was the centre of attention, and then I felt abandoned. When my special five minutes were up and I had given my feedback, all the attention of the group shifted to somebody else, and in that moment I suddenly realised what the client must feel when you have finished the reading and it's all over and suddenly they are back to a world where no one is all that interested in them.

Audience: I tried to get the other people in the group involved in my interpretation, out of a desire to make the "client" feel comfortable, because they were listening. I said to the others, "And what do *you* think about what I have said?" But it didn't seem to work.

Audience: I felt as if the privacy was gone when he did that. Even though I knew the others were sitting there listening, I could pretend the interpretation was private, until he drew them into the conversation. I didn't like it.

Juliet: So, in fact, involving the others had the opposite effect to the one intended. Even in an artificial situation like a student exercise, people want to feel that their words are private and that their material and experiences are very safe and contained. And the last group?

Audience: The only striking thing that came up for me was what to do when somebody says something that throws you. My "client" told me something about her childhood that really upset me.

Juliet: Perhaps the first desire when you feel thrown is to move quickly on to the next thing. The thing to do, perhaps, is to stay with the upsetting thing, and monitor what you are feeling.

Audience: It took me a while to feel I was in control of myself again. It's true, I did try to move on to the next thing as quickly as I could.

Juliet: Perhaps you need to allow yourself to be thrown and feel your own upset, and then think about whether there is something you could communicate to the client about it, rather than thinking, "I had better move on quickly somewhere else." This can be quite hard when you are in the session.

Audience: My "client" didn't let me off the hook! He brought the issue up again until I started dealing with it.

Juliet: I think that clients will do that, if you listen to them and if you let them. They do usually want and need something, and they will try to find different ways of getting it, or try to get you to talk about it even if they are not being direct. Don't feel that you have got to gallop through and give as much information as you can. Try to leave some pauses for breath, so that if the client wants to take you somewhere, the train won't be going so fast that you can't brake and change track and listen. There is a tendency, when you are a bit nervous (which often happens when one is first confronted with the client), to talk and fill all the gaps, and not leave any room for things to unfold more naturally.

Perhaps there is a possibility of finding some balance between being completely silent and displaying what is known as "verbal diarrhea". On that happy note I think we have to stop, because we have run out of time. Thank you all very much for attending the seminar, and for participating in the exercises with such willingness.

Part Two:
The Astrologer,
the Counsellor and the Priest

by Liz Greene

This seminar was given on 16 November 1996 at Regents College, London, as part of the Autumn Term of the seminar programme of the Centre for Psychological Astrology.

Chaotic times

I would like to begin by asking how many of you are practising astrologers. Most of you? Very good, that is what I had hoped. The reason I am asking is that the subject of this seminar is in some ways quite specialised. It is meant to help any of you who are working in this field to understand the psychological issues involved in the study of astrology, and the nature of the inner challenges which arise, both general and specific, in the course of astrological practice. As far as those of you who aren't astrologers are concerned, I am not sure what you are hoping to get from today's theme, but perhaps you will gain some understanding of why you are sitting here.

Audience: Have we got any priests in the group?

Liz: How many of you are priests? No one? That is a pity. I am not a priest, nor do I have any intention of becoming one. But I was hoping these chaotic times might have brought one or two out of the woodwork, out of sheer annoyance if not genuine interest, as the seminar's title couples them with us. It is, of course, possible to be a priest – even a Catholic priest – and find that astrology is not incompatible with the Christian ethos. I have had numerous clients over the years who have demonstrated this. But it requires a perspective on religious matters which is symbolic and inclusive rather than literal and exclusive, and that is unfortunately not especially common.

Pluto in Sagittarius

There are several reasons why I wanted to give this particular seminar at this particular time. The chief one is that, as all of you know, Pluto is now firmly entrenched in Sagittarius, and religious, spiritual, philosophical and moral issues are starting to become very heated up. Historically, this is the tendency every 246 years when Pluto passes through this sign.

Pluto in Sagittarius reflects a time when there is likely to be a great deal of questioning, religious anxiety, intolerance, fanaticism, and sectarianism – as well as a tremendous longing to find some kind of universal truth, moral and spiritual, which is cleaner and less corrupt than what preceded Pluto's advent into the sign. Pluto's passage through Scorpio tends, historically, to conclude with a deep collective cynicism and world-weariness, born of seeing too much darkness and hypocrisy in the world. Some kind of renewal of faith is urgently needed – some new world-view which can restore our belief in the goodness of life.

Because this is going on around us as well as within us, and will be going on for the next twelve or thirteen years,[3] all of us who are involved in this profession are under fire, both from the collective and from within ourselves. This transit does not just affect people "out there". It affects every individual internally, and we are not exempt merely because we know the name of the transit. Transits of this kind are not things that go on somewhere else, which one might happen to run into by accident. They reflect inner experiences and changes which occur in every human being.

---

[3] This was the time span when the seminar was given in 1996. Pluto enters Capricorn briefly from February to June 2008, and moves into the sign again for its full transit in November 2008.

But because they occur in every human being, the sum total is a collective experience. Pluto dredges the bottom of each zodiacal sign's pond, bringing all that is useless, outgrown, rotten and poisoned to the surface, so that the water can flow cleanly again and room can be made for new growth. Each of us is going to have to cope with the issues that Pluto's dredging process raises. Sagittarius' pond is concerned with how we perceive God, which is to say, what we envisage as the highest good, and what we interpret as the primary authority in the cosmos. Pluto in Sagittarius will challenge us about how we define right and wrong, on a personal as well as a collective level.

It should be apparent, in the light of this transit, that the kind of confusion, disillusionment, and sectarianism that is occurring within the body of conventional religions is going to open the doors to a great many alternative approaches, of which astrology is generally considered to be one. Of course, astrology has only been an alternative approach for a couple of hundred years. Before that it was mainstream. And it is not a religion, a philosophy, or a moral code, but rather, a unique model of the cosmic system, which can be integrated into most, if not all, spiritual, philosophical and moral approaches. Be that as it may, the collective presently perceives it as "fringe", and as part of the collective we too are affected by this perception.

I feel it is extremely important that, as astrologers, we know what we are doing at the moment, which means not only knowing what we are invoking by doing this kind of work, but also why we are doing it. Each of us individually needs to be conscious of what happens between us and the client – what really happens, not what we would like to think happens. What is actually constellated on unconscious levels, in both the astrologer and the client? What has brought the client to us, rather than to his or her vicar, doctor, or psychiatrist, or anyone else who might once have stood in the same position in which we as astrologers are standing now? And just what is that position?

The plan for the day

There is a rough structure which I would like to try to follow today, because we have a vast area to explore and we will no doubt periodically get sidetracked in fascinating moral and spiritual discussions which go nowhere. I would like to start by briefly examining the role the astrologer has played over the centuries, because history is not merely a dead past. It also shapes the present. The historical role of the astrologer underpins what we do and how we are seen now, and we carry our past with us, consciously or unconsciously. Examining our historical role will lead us into an examination of what kind of archetypal figures stand behind us when we do our work. I will try to explain what I mean by that as we go along.

The energies or archetypal patterns which underpin our work are a profound and important issue. There are a number of archetypal figures which have been associated with astrology for many millennia. These figures symbolise the essence and purpose of the study. Because of our inherent differences in temperament and individual birth horoscopes, we tend to align ourselves, consciously or unconsciously, with one or another of these mythic figures or modes of perception.

We may not be aware of it, but our birth charts and the qualities of character they reflect make us open to certain kinds of mythic patterns. These form the substance of the cosmic allegiance which we experience – or, if you like, the god we worship, whether or not we call it by that name. And because these patterns are archetypal, they also reflect how others see us, according to *their* birth charts. It is quite pointless to protest against what other people project onto us. Such projections are unconscious and mythic, and they will occur whether we like it or not. It is wiser to try to understand them and work with them if possible, rather than feeling angry because we are misunderstood.

To help us get a clearer sense of how this works on both a general and a specific level, we can look later at the charts of a couple of astrologers who have made important contributions to the study. Both these people are now dead. It is far more civilised, when discussing our colleagues, to use the charts of those who are no longer living and whose birth data is in the public domain, rather than taking apart people who are living but are not here to participate in the discussion. I have no intention of examining these charts in order to criticise the individuals' astrological perspective, or explore personal pathology. But these charts may help to illustrate how astrology is experienced by different astrologers, and why they try to offer the particular approach they are offering.

After that I would like to look in some detail at what actually takes place during an astrological consultation. We will need to look at what, in psychological terminology, is called transference and counter-transference, because astrologers are not exempt from this phenomenon. Many astrologers think that because they only spend a couple of hours with the client and have a bit of paper in front of them, the unconscious will sleep quietly, and the kind of subtle interaction that takes place in analytic work will not occur in the astrological session.

However, people do not obligingly leave the unconscious outside the door simply because one is an astrologer rather than a psychotherapist. When any individual seeks another person's help and advice, certain projections are set in motion, both parental and archetypal. From the moment that the client telephones to make the appointment, there is already a transference, and there may already be a counter-transference on the part of the astrologer as well. Telephone voices and letters suggest a great deal about the client, even if we register these things unconsciously.

Exploring the experience of the astrological session will lead us into the deeper personal reasons why each of us has taken up this study, and what comprises our unconscious psychological baggage. We will need to look at the unconscious power issues involved in our work, as well as the quest for redemption, the effort to heal our own wounds through other people, and the parental complexes which have drawn us into the helping professions. We also need to explore the ambivalent relationship we have with the collective in terms of being "respectable" or "unrespectable", and what we may secretly be trying to prove to others. You can see that we will be opening the proverbial can of worms today, or possibly even several cans.

In addition, I would like to look at the issue of synastry between the astrologer and the client, and the kinds of chart dynamics which invoke certain energies in the astrological session. Then we should hopefully have time to look at a chart or two from the group.

The historical role of the astrologer

The priest, the philosopher, and the *mathematicus*

Some astrological practitioners and schools do not seem to attribute much importance to astrology's history, as though the study sprang into being full-blown in this century and has no past. Others select an historical period with which they can identify, such as Britain in the 17th and 18th centuries, because of an affinity with the type of astrology developed at that time. But whatever our affinities, we would be wise to remember our ancient roots, for they are still with us and are sometimes contrary to the role in which we presently see ourselves. Not only do we lose a rich and valuable sense of belonging to an ancient and continuous tradition if we disregard those roots; we also remain unconscious of their effect on us and our clients.

The earliest role of the astrologer was that of a priest. The function of the astrologer in Babylon, which is where the study's beginnings lie, was to interpret the intentions of the gods, so that the ruler and the state could be protected and aligned with the divine will. Individual horoscopes were not cast in Babylon; this was a later Greek development. But phenomena such as eclipses and major planetary conjunctions were understood to have bearing on the fate of the nation and its ruler, and it was the job of the astrologer to make sense of these phenomena and issue advice accordingly.[4]

The astrologer was thus a *pontifex maximus* – a maker of bridges between the cosmic and human realms, or between the macrocosm and the microcosm. Babylonian astrology was embedded in a religious context, and the astrologer was usually a priest of the Sun-god, holding a political as well as a religious authority which is virtually impossible for us to conceive of now. The ruler was seen as the embodiment of the god on earth, and the astrologer knew the ruler's fate.

The Sun-god seems to be the special deity with which astrology was linked in the earliest period of its development, and the link

---

[4]For a thorough and profound examination of the ancient role of the astrologer-priest, see Nicholas Campion, *The Great Year*, Penguin, London, 1994.

continued in subsequent centuries. When we start to look more specifically at the archetypal background and mythic figures which are associated with the study, you will see a continuity of this ancient relationship between astrology and the solar realm. It reflects an underlying belief in one creator-deity who is the source of life, and whose will the astrologer is responsible for interpreting.

We are not priests of the Sun-god any more – at least not in any recognisable form. But even if we think we are merely going to help someone decide whether or not they should sell their house, the client may unconsciously expect something else. Despite the modern and sometimes exceedingly pragmatic role that we assign ourselves, the client may come with an unconscious assumption that we are going to be able to do what the astrologer-priests of Babylon did. We are expected to stand as a bridge between the individual and God, and communicate the will of God to the client – even if the client doesn't believe in God on a conscious level, and even if the astrologer is not concerned with religious or spiritual matters. And no matter how humbly and carefully we explain that we are simply reading a map of the solar system, we must nevertheless deal with this archetypal expectation, which may be our own as well as the client's.

We may not want this role; we may not feel we deserve it; and we may not believe in it. But the past is part and parcel of the work that we do, just as it is of the work of the medical doctor. Are there any medical practitioners here today? Good, there are a couple of you. You will no doubt be well aware that the ill patient is going to bring the same kind of expectation of divine intervention, because behind the doctor the patient sees Asklepios, and Asklepios can raise the dead.

Audience: It is one of the most difficult things about medical practice. The patient's expectations are always greater than our knowledge.

Liz: The expectations are archetypal, although the doctor is human. Any wise doctor knows that patients do not come just to have their aching joints examined, or their flu symptoms diagnosed. They carry a much more profound expectation – a divine intervention which will somehow allow them to live forever. The expectations placed upon medical doctors are extremely unrealistic. Many people do not bother to educate themselves about the care of their own bodies, nor do they acknowledge the inevitable limitations of medical knowledge. They go to their doctors hoping to receive a cure for life itself.

We get the same kind of impossible expectations, and for us it may be worse. Asklepios is often part of our backdrop of mythic figures, but other figures may also be relevant, as we shall see later, and we may have to deal with a whole crowd of archetypal projections. The archetypal background of astrology fuels not only the client's expectations but also our own, and we would be wise to remember that it is extremely dangerous psychologically to identify with an archetypal figure. We have to find a way to accept these archetypal projections without identifying with them.

Perhaps the role of the astrologer-priest is in truth what we are enacting. Think about it. If we are indeed bridge-builders between the divine and human worlds, what will such a role do to us psychologically? It is an enormous responsibility, isn't it? Is that what we are really doing? How many of you believe that this is our task? I see that most of you have put your hands up. I also believe it is our task, and I fear we are ill-equipped to do it – frighteningly ill-equipped, because we are not trained as priests. Most of us are not even trained as psychotherapists, which is a reasonable alternative. Some have made the effort to undergo such a training. But in many astrological circles it is considered unnecessary or irrelevant.

Historically, the astrologer remained a priest until the time of the Greeks, and continued to play this role in the East for much longer. When Alexander the Great returned from his conquest of India in the 4th century BCE, he was warned by the astrologer-priests of Babylon not to enter the city gates because the astrological omens were menacing. Alexander, being a Leo, felt he did not need to obey this good advice, and wound up dying of marsh fever. But despite the continuity of the astrological priesthood in Babylon and Persia, in pre-classical Greece the priestly training gradually changed into philosophical speculation, and the astrologers of the time were usually both philosophically and mathematically trained, although they were often involved with one or another of the mystery religions.

By the time the Romans had established their em
Western astrologer had lost the priestly mantle. The better Roman astrologers, such as Thrasyllus, were Platonists, and continued the philosophical and mathematical tradition of the Greeks. But the astrologer had become a *mathematicus,* which despite its high intellectual and philosophical requirements means something rather more humble. During the Roman period the fortune-telling element in astrology assumed greater and greater importance – in part because the Romans, especially after the Republic gave way to the empire, did not have the same sense of religious awe as the Greeks, and were more concerned with second-guessing Fortuna through the art of prediction. Being a more practical people, they wanted results, not philosophy. Although Plato scorned the use of astrology for fortune-telling, Thrasyllus the Platonist was not averse to making astrological predictions for the emperors Augustus and Tiberius – as a well-paid political advisor, not a *pontifex maximus.*

The rise of the mystery religions in Rome did not succeed in restoring the astrologer to his or her former religious role, although astrology formed an important part of both Mithraism and Orphism. And once the emperor Constantine had declared the empire Christian, the fate of the astrologer was more or less sealed. An attempt was made during the reign of the emperor Julian to create a caste of astrologer-priests in the service of the Sun-god, but Julian was murdered and his efforts to restore religious tolerance and inclusiveness to the empire failed.

As Christianity grew and flourished, there was, of course, no place for the astrologer as priest, although some of the early Christian Fathers, such as Augustine, were versed in astrology. Throughout the medieval and Renaissance periods, the astrologer could not lay claim to any priestly sanctity. If not being actively persecuted by Church authorities, he or she was a political advisor. Nostradamus, for example, played this role for Queen Catherine de' Medici of France. The great princes and cardinals of the Renaissance, and even certain Popes, depended heavily on their astrologers for decision-making. Some of these astrologers, such as Marsilio Ficino, were Platonists or Neoplatonists. But if one wanted a *pontifex maximus,* one turned to the

Church. Otherwise one was liable to get into considerable trouble. By the time the Enlightenment arrived, the astrologer's spiritual and philosophical authority had gone altogether. The astrological practitioner had become a backstreet fortune-teller, and what was once the prevailing world-view had now become mere superstition.

Conflict with collective religious authority

Throughout its history, the Church has created an enduringly hostile climate for astrology, despite the astrological proclivities of Popes such as Leo X. Why should this conflict have occurred? The obvious answer is that there was no room for two religious authorities. A decision had to be made about who was best suited to wear the mantle of the *pontifex*. Did the role lie with the priesthood of the Church, or did it lie with the priesthood of the Sun-god? Ever since Constantine was persuaded to deny his solar worship in order to make his empire officially Christian, it could not lie with the astrologer, because this would have undermined the authority of the Church. There is a fundamental incompatibility, not between the tenets of Christianity and the world-view of astrology, but between the collective authority of the Church and the individual authority of the astrologer – which is rooted in a direct relationship with the cosmos, as well as in astrological tradition.

It might be helpful for us to be conscious of this fundamental incompatibility, and understand what it implies. An astrologer may be deeply Christian, and may be able to reconcile the two and allow one to enhance and nourish the other. But the political structures of the religious body that we call Christianity – be they Anglican, Catholic, Lutheran, or Seventh Day Adventist – are in inexorable conflict with astrology, because we cannot answer to two religious authorities. Where does our authority come from?

Audience: From the empirical experience of generations and generations of astrologers. It is essentially objective. It is as scientific as it is possible to get. It is a body of knowledge, not a set of beliefs.

Liz: Yes, there is a difference between the spirit of inquiry which has led to astrology's continuously accruing body of knowledge and the unquestioning faith in dogma required by the Church. But scientific knowledge and religious faith are not always mutually exclusive. And astrology itself is not a religion, although its origins are embedded in a religious framework.

Audience: The Christian tradition recognises one God. The pagan religions believed in many different gods. Surely that is the basic conflict.

Liz: Are you suggesting that astrology is a pagan religion? Even if it were, the conflict between Christianity and paganism is not that simple. Many people use the word "pagan" to describe any pre-Christian religion, which implies that all paganism was the same. This is not only unjust; it is also ignorant. The Babylonians believed in a multiplicity of deities, and worshipped the planets as gods. But the astrology which we now practise is essentially Greco Roman. The Greco-Roman astrological world-view was monotheistic, steeped in Pythagorean and Platonic philosophy and Orphic teachings. This highly sophisticated cosmology recognised one deity with many faces. The plurality of the gods was symbolic, representing different dimensions of a single cosmos and cosmocrator. The astrology that we work with has always been monotheistic – as much if not more so than a Christian heaven peopled with a plurality of angels and saints. How many of you are practising Christians as well as astrologers?

Audience: What do you mean by "practising"? Going to church, or believing in the Christian teachings?

Liz: Believing in the fundamental tenets of Christianity. Only a very few of you have put your hands up. Do you experience a conflict between Christian teachings and astrology? No? Do you experience a conflict with the authority of the Church, or do you just keep your astrological work quiet and avoid the issue?

Audience: I keep it quiet.

Liz: Why?

Audience: I keep it quiet around orthodox Christians because it causes too much trouble if I talk about it. But actually, I go to a Christian Spiritualist Church to worship, where I am accepted as an astrologer.

Liz: So on the fringe of Christianity you have found a place where astrology can co-exist with Christian teachings. But in the mainstream you would keep quiet about it.

Audience: Yes.

Audience: I also keep quiet about it, because the few times I have ever raised the issue, I have been heavily criticised and harassed.

Liz: I think that we need to look very carefully at what this collective conflict does to us on a psychological level. How many of you are practising Jews?

Audience: I am not a practising Jew, although I take some of the religious tenets very seriously. But there is a Kabbalistic tradition in Judaism which is also astrological. I suppose I would keep quiet around orthodox Jews.

Liz: How many of you are practising Muslims? No one? The same conflict applies with Judaism and Islam. It is a conflict with the religious institution, rather than with the essential spirit of the religion. I take your point about the Kabbalistic tradition. There is also an esoteric tradition in Islam and in Christianity. It is the mainstream institutions which seem to provide the source of the conflict. By challenging the authority of the collectively acknowledged *pontifex*, we are separating ourselves from the collective and are therefore outcast. This carries certain psychological repercussions. Apparently all of you have rejected orthodox religious structures, although some of you may retain a faith in the religion itself. On the conscious level, that may work very well.

But we cannot throw away our collective religious heritage like a suitcase from a train window, any more than we can throw away our parental inheritance. One's world-view may be highly individual. One may reject the teachings in which one was brought up, or espouse a hybrid or esoteric version of them. But the culture in which we have been born and grown up is psychologically part of us, and if we take up the role of the priest in our astrological work, consciously or unconsciously, we are challenging collective religious authority.

The astrologer as outsider

Audience: I think it is a very big strain to practice as an astrologer and also try to function as an ordinary person who is part of the collective. It is stressful. I always feel vaguely guilty, as if there were something I ought to be ashamed of.

Liz: You are underlining very clearly the point I am trying to make. There may be profound guilt involved in the invocation of the ancient astrologer-priest's role. It creates a sense of being an outlaw, whether we acknowledge this or not. Inserting ourselves between the divine and human realms places us in the role of priests, whether we like it or not, and thus we are heretics in the context of the Judeo-Christian culture into which we have been born. That is going to affect us on profound levels, even if our friends are all part of the subculture and we never have any dealings with those who might censure us. Even if one comes from a family of astrologers, this conflict will still take its toll. What effect do you think it will it have on you as an individual?

Audience: Inflation. Sometimes I find myself going around thinking, "I know better than all these ignorant people."

Liz: Yes, that is a characteristic problem in all the esoteric fields of study: "I know something you unevolved lot don't know." But inflation is generally a compensation for its opposite. One of you has mentioned guilt and shame. This conflict with collective religious authority, which is older and deeper than astrology's conflict with science, can trigger the astrologer's personal wounds, and activate uncomfortable feelings of inferiority and isolation. Wounds which begin as a family matter are exacerbated if the whole collective seems inimical.

We know that aspects such as Sun square Saturn, Sun conjunct Chiron, Moon opposition Chiron, and Moon square Saturn tell us a good deal about the individual's personal history and personal conflicts. So do placements such as Saturn or Chiron in the 10th. We would ordinarily interpret any of these aspects on a personal and family level, and recognise that they frequently describe feelings of insecurity, vulnerability, and fear of rejection. Difficult Pluto aspects can also reflect feelings of isolation and alienation, and we can learn a lot about the family history from such aspects. Virtually everyone has placements like this somewhere in the chart, and insecurity and loneliness seem part of the human condition. But such feelings of personal isolation and insecurity become inflamed if we are also dealing with a sense of isolation from the collective. The archetypal conflict around religious authority, which goes back so many centuries, will press on that raw nerve, and can aggravate the astrologer's sense of alienation and vulnerability.

For the astrologer, Moon-Chiron or Sun-Saturn or Pluto in the 10th is not just a personal or family issue. The moment we make a statement of separateness from the collective by working as astrologers, we are invoking something which will have an effect on the way we experience such aspects. It is as though we are taking the aspect and putting it into an arena where it is subject to additional pressures. Often the compensation for the uncomfortable feelings that are triggered is inflation. In order to cope with the archetypal sense of being an outsider, spiritually and psychologically, we may compensate with the fantasy that we are spiritually superior, or are in possession of secrets which make us special. Then the experience of collective rejection does not seem so painful.

If the collective rejects us, or metaphorically tries to burn us at the stake, we have got to come up with something to stop us feeling bad, inferior, and lonely. We may say to ourselves, "It doesn't matter, because we know something they don't know. We are in the vanguard of the spiritual evolution of the planet. We are here to teach others." But maybe we are not so special. Maybe we are just humans lumbering along, bewildered by life like the rest, but we happen to be very fortunate in discovering an area of study which gives us a bit more insight into our dilemmas.

Inflation creates its own isolation. We become like the downtrodden waiting for the Day of Judgment. The unevolved "scientific community" is oppressing and persecuting us. We can easily become evangelical, and I know some astrologers who are. We don't usually pontificate at Speaker's Corner or wander up and down Leicester Square with a sandwich-board. But we may participate in television programmes in which we are subjected to tests we cannot possibly hope to pass. Or we put ourselves in positions where we are humiliated by a skeptical public or an unpleasant journalist or television presenter, in the hope that we can "convert" the public.

We may also let ourselves be drawn into arguments with somebody who says, "Prove to me that this rubbish works." For some unaccountable reason we stand there and actually try to convince such discourteous twits that we are really nice, sane, decent people. We waste time and energy trying to persuade the collective that we are not inferior. We are not heretics; we are not charlatans; we are not gullible fools; we are not in league with the devil; and we are not mad. We expend enormous effort explaining ourselves to those who were never prepared to listen in the first place.

Collective insecurity works at a subterranean level, and I doubt that anyone in this room is exempt from the sense of being an outsider – no matter how rational and detached we think we are. In choosing to pursue this study, we set ourselves on a collision course with a world-view which has dominated for the last two millennia. It is not a collision with science; it is a much older conflict. It began when we lost our honoured position as priests, and became backstreet fortune-tellers struggling against a prevailing cosmology in which there was only one religious authority, which was not that of the planets. This is part of our inheritance. We carry two things from the past – a priestly role which is honourable yet also terrifying in the weight of its responsibility; and an aura of something dark, dirty, and heretical.

The dark and dirty bit may have something to do with why so many astrologers have such a difficult time asking for a fair fee which reflects the amount of work and effort they have put into their training. This is another area we need to look at later in the day. Why do so many astrologers struggle with the material world, unable to make a living at their work despite years of study, a highly ethical attitude, and a "quality product" to offer? I know many experienced astrologers who are terrified of saying, like any architect or plumber or accountant, "I charge £75. an hour and I am worth it." Even the local vicar gets a free house in which to live.

But if one is a heretic, one cannot ask for such a thing. Instead, one begs for acceptance from people. One is desperate for acknowledgement. We want our clients to validate us, because the client is a representative of the collective. In essence that is correct – we are trying to help the client, and we depend on feedback to ensure that we are on the right track. But sometimes we go too far, and lose our sense of self-worth. We forget the value of what we have to offer. The client comes to us and says, "Is this going to work? Is this going to help me? Prove to me that you can do something for me." And we fall into the uncomfortable position of needing their reassurance that we are giving them what they want before we can believe that we are worth the money we have requested for our services. This is the place of the outsider.

If any of you want to interrupt and say something as I am going along, please do. I am being deliberately provocative, and exaggerating these issues somewhat because I feel they need to be recognised.

Audience: If we ourselves feel that we are in a backstreet prediction game, if we partly believe that, then there is always going to be something uncomfortable about asking for money, because we know we aren't doing what we should be doing as astrologers. If we are not clear that our position is to put the person in contact with the cosmos, and we try to give them predictions instead – which may or may not be valid – then we are asking for money on their terms rather than on our own.

Liz: You are talking about betraying what you believe your work to be about.

Audience: Yes, either deliberately in order to make money and get clients, or just by not being clear about our values.

Liz: Yes, there is usually a lot of guilt generated by any self-betrayal, conscious or unconscious. There is another kind of guilt generated by loyalty to our ideals and values, which reflects a conflict with the collective. It seems we cannot win on this one. Later I want to explore how each of us defines his or her astrological work. Many astrologers do not see themselves as psychological counsellors, let alone priests. They see themselves as consultants who can offer advice to a client about worldly matters. There is a place for practical predictive work, although it is no less heretical, in collective terms, than a psychological approach. However, if you don't feel making predictions is your role, but you are doing it because it is what people want, then you are caught between a rock and a hard place.

Audience: Sometimes there is something obvious in the chart, and you can offer practical advice. But very often you can't see anything of that kind. The client is asking for something, and you can't give it to them. You can put them in touch with something deeper, but you feel as though you are letting them down by not giving them what they want.

Audience: When we try to interpret the heavens, or what the universe is trying to tell us, we bring our own personalities into our interpretations. So the very Saturnian type of astrologer will give Saturnian advice, and the Uranian type will give Uranian revelations. This is inevitable because we stand in that midway position between the universe and the client, and we colour it in both directions.

Liz: Yes, we all have an individual chart and an individual psyche, and we also have our own favourite gods. It is not possible to be totally neutral and objective. But we can try to be conscious of our allegiances. This can make us think twice before we offer an interpretation. We may also be unable to work with certain kinds of issues. Then we have to be honest enough to say to the client, "This is an area in which I can't give you much help. I have a colleague who specialises in this kind of astrological work. Here is his phone number."

Audience: Whatever your individual vision, you usually get clients who are somehow in tune with it.

Liz: If we work by referral rather than by advertisement, then yes, we get clients who are attuned to our approach. We attract people who want what we have to offer, and in the main, once we have created an energy field as a practitioner, we don't often attract clients who are looking for a different kind of astrologer – unless there is an unconscious conflict at work.

The archetypal background

I would like to look now at the archetypal background of our work. The mythic figures which have relevance to the study and practice of astrology have been associated with it since it was first developed. They are gods or demigods who were said to have taught human beings astrology, or who created the cosmos and were deemed responsible for its orderly functioning. These figures are archetypal, which means that they symbolise a mode of perception. When we perceive reality "through" such figures, our interpretations of life – including the attitudes we bring to our work – are coloured in a certain way. It is worth exploring these images because they can help us understand the deeper motivation behind the individual astrologer's approach and allegiances.

Divine male images: Prometheus and stolen fire

Let's start with the obvious, which ought to be especially obvious for the astrologer with a strong Uranus in the birth chart. You are undoubtedly all familiar with Prometheus. He is the figure most discerning astrologers link with the planet Uranus, and he is not only a thief but also a culture-bringer. In status he stands midway between the lofty Olympian gods and ordinary humanity. He is a Titan, so he has a celestial spirit in an earthly body. In many ways he is the prototype for the astrologer, as he teaches astrology to human beings, amongst other arts and sciences. In fact he teaches all facets of knowledge which reveal the unity and workings of the cosmic system.

I have spent a lot of time in other seminars talking about Prometheus, so I will not dwell on him for long.[5] But there are one or two points worth reiterating. There is a wonderful line in Aeschylos' play, *Prometheus Bound,* where Prometheus speaks about all the things he has done for humankind. He ends with a profoundly Uranian declaration: "I have made men cease to contemplate their deaths." This vision of what Plato called "the eternal realities" is often invoked during astrological work, and in this sense the archetypal figure of Prometheus is part of the psychological inheritance of the astrologer. The revelation of an orderly cosmos, and the discovery that events do not happen by chance, can be as illuminating to the client as Prometheus' stolen fire was to human beings.

Prometheus is a bridge-maker, because he carries something from the world of the gods to the world of mortal incarnation. The fire that he carries is itself the bridge, awakening human beings to possibilities they had not recognised before. What else does the priest do, if not lift our eyes to that which lies behind the temporal, that which is eternal and part of the eternal design? Prometheus does not do this through faith; he does it through knowledge. He is Uranian, not Neptunian. But he is a true *pontifex maximus,* and the astrologer who is aligned with his vision of human potential must accept the consequences of the act of stealing fire.

We are all infected by Promethean vision. By pursuing knowledge of the cosmic system, and passing that knowledge on – particularly if it is for the purpose of raising consciousness – we align ourselves with this mythic figure. That means we are going to incur his punishment, on one level or another. He is punished because he has

---

[5]See Richard Tarnas, *Prometheus the Awakener,* Auriel Press, Oxford, 1993, and Liz Greene, *The Art of Stealing Fire: Uranus in the Horoscope,* CPA Press, London, 1996 (2004), for an astrological interpretation of the Prometheus myth.

stolen something that only the gods are allowed to possess. Whether we interpret the gods as the collective unconscious, orthodox religion, or the instinctual forces of nature, Prometheus acquires and disseminates forbidden knowledge, and is punished for his offence. If we translate that into psychological terms, what does it mean for the astrologer?

Audience: It means that we have no right to know what we know.

Liz: Yes, we are privy to a cosmic mystery which has come into our possession illicitly. We are not "supposed" to have this knowledge, and we are not supposed to pass it on. What kind of punishment do we invoke? How do the gods retaliate?

Audience: We become outsiders.

Liz: We also become thieves. We experience what we are doing as vaguely immoral.

Audience: That is probably why we continually justify what we do. I sometimes have a feeling that I "should not" know what I know about astrology. When I look at someone's chart, and see how much there is to be seen about such deep things in the person, I wonder why I should be entitled to know all that. And I can't possibly tell people who don't know anything about it. It's true, I do feel it's vaguely immoral. I feel I don't deserve the knowledge, even though I have worked hard and studied and didn't get it through some kind of revelation.

Liz: What you are saying is very honest, and it also demonstrates my point. Feelings of guilt and isolation from the community seem to be the psychological expression of Prometheus' punishment. How do we help to create our own isolation?

Audience: We punish ourselves only if we believe that what Prometheus does is not right. If we shed that belief...

Liz: Can we shed it? Prometheus is not a thief from the point of view of human perception – how could he be, when he has transformed human life? – but from the gods' point of view he has set himself against natural law. The gods are images of natural law – or, put another way, images of the collective unconscious – and consciousness defies the natural order of things. The fire which the Titan gives to human beings is meant to be the secret of the gods. I do not think this is a "belief". It is an archetypal reality.

Prometheus, like the other images we will be exploring, may be one of the unconscious projections of the client. Individuals who hope to be given the key to the future, the key to how and why it all works, are projecting this mythic figure on the astrologer. This may be emphasised in those who are not well connected to Uranus in their own charts, and who want the astrologer to play this role for them and provide the overview and vision which they themselves cannot seem to develop. Often the astrologer serves to activate Uranus in the client's chart – not literally, although sometimes there are strong Uranian synastry contacts, but metaphorically, because we may provide a new and more comprehensive world-view which allows the client to see his or her situation from a clearer perspective. It is also common to see strong transits or progressions to the client's Uranus, or transiting Uranus making strong aspects to natal planets, at the time of the astrological consultation. A person's first encounter with astrology – and that applies to us as well as our clients – is often heralded by the shadowy figure of the great Titan carrying his stolen fire.

In the main, the unconscious person is fated by his or her character and complexes, as well as by the movements of the collective unconscious. That is the "natural" state of human beings. We blunder along and things happen and we don't know why. The moment we develop consciousness of the kind that an astrological perspective offers, we are no longer "natural". Consciousness is unnatural and artificial, because we work to achieve it. Consciousness alters the balance of the psyche. We are interfering with the organic unfoldment of life, and are defying nature. We are doing something that flies in the face of the natural order. And nature will fight back, within us as well as outside us.

Audience: You seem to be talking about the realisation that there are divine powers within the human being which make us godlike.

Liz: Yes, that is one of the things Prometheus symbolises – the recognition of the divine potential within human beings. From this perspective, we have the right to his fire without the mediation of collective religious authority. The knowledge of the ancient astrologer-priest was not deemed illicit, because the priest had earned the right to the knowledge. How? One consecrated one's life to the god, and received the gift of fire with the god's consent, rather than stealing it.

We will look at this issue of consecration more carefully later. From the collective perspective, what we are doing is illicit. From the priest's perspective, we are imparting knowledge because that is our job. This job is what Plato understood as education: we attempt to invoke a knowledge of the eternal realities that has always existed in the client's soul. But we still offend nature. I sometimes wonder whether the material misfortune, emotional unhappiness and social ostracism that so many astrologers experience have something to do with the punishment of Prometheus, enacted unconsciously and therefore literally and compulsively.

Audience: I keep thinking about the fear of knowledge. When you work with fire, you can burn your fingers. If I remember the myth correctly, Zeus punished humanity by sending them Pandora's box. So now we have illness, old age, death, and misery along with Prometheus' fire. Maybe this is why people are afraid of astrology – self-knowledge hurts.

Liz: Yes, consciousness always burns, and although it may not bring literal illness, old age, death, and misery, it brings a deeper awareness of these conditions, and therefore life can hurt us more. The mature person is often more vulnerable than the young one, because unconsciousness carries its own protection, like a kind of psychic rhinoceros hide. When we are unconscious we don't recognise the consequences of who we are and what we do, so we have less ambivalence and suffer less internally. When we are conscious, we suffer chronic ambivalence. This too may be part of Prometheus' punishment.

The client may find through an astrological consultation that his or her apparently irreconcilable conflict is reconcilable after all, but the same grace may not be available for the astrologer who gave the client the advice. We may not be able to make our own lives perfect through the knowledge we possess, and we may have to give up the fantasy that we can. That may be another way in which Promethean suffering manifests itself in our lives. There is an understandable tendency amongst astrologers to hope that, if one learns enough, one will be able to avoid going through the kinds of things that other people go through. We want our work to exempt us from ordinary human suffering. Far from exempting us, it may make matters worse.

Audience: Would you say that this applies to psychology also?

Liz: Yes, I believe so. It applies to any kind of increase in consciousness. There is a tendency on the part of the lay person to assume that anyone who practices as a psychotherapist is, or should be, devoid of conflicts and problems. It is possible that the psychotherapist also harbours this secret feeling, and this may account for much of the guilt-induced self-destructiveness which can be observed within the profession. Yet any sort of deep understanding of and compassion for other human beings seems to arise only through being injured by life, and often the healer or teacher cannot find a way to alleviate his or her own loneliness and alienation. Prometheus is extremely important for the psychologist as well as the astrologer.

This does not mean we should try to identify with this mythic figure. But we need to be aware of when the Promethean vision motivates our interpretations, and when it constellates our guilt. We are not Titans, nor are we redeemers of humanity. We are made of the same stuff as our clients, and can only claim a difference in that we know how to read funny little squiggles in a circle on a piece of paper. Anyone can learn to read these squiggles, given sufficient time and effort. Astrological knowledge is Promethean because it pulls aside the veil and reveals the orderly workings of the cosmos. Thus it is illicit knowledge, from the perspective of the collective. But we might also remember that Pandora's box contained hope as well as woes.

Apollo and solar consciousness

As the representation of solar light and consciousness, Apollo was perceived as a cosmocrator. For this reason he is important to us as an archetypal figure. Apollo is often shown with a snake, which is an image of the great serpent Python which he conquered. Python is a symbol of the underworld powers over which Apollo alone among the celestial deities had control. The snake is also the Great Round, the eternal circle of the heavens and of fate. We will meet this snake again as the companion of Asklepios, Apollo's son.

Apollo is a complex god with many faces, among them prophecy and music. Above all, he is Helios, the centre of the solar system and the cosmocrator who regulates the orderly movements of the heavens. For this reason he was often associated with astrology, and in many statues and frescoes he is shown holding the band of the ecliptic like a giant hula-hoop, or wearing a kind of sash on which are inscribed the signs of the zodiac. Apollo is also the slayer of family curses, the god who presides over what we might now call individual consciousness. Where Prometheus brings knowledge of the cosmos, Apollo brings knowledge of oneself. "Know thyself!" was carved over the doorway to his shrine at Delphi. The divine light-bringer offers psychological as well as physical light, and through knowledge of the planetary movements the darkness of inherited guilt and conflict is dissipated. When we focus our work on illuminating the client's dilemma, bringing light into the individual's darkness and helping to dispel the grip of the family past, we are aligning ourselves with that energy of which this remarkable mythic figure is the chief embodiment.

Does this archetypal image, like that of Prometheus, carry consequences? I believe it does. Apollo's struggle with the serpent Python, which is a single event in the myth, occurs repeatedly in those who are aligned with solar consciousness. Apollo is no friend to the underworld powers. His conflict with the Furies in the Orestes myth is irreconcilable until the goddess Athene steps in to break the deadlock. Life is not entirely a bed of roses for the "gentleman of Olympus", because the chthonic forces always seek to overturn his position, particularly through family and community relationships. In myth, Apollo has no partner and has bad luck with his children. The women whom he pursues reject him – Daphne, for example, prefers to become a laurel tree rather than submit to his embraces. His son Phaëton is destroyed when the solar chariot runs out of control. Asklepios is struck down by Zeus. Orpheus is torn to pieces by the Maenads. Apollo is a radiant but lonely god.

The god himself does not appear to suffer. But there are similarities with Prometheus in that this figure is essentially alone, as is the individual who separates himself or herself from the collective through consciousness. Nor is Apollo an outlaw; he is honoured by both gods and humans. He is surrounded, moreover, by his Muses, who symbolise different aspects of the arts. Urania, the Muse of astrology, is one of these. They are not partners in the sense of being equals, but they reflect the creative power of the god. Yet those astrologers who espouse a solar vision – the unique value of the individual and the healing power of individual self-expression – may also have to accept the sense of alienation from family and community which such a perspective brings.

Chiron and the wounded healer

Audience: I just wondered how much Chiron's theme comes in here. He and Prometheus both suffer, and Prometheus is responsible for allowing him to become mortal and die.

Liz: Yes, I was about to move on to Chiron. This is another extremely important mythic image to which, like it or not, we have a profound link. It is the mythic figure rather than the planet which I would like to explore. Chiron, like Prometheus, is a teacher of astrology. Among his astrological pupils was Asklepios, whom we will get to shortly. Chiron is indeed linked with Prometheus, because Prometheus gives the Centaur his own place in the underworld so that he can be freed from his suffering. Chiron is not an eternal spirit. He dies according to his own wish, because he cannot stand the pain anymore. Or we might say that he is transformed, because he lets go of his immortality and therefore of his pain.

There are many beautiful representations of Chiron in frescoes and mosaics, mainly from the Roman period. Usually he bears a child on his back, reflecting his role as teacher and educator. Although usually portrayed naked, he is occasionally shown dressed in an ordinary *chiton* like any Greek businessman. This indicates his civilised nature, although it must be rather difficult to find the right cut of *chiton* if one is half-horse. The figure of the wounded healer is well-known within the helping professions. One of the ways in which we understand this mythic image is that we cannot experience compassion if we have not been hurt ourselves. If we don't know what pain feels like, we cannot recognise or respond to it in others. Therefore we have something to offer other people who are wounded only if we have been wounded ourselves, and can be honest about the nature of the wound and the kind of pain we carry.

There is a common assumption, amongst helpers as well as the collective, that anyone who goes into the helping professions does so because of innate altruism and idealism. But of course it is not so simple. I do not doubt that altruism and idealism exist, often in large quantities, in those who are dedicated to helping others. But we take up this work also because life has hurt us, and there is a tremendous desire to understand why this suffering has taken place. In our efforts to understand the suffering, we begin to recognise it in other people as well, and we feel that something creative and meaningful can be made out of our own pain if we can help alleviate that of other people.

The desire to alleviate suffering through understanding is not universal. There are many people who offer their help through a more emotional and intuitive path such as spiritual healing, or caring for the ill and elderly. But astrologers are driven by an intellectual quest, a need to find some kind of cosmic order which can give meaning, if not an answer, to the mystery of human suffering. This is where we see the Centaur at work, for in myth he is not only a healer – he is a philosopher-sage and a teacher of astrology.

The unconscious impetus behind the astrologer, as with any other helper, may not be only altruism, vision, and idealism – it may also be pain. That is what the myth of Chiron describes. Prometheus steals his fire because of idealism; his pain comes later. These two different mythic figures describe two different archetypal backgrounds to our work. Both are relevant. Prometheus is a visionary, who benefits human beings because he sees their potential. Chiron heals because he suffers, and he suffers even before he is wounded by Herakles' arrow. He is half-god and half-beast, alone and outcast from both humankind and his own wild tribe of centaurs. He stands at the interface between the primal forces of the collective unconscious and the civilised structures of social consciousness, and he is injured and made wise by both. The ramifications of this myth for the astrologer are very profound, because they hint at the deeper reasons why we do this work. What started all of you on this journey? How did you get here?

Audience: It's a long story.

Liz: I expect it's a long story for every one of us. But it is worth thinking about the beginning of that story – whether it begins with some experience of suffering for which you had no explanation, and which propelled you into the desire for deeper knowledge. Otherwise, why didn't you just go to your local vicar? He or she could have told you that whatever happens to you is God's will. Why did you choose to learn astrology to make sense of your life?

Audience: I wanted something more than the reassurance that God was behind it. I suppose I wanted knowledge, because knowledge gives me a kind of empowerment. Being told it's God's will puts you in a very passive position, like a child.

Audience: We need to understand.

Liz: That seems to be the crux of it – we need to understand. This is the quality of Chiron, who cannot lie down and quietly accept life's blows, but instead seeks insight into the meaning of it – even if this does not heal the wound. We also need to feel that we can make something creative out of our wounds. We must believe we have something to offer life, in spite of being wounded. We wish to be people who walk upright, not injured victims who crawl. As you say, this is empowerment. If we have knowledge, our hurts do not render us impotent, maimed, and ineffectual. We can still contribute something positive, and can still have personal potency in spite of the wound – or perhaps even because of it.

Audience: You are saying we need a context for the wound, so it becomes something more than a wound.

Liz: The spirit of Chiron makes us want to understand the context in which we have been hurt. The impulse to teach, to offer what we have learned, is peculiar to this mythic figure. He is the archetypal teacher. Other mythic figures give knowledge – Hermes, Prometheus, Athene – but teaching is not their main job. Their conferring of knowledge is incidental to their function. There is something quite remarkable about the impulse to teach. We have been hurt by life, and in response we learn astrology so that we can make sense of life. We need to understand But why do we feel we must pass on our knowledge to other people?

Audience: It binds us together with other sufferers.

Audience: It brings us back into a sense of collective participation. We aren't isolated any more.

Audience: It regenerates us.

Liz: Yes, we are invoking an experience of mutual compassion and mutual understanding, and then the wound does not hurt as much. Wounds are truly terrible when they are experienced in isolation. When we know that someone else has been wounded, we can say together, "Yes, I know what that feels like. I know what it is like to lose someone. I know what it is like to be lonely. I know what it is like to have a physical handicap. I know what it is like to be human." This makes an enormous difference. It isn't the same as suffering alone. In that moment of communion, we experience healing. We are trying to heal ourselves through a connection with other human beings. In this way we cut across the suffering caused by our isolation, by our heresy, by our illicit knowledge, by the mess that Prometheus has landed us in because he is a thieving outlaw. We are restored to our priestly roles. A priest needs a congregation. Why does a priest preach? Why does he or she need to talk to people about God? Every time the priest inspires someone else's faith, his or her own faith is renewed.

Audience: It is interesting that you use the word "connection", because the root of the word "religion" means to reconnect.

Liz: We astrologers do isolate ourselves, because of both our history and our connection with Promethean fire. The Promethean spirit is deeply alien and cut off from life. Through practising this art, which may be seen as a form of education, we reconnect with both other humans and the cosmos, so we are not quite so alienated any more.

Audience: I feel very lonely in this work. Ten years ago somebody said to me, "If you carry on doing this, you are going to be alone." Now I understand exactly what he was saying.

Liz: That is the punishment of Prometheus and the innate condition of Apollo and Chiron. Belonging in the instinctual sense is inevitably destroyed by any knowledge which separates us from the collective. As long as we have groups like this to go to – and there are many astrological, spiritual, esoteric, and psychological groups – we can escape some of that sense of isolation. In some ways the comfort is illusory, because we have merely found a subculture of other people equally isolated from the collective. Yet it may be enough.

Any move toward individual consciousness involves the experience of aloneness. If we are dishonest about this, and imagine that we can escape it by joining the Astrological Association, the Astrological Lodge, the Faculty of Astrological Studies, the CPA, or any other like-minded group, we may be deeply disappointed, because we will still have to face the consequences of our illicit act. In many esoteric and spiritual groups there is enormous hunger. The hunger is only partly for the teaching. It is also for a connection with a body of fellow sufferers and seekers, amongst whom one can forget one's isolation. One finds a surrogate collective, perhaps even a surrogate family, to replace the one from which one has been alienated.

Audience: Isn't that true for every human being in some way?

Liz: On the most fundamental level, yes, it is true for every human being. But I think it is a different kind of aloneness. Many people grow up thinking and feeling in a tribal way, and they "fit". They belong because they are not yet individuals. Even when a crisis hits, they can always turn on *Coronation Street* or *Brookside* or *Eastenders* and receive the given wisdom of the collective. Loneliness for such people means being without a partner or family or friends. The loneliness of consciousness exists even when one is surrounded by partners, family, and friends. Ordinary human loneliness afflicts us all, and can be alleviated by companionship. The loneliness of individuality is mitigated by companionship only to a degree, because it is of a different kind.

How do we articulate the isolation that consciousness brings? It is almost impossible to communicate how it feels. How many of you have been in depth psychotherapy? Most of you? Then you know that the reality of the unconscious will always affect your experience of other people. Your perception of their motives and behaviour, as well as of your own, becomes multi-levelled. Someone says something and you know perfectly well that there is a hidden agenda behind the words, because you can hear it, smell it, and feel it. The agenda may not be negative. But nothing is quite as it seems on the surface. And your knowledge of the person's horoscope may make matters worse, because you are then aware of important things about others of which they themselves may be oblivious.

If the people around you have absolutely no awareness of these deeper levels of reality, how do you explain your reality to them? You can say to your hostess at a dinner party, "I'm sorry I spilled wine all over your sofa, but it's probably because I have unconscious feelings of hostility toward you. I expect I am projecting my mother on you." Or, "I'm sorry to hear your son is doing badly at school, but it may be because he feels the weight of your unconscious expectations and is asserting his identity by retaliating." This is not a good recipe for social popularity. In the end it is like having a gag put across one's mouth. Consciousness isolates, and nowhere more intensely than within the very relationships that are supposed to take away our isolation.

Audience: My problem is learning to shut up about these things. I keep blurting out exactly the kind of thing you are talking about. Then I feel very hurt when the other person doesn't want to hear it.

Liz: That is Stage One. Stage Two involves getting rather Byronesque and a bit paranoid. One feels slightly inflated and very special, because one knows things others don't know. Stage Three involves learning to laugh at oneself, which usually accompanies the realisation that one is not so special after all. Stage Four involves making peace with what one is and what one has chosen. We may have to learn the hard way not to be compulsive about communicating what we know. That is another way of saying that we may have to learn to live with a certain degree of isolation.

Jupiter and divine law

Now I would like to move on to Zeus-Jupiter. You are probably all familiar with portrayals of him seated with his eagle and the sceptre of rulership in his hand, looking every inch a king. But what does he really rule? Certain mythic figures are regularly portrayed bearing the celestial globe or the wheel of the zodiac, and Jupiter is one of these. This is not because Jupiter teaches knowledge of the cosmic order to human beings. He *is* the cosmic order. He is the cosmocrator who ensures that the whole system continues to operate according to divine law. Jupiter, like Apollo, can symbolise the mind of God, the divine will behind all manifestation. The Greeks favoured Apollo in this role, but the Romans favoured Jupiter – perhaps because he is more imperial. Also, he had a more interesting love-life.

Jupiter's relationship with astrology should be no surprise. After all, we associate the planet with the 9th house, which is concerned with philosophy, religious and spiritual matters, and all "universal" systems of thought which can help us to extract meaning from life experience. This is a different approach to astrology from that of

Prometheus. It does not concern forbidden knowledge, but reflects an intuitive revelation of the bounty and essential goodness of the cosmos.

The astrologer with a strong 9th house, a dominant Jupiter, or an emphasis in Sagittarius may experience his or her work as a means by which the greater pattern can be revealed, and through which one can reconnect with the bountiful and generous source of life. This is the joyful dimension of our art, and it conveys the sense that we will be looked after by an intelligent and beneficent source. On the psychological level, the study of astrology can sometimes be a kind of Great Father, a world to which we can turn when in distress because we are reassured of our place in the universe and the eventual resolution of conflict and pain.

Jupiter is also the dispenser of gifts, and the motives which propel us to do this work are not limited to pain, compassion, or an impersonal humanitarian vision. Chiron, Apollo and Prometheus are not the only perspectives which drive us to pursue this art. We may also revel in the pleasure of enlightening others and revealing a universal context for their everyday dilemmas. We may be Jupiterian without being Promethean. Reforming the world may not be every astrologer's cup of tea, but the revelation of its hidden design may provide inspiration, faith, humour, generosity, and a willingness to endure many hardships because we know we can learn from them and become better people.

Jupiter too has his ambivalent side, and it is connected with inflation and an excessive sense of self-importance. Having an adoring group of acolytes at one's feet can be very pleasing to a swollen Jupiter, especially if they are sexually attractive and pay well, and the astrologer who identifies with this role may have more in common with the pop star and the film actor than with the doctor and the psychotherapist. Astrology has its showy side. Its representatives invariably offend those Saturnian astrologers who want very badly to be seen as respectable by the scientific community, and who may have forgotten, beneath the weight of Promethean idealism and Chironian pain, that astrology can also be great fun.

At a European astrology conference some years ago, I overheard the organisers discussing whether or not a particular famous newspaper astrologer (who shall remain nameless, but who has a Sagittarian

Ascendant with Jupiter conjunct the Sun in the 1st house) should be invited to speak at the next Congress. The decision not to invite her was unanimous. The reason? Because she was too glamorous and wore low-cut dresses when presenting lectures. In a similar vein, at an analytic congress, a male analyst of my acquaintance turned up in a bright yellow sports jacket to give a lecture. He looked very attractive in this jacket, rather like the proverbial bird of paradise amongst chickens. A pair of elderly ladies of the sober, caring type could not refrain from pointing out to him that such garb was unsuitable for an analyst. What kind of clothes *are* suitable for an analyst? Although these incidents may seem insignificant compared with the grandeur of the archetypal realm, they are highly symbolic. It is in such small encounters that we may see the archetype peeping through, and the responses which it constellates in others.

Jupiter run amok can sometimes immerse us in sleaze. But all work and no Jupiter makes Jack, and the astrologer, a very dull boy or girl indeed. The world-view of the dark side of Jupiter can lead to slickness, financial trickiness, and a kind of infantile Oedipal rivalry with colleagues. Yet this great god, king of heaven and giver of gifts, is as important to us as any of the other images we are exploring. Without his joy, creative fertility, and eternal youthfulness, we lose our way among the thorns of incarnation, and forget that, above all else, we as well as the client may need to discover that the world is actually a good place to be after all.

Semi-divine male figures: Orpheus and the sacrifice of desire

Now we must come down from the Olympian heights and consider two more male figures. These are semi-divine humans, fathered by a god but incarnated in mortal flesh, and therefore subject to the same mess as the rest of us. Both were said to be the sons of Apollo, although there are alternative stories about their human parentage. One if not both may also have an historical basis, and may have been accorded a mythic status not dissimilar to the one we accord to the historical Jesus. Finally, both conveyed divine wisdom to their followers, amongst which was astrology as the expression of the orderly cosmic system.

Orpheus probably existed, although it is impossible to prove. There are enough similar stories from varied sources to suggest that there really was a bard wandering around Thrace at a certain point between the 6th and 5th centuries BCE, who was an initiate of the Dionysian mysteries and taught cosmic wisdom to a group of disciples. Although many myths give him mortal parentage, he was also accorded the honour of being the son of Apollo. He expressed his wisdom through poetry and song, and also through astrology. The Orphic cult which formed around his teachings had great influence on the development of early Christianity, and iconographically Orpheus and Christ are sometimes interchangeable. For example, one late Roman medallion portrays Orpheus, with his lyre, hanging from a cross. In myth he is a seer and a mystic, and he is an important figure for any astrologer working intuitively and poetically to understand and communicate the heavenly design.

Orpheus was a favourite figure in ancient iconography, and there are many representations of him. He is often shown surrounded by the animals he tamed with his music. Occasionally he is portrayed surrounded by the signs of the zodiac, or by twelve animals which symbolise the twelve signs. The animals represent wild nature, within the human being as well as in the world, and the poet-astrologer's capacity to subdue their savagery reflects the healing power of the cosmic "music" which he sings.

Orphic teaching was highly moral, and also highly eschatological – in other words, it was concerned with the redemption of the spirit from the darkness of mortal incarnation. This dualist world-view has a good deal in common with Christianity, and is still reverberating in the collective, not least in the world of astrology. The Orphics didn't say, "The cosmos is orderly and the planets make patterns which are reflected in human life. Get on with it." Instead, they declared, "The cosmos is orderly, the planets make patterns which are reflected in human life, and you must align yourself with the higher level of these patterns if you wish to find spiritual enlightenment. You must conquer your lower nature and espouse an ascetic life which is anti-instinctual and anti-material. Then you will not be subject to the darker aspects of the planetary order. You will be an initiate of the mysteries, fit to transmit their wisdom to others."

This is all rather familiar, although some astrologers might not realise it was Orphism which started this ball rolling. Asceticism and sacrifice of the desire-nature enter the world of astrology coincident with the rise of the Orphic cult. In myth Orpheus himself came to a bad end. The women who celebrated the Dionysian mysteries that he reformed were offended at his repudiation of the feminine and his denigration of the instinctual side of the cult. So they tore off his head, which, according to the story, went on singing and became the cult object of a famous shrine.

Among other things, the story of Orpheus and the precepts of the Orphic cult present us with the moral dilemma of how much the astrologer's personal behaviour and lifestyle affect his or her effectiveness in the role of *pontifex*. The Orphic world-view contains many paradoxes and raises many questions, and there is a profound warning to be read in the symbolism of Orpheus' death. The split between spirit and matter is the source of a great many difficulties in our work, because when we align ourselves with the eschatological perspective of Orpheus we view the chart in a dualist way. We see some planets and configurations as "higher" and others as "lower", and we feel it is appropriate to bring moral dictates into the astrological session. We may believe the individual must "transcend" certain dimensions of the horoscope, and although there may be few astrologers who entirely espouse the strict lifestyle of the Orphic priest, there are many who follow it to one degree or another – or feel they ought to.

The Orphic world-view tells us that the degree of our willingness to sacrifice personal desires has bearing on how effective we are as astrologers. This could open up a discussion that would keep us here for weeks, because although the particular moral precepts of the Orphic cult may seem excessive now, the underlying issue is still relevant. We need to consider the importance of morality in relation to astrological work – the morality of the astrologer and the morality the astrologer conveys to the client. Orpheus is part of our archetypal background, and like the other mythic figures, he may be the primary figure for particular astrologers, colouring their perception of the meaning and purpose of their work. How many of you believe that the moral tone of our personal lives affects the kind of astrologers we are? All of you have put your hands up. Very good. The problem is, which morality do we espouse?

Audience: I think it has something to do with integrity. Integrity is knowing and living by our own rules.

Liz: Yes, one definition of integrity is living by the principles that one espouses. But we are in very tricky terrain. What are those principles? How does the astrologer acquire them? From a guru? From parents and family? From friends? From a spiritual revelation? From psychotherapy? Are these principles of the "conquer your Venus in Scorpio square Pluto because it is part of your lower nature" variety? Are they of the "marriage is forever and I will tell every client who is thinking of leaving his or her spouse that it is morally wrong" variety? Are they of the "I am a Labour supporter and any other political perspective is selfish and wrong" variety? Do we have the right to impose our personal morality on the client? Do we have sufficient wisdom to know when the client is in violation of a spiritual truth? And if we have a client who tells us in confidence that he or she is thinking of robbing a bank, or is secretly a member of the IRA, is it right to interfere? For that matter, is it right *not* to interfere?

Audience: You don't believe in making it easy for us, do you?

Liz: No. It wouldn't be any fun otherwise. But if we are to practise what we preach, which is how one of you defined integrity, we are forced to recognise that no one is in a position to tell us as individuals what morality we should espouse; nor are we in a position to tell our clients. No one can do that because the birth chart is a highly individual thing, and the kind of value system that the birth chart reflects will equally be a highly individual thing, and cannot be reduced to universal precepts which are right for everybody. I am not talking about what constitutes morality in a social sense. That is pragmatic in nature. If we allow people to beat each other up and murder each other, we are faced with social chaos, and therefore we create laws which forbid certain kinds of behaviour. The morality to which I am referring is far subtler.

The primary theme which runs through the Orphic myth and teachings is that something must be given up in order to be a priest-teacher. Something must be purified, cleansed, or sacrificed. There must be a willingness to consecrate. Consecrate means to make sacred. One must consecrate one's life in order to be a priest. What does that mean on a personal level? How do you consecrate your life?

Audience: You give up personal investment in what you are doing.

Liz: That is a beautiful ideal. But is it humanly possible? One can aspire to it, like the speed limit on Italian motorways, but how do we accomplish it? And what, after all, is fundamentally wrong or bad about the personal needs and wishes of the astrologer?

Audience: Nothing, I suppose, except if we put them before the needs of the client.

Liz: And what if the client's needs mean he or she rings you every night at 11.30 wanting advice, and takes to dropping in regularly for heart-to-heart chats, and doesn't feel inclined to pay your fee, and also takes a fancy to your boyfriend? Ideal and reality, as usual, may be rather far apart. We are back to the problem of identification with an archetype. It is *hubris* to think we can be Orpheus, because he is a mythic figure. If we try to be Orpheus, we will probably wind up in a psychiatric ward, which is the symbolic equivalent of losing one's head. At best, we will wind up with nobody wanting to consult us, because we will go around in hair shirts, emaciated from having eaten nothing except lettuce, smelling terrible, and convincing the general public what they already believe – that we are raving loonies. The Orphic vision needs to be accommodated to reality, which means, first of all, the individual reality of the astrologer, and second, the individual reality of the client.

Audience: I think this sort of aspiration towards purity is quite dangerous psychologically. And it isn't a constructive quality to bring into a consultation, because it means separating yourself from the ordinary humanity of the client.

Audience: I don't think you need to align yourself with a non-human figure in order to practice astrology.

Liz: No, we do not need to align ourselves. It would be much better if we didn't. But it is unlikely that we can avoid being affected by these archetypal patterns. The language of astrology is itself archetypal, and one needs a very long spoon to sup with an archetype. The alignment happens at an unconscious level. It is another way of saying that the individual astrologer, because of the particular nature of his or her chart, espouses a certain world-view, and perceives reality through that lens. Prometheus, Chiron, Apollo, and Orpheus are lenses through which we experience and interpret life. I am using the mythic images to describe these modes of perception because they are evocative, and their stories give us insights which a more rational analysis might fail to provide.

Identification with an archetypal figure constitutes a dangerous inflation. We need to learn *not* to align ourselves in that way, by discovering when we are doing it unconsciously. The individual who borrows a sense of potency through such identification is usually attempting to compensate for a severe lack of self-worth. But rather than increasing self-worth, archetypal identification creates an impossible divide between the individual and external reality. What we call madness is often linked with this increasing loss of connection with external life, and a corresponding inflation within. These mythic figures describe the archetypal patterns which inspire our work. They are images of a particular function in life. In the same way, the craftsman is aligned with Hephaistos, and the writer with Hermes. It doesn't mean we should set up an altar in the bedroom with a statue of the god. It means we need to understand the source of our inspiration, because it colours both our world-view and the way others perceive us.

Orpheus reflects a particular way of tapping the wisdom of the cosmos, which is poetic, intuitive, and passional rather than rational and pragmatic. The seven strings of his lyre symbolise the seven planets, whose cycles create the "music of the spheres". His capacity to tame the beasts and make the stones weep with his music reflects the healing potential which such a vision of cosmic order and harmony can release. Knowledge of the "music of the spheres" was meant to awaken the spirit from its numb apathy within the prison of mortal incarnation. Orpheus is a medium rather than a creator-god, channeling solar light through poetry and rendering himself a fitting vessel through asceticism, self-sacrifice, and denial of personal desire. I am sure you can all see how powerful a mode of perception this figure symbolises for those involved in the study and practice of astrology.

Asklepios and the art of healing

We can complete our little survey of male archetypal figures with Asklepios, because he too is part of the mythic background of astrology. He is a semi-divine figure, partly human and therefore subject to death like the rest of us. He is relevant not only because he is invoked when our work concerns the psychological health of the client, but also because he breached the law of life and death by raising a dead man to life. For this crime Zeus struck him down. He acted out of compassion, but behind the compassion was also *hubris,* so his punishment, from the perspective of the gods, was just.

Asklepios' tragic end is a disturbing image of the necessity of recognising our limits. We cannot heal everything, and it is *hubris* to try. As astrologers we are not usually involved in attempting to raise the dead, at least not at CPA seminars, but we might take this act as a symbol of attempting to alter necessity and undo that which is irrevocable. Death belongs to the realm of Hades-Pluto, whose word is incontestable, even by Zeus. Thus there are experiences and dilemmas in which both we and our clients find ourselves which no amount of astrologising or psychologising can alter. Pluto's domain often involves coming to terms with the unchangeable, especially with regard to family inheritance, and it is perhaps in this sphere that Asklepian *hubris* proves most tempting to the psychologically inclined. We want our clients to be happy and fulfilled, and we try to find solutions to difficult configurations in the birth chart. But the birth chart itself is a kind of necessity, and all human beings must learn to live creatively within the limits they have been given.

Asklepios was said to have been taught healing and astrology by Chiron, and in turn he himself became a teacher of astrology and cosmic wisdom, as well as being the god of healing. In the *Corpus Hermeticum,* that remarkable collection of Neoplatonic and Hermetic writings from the 1st and 2nd centuries CE, Asklepios is presented as the pupil of Hermes Trismegistos, and in turn becomes a teacher himself in many of the texts. Asklepios is generally shown bearded in Greco-Roman art, but occasionally his likeness to his father Apollo is emphasised, not only in his youth and beauty, but also in the *omphalos* which is frequently seen at his feet. A larger version of this *omphalos* or "navel stone" can be seen at Delphi, the chief shrine of Apollo. It symbolises the linking point between heaven and earth, the navel of the great Earth-mother which connects all that lives in mortal incarnation with the eternal world of the heavens and the Sun-god. Asklepios, like Apollo, is usually portrayed with a snake (or sometimes two snakes) wrapped around his staff. The caduceus entwined with two snakes has today become the traditional symbol of the medical practitioner.

As a god of healing, Asklepios is relevant to all astrologers who seek to facilitate the psychological health of the client. He is also often present in the astrological session because the client in search of healing will project this archetypal figure onto the astrologer as well as the medical doctor, and expect everything to be made better if the astrologer's prognosis is correct. As is fitting for a child of Apollo, Asklepios is a bright and positive image, and any astrologer motivated by a desire to heal others' suffering will be strongly aligned with this figure. The more we are aligned with him, however, the greater the risk we run of overestimating what we can achieve through our work, and the more likely we are to be seduced by the client's unconscious expectations of a miracle. The capacity to accept that which cannot be changed lies with other figures, very different from the masculine images we have been exploring, and we now need to turn to them.

Divine female images

There are a number of female figures which are associated with astrology, and most of these are much older than the masculine images which we have just examined. Their symbolism points us in a very different direction. Apollo, Prometheus, Chiron, Asklepios, and Orpheus are essentially concerned with the spirit, and with the place of the human being in the larger cosmic system. All are on the "side", if that is the right term, of evolution and consciousness, as might be expected from figures connected with the heavens and with solar fire. Astrology in this context is a means of connecting with the spiritual source, and of aligning oneself with the goodness and order in the cosmos. From this perspective astrology is a transformative art. The astrologer who draws from this source is essentially focused on the potentials of the human spirit, and not on the limits of fate which circumscribe each human life.

With the feminine images, excepting the Muse Urania whom we will come to shortly, the roots, feeling-tone, and meaning are, at first glance, antithetical to what we have already explored. These female figures are linked with the cycles of the Moon, the inevitability of death, and the secrets of the underworld. They are all forms of the Great Mother, and they dispense the share or allotment given to each creature in mortal incarnation.

This is as healing a perspective as that of the male deities, but it is not concerned with spiritual potential as much as with an acceptance of life on earth. The astrologer who draws from this source is essentially focused on life here and now, and on helping the client come to terms with the inevitable cycles of time and change. The positive dimension of the archetypal perspective which these figures reflect fosters tolerance, patience, and compassion, as well as the wisdom to recognise the quality of the moment and the necessity of letting go. The negative dimension fosters fatalism, passive acceptance of planetary patterns, and an emphasis on sickness and suffering. The astrologer who is unconsciously identified with these figures may also seek to keep the client in an infantile and dependent state, rather than encouraging him or her to develop an independent decision-making capacity and sense of personal responsibility.

The Moirae

The oldest of these feminine images is Moira or Fate. The three Moirae are frequently portrayed on Greco-Roman sarcophagi. Clotho is shown reading the book in which the fate of the deceased is written; Lachesis is shown winding the life-thread around a spindle; Atropos is shown inspecting the celestial globe which contains the planetary patterns presiding over the dead person during his or her life.

The Moirae symbolise that which has been written at birth – the limits circumscribing every mortal life, from which we cannot escape. Our allotment is inherent in our bodies, in our genetic inheritance, and in the family psyche from which we have emerged, as well as in our racial and national background. The sins of the parents are visited on the children, and the children must carry their share. *Moira* is the Greek word for allotment, share, or portion. I don't want to spend too much time on Moira (in myth she is a single figure as well as a triad), as I have already written a good deal about her in *The Astrology of Fate.* But this archetypal image wields enormous power, not only on us but also on the client who expects the shape of his or her fate to be revealed in an astrological session, and who unconsciously perceives the astrologer as the actual maker of fate – Moira herself.

Respect for the limits which circumscribe the individual can help the client come to terms with what is, rather than what he or she might ideally want life to be. It can also help the astrologer find constructive meaning in each configuration in the client's chart, interpreting it in terms of its reality rather than playing the "escape your square by using your sextile" game. Astrologers who are aligned with Moira are rarely impressed by the "transcend your lower nature" message, and are more likely to see the innate value in so-called "dark" configurations than are those who are more Orphically inclined.

The danger in being too identified with this world-view is that we may forget the remarkable power for change and transformation which consciousness can wield. There are things which perhaps we should not accept passively or perceive as fate – at least not on any outer level, and maybe not even on the inner one. Those astrologers who think in terms of karma are not always as spiritually inclined as they might think. Sometimes this term can mean, "Just accept the situation. There is nothing you can do except suffer." This is not necessarily enlightened spirituality. It may also be the unconscious dark face of Moira, and it may conceal a secret drive to feel power over the client.

Because Moira and her cousins – Artemis, Hekate, Fortuna – are associated with magic, sorcery, and the underworld, they can carry a dark and sinister connotation. It is this element which contributes to the slightly murky image of the backstreet fortune-teller which so plagues us today, and which propels so many astrologers into attempting to convince the world and themselves that astrology is a science. It should be obvious that the chthonic qualities of the underworld female deities can scare us into an overly solar and rational world-view. Then we may begin to fear that which we cannot change, and start believing that everything in the horoscope is transformable into something else.

Moira is part of our archetypal inheritance as astrologers, and she can appear very sinister indeed. Her domain is the underworld, where the fates weave and spin – a world of shrouded secrets and forbidden fruit. Moira's domain is illicit in a different way from Promethean fire. She is a symbol of mother as the giver of fate. As an archetypal image, Moira will constellate mother-issues in both the astrologer and the client – particularly those involving dependency and the power of the mother to castrate and destroy her offspring. If we unconsciously align ourselves with her, we may find that the client polarises by repudiating what we are trying to offer, because he or she feels overwhelmed and overpowered by the insights we are seeking to offer.

Moira constellates anxiety in all those who depend on the power of the rational mind, and often the skeptic of astrology as well as the scientific astrologer are unconsciously plagued by a deep fear of her. Although we may identify ourselves with solar light, Orphic transcendence, Asklepian healing, and Uranian vision, we must still contend with this great and ancient figure, first of all the gods, who emerged from Mother Night and over whom no creature, mortal or divine, has ultimate power. The best Apollo could do in myth was to make the Moirae drunk, to extend the lifespan of his friend Admetus. But although Admetus gained a bit more time, he died in the end anyway.

We do not like the feeling-tone of Moira intruding on modern astrology. When we see an astrologer on television dressed up in star-studded robes, we cringe, and do not wish to be identified in any way with such a figure. There is a daily programme on Italian television called *Luna Park,* on which a woman called "la Zingara" (the gypsy), dressed in the inevitable clanking jewelry and robes embroidered with cryptic signs, sits poker-faced with a pack of Tarot cards, and eager young couples win or lose millions of *lire* according to whether they choose *la luna nera.* This programme highlights what happens when the mantic arts (of which astrology is one) are coloured by the image of Moira in the mind of the public.

Today we have a great terror of Moira, because we value individuality and human potential so highly. Moira levels us all, and relegates us to simply another one of the myriad kingdoms of nature, all doomed to die. Each of us will have our own personal issues about this dichotomy between the masculine deities and Moira, because horoscopes contain not only aspects like Sun-Uranus and Mercury-Jupiter – they may also display aspects like Moon-Pluto.

Artemis-Hekate

Artemis is generally shown in classical art as a young maiden in a short *chiton,* carrying a bow and arrow. The Romans knew her as Diana. She was the virgin Moon-goddess, sister of Apollo and mistress of wild animals. But in pre-classical Greece, especially in the Ionian cities of what is now western Turkey, Artemis was not the coy maiden in a gym-slip with whom we are so familiar. The great Artemis of Ephesos, who was worshipped all over Asia, was portrayed with a mural crown and many breasts. She was a promiscuous goddess and her shrines were served by temple prostitutes. The mural crown (representing city walls) symbolises her power over human affairs. Her many breasts connote her boundless fertility and capacity to nourish. She was also known as Kybele. Although she is more than five thousand years old, the most famous portrayals of this chthonic Artemis date from the imperial Roman period. There are many versions of this strangely beautiful and slightly sinister hieratic figure. All bear a collar of zodiacal signs.

These representations also show a disc behind her head. This might be lunar, but it is more likely solar, partly because the Moon was usually shown as a crescent, and partly because the disc is covered in small griffins – creatures which were always associated with the Sun and were thought to carry the souls of the dead to the heavens. This solar disc, combined with the zodiac necklace, proclaims Artemis of Ephesus a female cosmocrator, who presides over not only the phases of the Moon, but also the orderly patterns of the planets and even the Sun itself. She is the All-Mother, and her antecedents as the origin of all life are far more ancient than those of the Sun-god. She is another version of Moira, the great goddess of fate.

The chief quality which distinguishes her from Moira is her specific affinity with the life of nature. She is a more approachable figure than Moira, concerned with the continuity of the life-force rather than with its allotment. Artemis is Mistress of Beasts, and this tells us something about the respect for nature – human as well as animal – which is part of this archetypal perspective. Artemis is the enemy of all those afflicted by *hubris,* but she is the friend of every young or wounded animal, and this is the positive face which she can contribute to our psychological perspective. The mother of all life also nurtures all life, and no creature is too insignificant to merit her care. It should be apparent that the archetypal image of Artemis, when we draw on it for inspiration, fosters great compassion, particularly in those spheres of "ordinary" life where so many people are wounded or lost. No spiritual superiority or intellectual prowess is required to merit the protection of the Mistress of Beasts. Being a living thing is sufficient.

Artemis is also associated with magic, and in this context she is known as Hekate. Hekate is a lunar deity, often portrayed with three faces which symbolise the phases of the Moon, and as a goddess of the underworld she presides over the realm of magic and sorcery. She may be related to that mysterious quality of intuition which many astrologers utilise – admittedly or not – when working with a client, and which also earns us a bad reputation because it allies astrology with magic and the occult. How many of you believe astrology has any connection with the occult?

Audience: I don't. I think we should do everything we can to separate them in people's minds. I associate the occult with power, and astrology is something we learn, a rational study based on observation and experience.

Liz: That is a fair comment. But there is a reason why, in public consciousness, we are always identified with "occultists", whatever those are. We may need to look at this issue more closely. Just as we are plagued by Moira, we are also plagued by Hekate, and we would be wise to try to understand why. Hekate reflects the dark, underworld side of our work. As astrologers we quite rightly wish to dissociate ourselves from magic, but magic in its most profound sense involves manipulation of the energy patterns which underpin life. Magical ritual is a disciplined, conscious, and focused application of this kind of manipulation, and whether we like it or not, the setting up of the chart and the act of interpreting it with the client comprise a form of ritual.

Psychotherapeutic work is a form of magic in this sense. When we interpret a chart, that too is a form of magic because we are intervening in the "natural", unconscious state of the client and invoking consciousness as a means of transforming (a nicer term than manipulating) the energy patterns underpinning the person's life. We may not be doing any manipulating – at least not in any sinister, power-driven way – but we may contribute to the initiation of the process of transformation simply through bringing issues into the light, and therefore we are involved in something magical. And this gives us power, the power of Hekate, who holds the secrets of the hidden side of life. We can protest and disown this, but nevertheless we are involved in it, and we need to recognise that dimension of seership which Hekate symbolises.

Hekate, because she is lunar, also reflects the inexorable process of the cycles of time, and this "secret" – one which a more material consciousness often denies – may appear magical to those who do not understand it. Astrologers know that all things move in cycles. Whether the cycle is the twenty-four-hour return of each zodiac sign to the eastern horizon, the twenty-eight-day lunar return, or the two-and-a-half-century Pluto return, everything comes round again, and there is nothing new under the Sun. The wisdom of Hekate is concerned with knowing the secret of time and the cycle-imbued qualities of the moment, and on this understanding of the moment all magic depends. That is why magical rituals are timed so precisely. One cannot perform them on any day of the week. Alchemy is also a form of magic dependent on astrological timing, and we are involved in psychological alchemy. We interact with the client on emotional and intuitive as well as intellectual levels – at the precise moment when the client sees fit to consult us, which reflects the secret of his or her inner timing.

We may not like the image of Hekate, and may not wish to be associated with it. They didn't like her even in ancient times, because Hekate in popular consciousness was always connected with witchcraft, spells, and other exhalations of the nether regions. We have a hard time today convincing certain particularly obtuse lay persons that astrology and witchcraft have nothing to do with one another. I am not suggesting that there is any overt link, either in practice or in intent. But Hekate, like Artemis, is connected with a certain kind of knowledge of the dark side of life, and this knowledge is secret – not illicit in the Promethean sense, but hidden from those who walk in the daylight world. Hekate was also the goddess of crossroads, where the bodies of executed criminals were buried to prevent their ghosts from walking. While remaining mistress of the dark forces, she also protected humans from them. We are neither witches nor occultists. Nevertheless Hekate may sometimes be present in the astrological session.

Fortuna

Fortuna is a uniquely Roman deity in character, although she has antecedents in the Etruscan pantheon and in the Greek Tyche (destiny)   and, of course, in Moira herself. She was called Fortuna Primagenia – "first-born" – and in this guise is shown suckling the infant Zeus. She is thus, like Moira, a parthenogenic cosmocrator, a power already present in the cosmos before the bright Olympian gods take rulership of the heavens. Fortuna is generally portrayed with a cornucopia to reflect her beneficent role as the bringer of riches, but she also carries a wheel (a flat disk with a nub at the centre). This is the "Wheel of Fortune" which has come down to us as one of the Major Arcana of the Tarot. This wheel is an important astrological symbol, because its origins lie in the circle of the Sun traversing the heavens. The circle with a point at the centre is not only our astrological signature for the Sun; it was also Apollo's symbol and appears with his image on many Greek coins. The hub at the centre is the *omphalos*. Many temples and shrines to both Apollo and Fortuna were built as circular structures, linking the two deities through the symbolism of the Sun's passage around the heavens. Fortuna is thus both a solar deity and also an image of the earthly plane through which solar power manifests.

The Latin word *fortuna* is derived from an Etruscan word which means the yearly passage of the Sun. As the solar light moves through the different zodiacal signs and mansions of the heavens, so do the fortunes of all living things ebb and flow. The Etruscans had a goddess called Nortia, an early form of the Roman Fortuna, and annually at a festival to celebrate the birth of the new year the Year Nail was driven into the wall of the temple of Nortia to symbolise the inevitability of fate. The relationship between Fortuna and astrology is a deep one, although she is not generally represented with a zodiac. Her wheel, however, is precisely that.

During the period of the Roman Republic, the cult of Fortuna reached an apotheosis, and many great temple complexes were built in her honour. One of the most impressive is at Praeneste (the modern Palestrina), set on a hillside south of Rome. A particularly striking feature of this great shrine complex is that everything is built in multiples of seven. There are seven terraces, and a tholus or circular shrine with seven columns. When visiting this site, I asked the superintendent of archaeology what the seven might mean – knowing full well that he would probably avoid the obvious answer. He nattered on about the seven days of the week, whereupon I suggested that the structure of the shrine, like the days of the week, was based on the symbolism of the seven planets. He smiled, nodded, and said, *"Ecco!"*, which in this context means, to quote the words of Francis Urqhart, "You might think so, but I couldn't possibly comment."

Fortuna also has a good deal to do with the collective association of astrology with fortune-telling. The flourishing of down-market astrological prediction during the Roman period owes much of its strength to the popularity of Fortuna. The darker face of this figure is connected with a world-view which perceives life as a kind of giant cosmic lottery, about which we can do nothing except wait for the main chance. Astrological prognostication of this kind is not concerned with either transformation or a compassionate acceptance of life as it is. It is meant to help the individual recognise the cycles of good and bad fortune so that he or she can take advantage of the former while avoiding the latter as much as possible. There is no morality in Fortuna, although there was a profound morality in the Greek philosophical conception of Moira. In Fortuna's world, the wicked rise and the good are crushed beneath the wheel.

When we are aligned with Fortuna, we offer our art as a means of interpreting what is to come, so that the client can take advantage of good fortune and protect himself or herself against bad fortune. Many modern astrologers identify with this role, and do not pretend to aspire to a deeper or higher level of interpretation. When performed with integrity it is a valid and useful role, offering sound advice and providing some protection against the vicissitudes of life. Its dark face is concerned with the fostering of a passive attitude, where the individual takes no responsibility for the planets as inner psychic factors, and can therefore do nothing to influence the impersonal turning of the wheel.

The client too may unconsciously espouse this perception of astrology, and assume that we will provide definitive advice about decisions and events. He or she may become resentful if we begin to speak psychologically, or imply that there might be an inner correlation to an outer event. The majority of lay people who read their Sun-sign predictions in the newspaper see astrology through the lens of Fortuna. As a collective we have not moved very far from the world of imperial Rome, with its pragmatic and utilitarian outlook and its emphasis on controlling external reality. There are many astrologers who feel strongly that this is their role. Fortuna is a powerful image, and unconscious identification with her makes the astrologer the giver of riches. This may be very tempting for an insecure astrologer who needs to feel powerful and important in the world. But it may not always help the client.

Urania

Finally we come to Urania, the Muse of *astrologia*. The nine Muses, according to Hesiod, were the daughters of Zeus and the Titaness Mnemosyne (Memory). They were the companions of Apollo, and according to some sources were his daughters, although according to others he remained a bachelor god because he could not choose which Muse he loved most. They were guardians of the oracle at Delphi, and like Apollo had the gift of prophecy. The Muses symbolise the Sun-god's capacity to create beauty and harmony through individual human inspiration. Apollo also has a darker feminine face – the great serpent Python, who symbolises the chthonic wisdom of the underworld. Although Apollo conquered the Python, his priestesses were called Pythonesses.

The Muses inspire human beings, and Urania brings the inspiration of astrology as a revelation of cosmic order. This tells us that astrology was perceived as a creative art, although the observational and mathematical skills necessary to work with it (which we now call astronomy) were also part of the domain of Urania. In most mythological dictionaries Urania is erroneously called the Muse of astronomy, although as we all know, astrology was astronomy's parent and *raison d'être*. She is generally portrayed holding the celestial globe, and sometimes a pair of compasses.

Urania is in some ways a female version of Uranus, transformed from an inaccessible creator-god to a symbol of inspired revelation of cosmic unity. She is an approachable, anthropomorphised Uranus, and because she is female and under the patronage of Apollo, she serves the Sun and therefore the individual soul and spirit. She also has links with Aphrodite Urania, the daughter of Uranus and a cosmocrator in her own right. Aphrodite Urania is sometimes shown together with Apollo in her guise as the morning and evening star. In this role she is also called Phosphorus, meaning "light-bearer", and although her sensuality and beauty reflect her close relationship with the earth, she is also solar and celestial.

The feminine celestial figure of Urania is particularly important because she bridges the divide between the heavenly male deities and the chthonic female deities, and presents us with an image which unites spirit and body, macrocosm and microcosm. She is a celestial figure yet she directly inspires individual human beings. Because astrology was always understood to reflect both above and below, it is a great mediating system, relevant to every level of life. This Uranian spirit in a Venusian body, bearing the celestial globe, is a fitting image to bring together the apparently antithetical realms of celestial and chthonic forces which form the archetypal background of our work.

Audience: Some of us are plugged into the whole bloody lot.

Liz: I suspect all of us are, to a greater or lesser extent. We have to answer to many gods. But behind this multiplicity of figures is a dyad, the masculine part of which is related to transformation through consciousness, the feminine part of which is related to acceptance of the cycles of fate. Perhaps we really serve only one god, who bears a double face. Or perhaps we should start lighting candles to Urania.

What motivates us: charts of astrologers

Let's move on now to the charts of two well-known "founding father" astrologers from this century, to help anchor the rather diffuse issues we have been exploring. It may seem a long way from the mythic realm to an analysis of individual charts. But it is important to understand how the archetypal background affects the ways in which we see our work, as well as the ways in which our clients see us.

An astrologer-philosopher: Dane Rudhyar

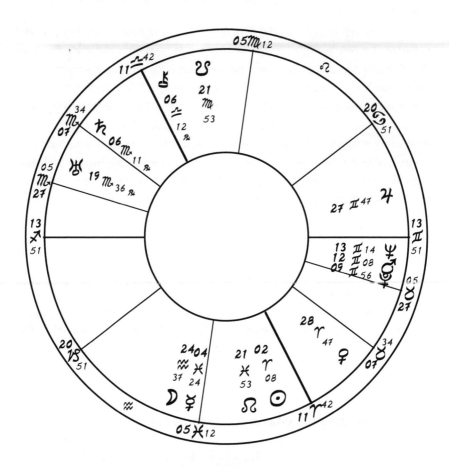

Dane Rudhyar
23 March 1895, 12.42 am, Paris
Placidus cusps

This is the birth chart of Dane Rudhyar, who is honoured throughout the astrological world for the contribution that he made to astrology. Some of you may already be familiar with his chart. I would like you to try to get a sense of Rudhyar's archetypal allegiances. I don't want to pick the chart apart on a personal level – there is no point in that, and he is not here to answer for himself. But it may be valuable to explore what gods this individual mediated in his astrological work.

Where did his vision come from? How did he understand his work? We don't all see the same astrological vision as Rudhyar, nor do we approach our work in the same way. Those of you who have been inspired by him, however, may learn a good deal about your own motivation.

One of the things which virtually leaps out of the chart is the powerful T-cross, involving the Sun in 2° Aries, in the 3rd house but conjunct the IC, Chiron in 6° Libra, in the 9th but conjunct the MC, and Jupiter in 27° Gemini in the 7th. Because this T-cross straddles the meridian and involves both the Sun and the chart ruler, it dominates the chart. I would also call your attention to the conjunction of Pluto, Mars and Neptune in Gemini. Pluto and Mars are in the 6th but conjunct the Descendant, and Neptune is exactly on the Descendant. It is useful to bear in mind the dichotomy which I was just talking about – between the solar and celestial mythic figures and the lunar, underworld figures of fate. What kind of astrologer is this?

Audience: This man would put great emphasis on the liberating power that a system of knowledge like astrology can give. Knowledge of a universal kind can help to free us and heal us. He would have to be a teacher.

Liz: Yes, the archetypal figure of the philosopher-teacher fairly screams at us from this chart. The Sun is in the 3rd, which as you all know is one of the two houses concerned with communication and learning. It is in Aries, a sign imbued with a strong crusading spirit. In Rudhyar's vision, knowledge – of self and of the "eternal realities" – can change the world. Sagittarius is on the Ascendant, with the chart ruler in Gemini in the 7th. Whatever he learns, he must pass on to others. The spinal column of the chart is the Sun-Chiron opposition. Chiron appears here not just as a vague mythic background, but as a powerful force in the horoscope. It is in the house concerned with the individual's world-view and perception of the cosmos. Rudhyar's understanding of life was strongly coloured by the theme of healing human suffering through understanding.

Audience: So his experience of Chiron would not be theoretical.

Liz: It isn't theoretical for any of us. But it was undoubtedly part of his conscious goals and motivation as an astrologer. He was deeply aligned with this mythic figure in terms of what drove him and fueled his quest for knowledge.

Audience: He also looks like somebody who would challenge the fate-ridden dimension of traditional astrology. He was born under that important Neptune-Pluto conjunction which took place in the last century. Mars is sandwiched right between Neptune and Pluto, and says, "We need to challenge these fatalistic forces!"

Liz: I have the same feeling about this configuration. Mars is the Sun-sign ruler, and it is hemmed in by two outer planets which are feminine and connected to the cycles of fate. Rudhyar's fundamental nature was fiery and individualistic, orientated toward the spirit and the world of the imagination. This Pluto-Mars-Neptune conjunction at the Descendant suggests that he perceived human beings as suffering under the burden of fate, and felt he must redeem them through knowledge. Left to their own devices, they are not able to get beyond the darker psychological and collective issues that bind them and make them victims. His teaching is meant to enlighten, or, as you say, to liberate.

Education through astrology must have meant the same thing to him as it did to Plato – a means of calling out the remembrance of one's spiritual home. This is an astrologer who was also aligned with Apollo and his children, especially Orpheus. And he is rather Promethean – his Moon is in Aquarius. He is not one of Hekate's tribe. Yet he cannot escape Hekate's world, because of the aspects to Mars, and because of Chiron opposition the Sun. He would fight to free people from the regressive forces of passivity, ignorance, and unconsciousness because this is his own mythic struggle.

Audience: There is something about that struggle with the underworld that brought him into contact with astrology in the first place.

Liz: That is what these archetypal allegiances really describe. We go through certain experiences, which make us seek answers or resolutions in certain ways. The experiences and the answers are part of the same fabric, part of the same theme. I know very little about Rudhyar's personal life. But I have no doubt that the Pluto-Mars-Neptune configuration, combined with Sun-Chiron, contributed to a profound sense of hurt, impotence, isolation, and powerlessness in early life, which in turn impelled him to seek answers in extraordinary places.

There may also be religious issues in the family background that wounded him and made him seek unorthodox truths. Chiron in the 9th is not very good at accepting the tenets of orthodox religion. Sooner or later one is injured by the dichotomy between what conventional religious approaches practise and what they preach, and one must find another, more individual path. We can look at the issue of personal wounding and say that a sense of hurt and disillusionment propelled him into astrology, and into his particular inspirational approach to astrology. There is a conflict in this chart between the fighting spirit of Aries and the passivity and frustration of Mars-Neptune-Pluto. He had his own personal dragon-fight to contend with. How did he deal with it? He translated it into a fresh, inclusive, humanistic approach to an ancient system of knowledge, and offered his understanding to a collective which he perceived as being in desperate need of it. And we have all benefited from what he has done.

How many of you are familiar with Rudhyar's work? He is sometimes credited with being the father of psychological astrology. He was actually more of a philosopher than a psychologist, but nevertheless he placed major importance on the issue of our psychological perception of experience. He lifted astrology out of its fatalistic, fortune-telling past, and placed the individual at the centre of the solar system. What more apt message could a person with such a chart convey? Many people find Rudhyar's work difficult to read, because he is often abstract and universal, and he doesn't tell us in a simple, detailed, cookbook way how to interpret the chart. One may be left thinking, "How do I apply this stuff?" Often the value is inspirational rather than practical. But any Sagittarian Ascendant could tell you that the practical must be preceded by a holistic overview; otherwise one loses the forest for the trees.

Audience: There is a resemblance between his chart and John Addey's.

Liz: I'm afraid I didn't bring John Addey's chart with me today, so we cannot do a comparison. But both men owe a great deal to the Platonic vision of astrology, which may be related to the strong fire-air emphasis in both charts. It should be obvious that the astrological overview that appeals to us as individuals is the one which resonates with our own chart. How could it be otherwise? The same applies to psychological schools of thought. The particular path that any astrologer follows is not the Ultimate Truth, but rather, the one which is right for that astrologer. It will be rooted in the archetypal background that in some way touches his or her own soul. Rudhyar's chart makes this clear. Many people find his work difficult, and prefer other authors.

Audience: It is very difficult to put his work into practice. There is no earth at all in this chart.

Liz: No, there is no earth. Undoubtedly he felt that his role as an astrologer was to inspire and expand consciousness, and the practical application could be worked out according to each person's experience and orientation. Fiery natures tend to be somewhat cavalier about practical details. This chart teaches us an important lesson. Each of us, as individual astrologers, cannot be any other astrologer. We can only be the individuals we are, with the charts that we have been born with and the interpretations and perceptions we have developed based on our unique life experience. We must do the best we can with as broad a base of learning as possible, but we must always remember that our understanding emerges from a subjective world-view, and is not a universal perspective on astrology.

Audience: To me Rudhyar's books seem inspirational. They are very poetic.

Liz: He *was* a poet, and also a musician. I don't know whether he had problems with Maenads, as was the case with Orpheus. Rudhyar was a visionary, and the imagination was the bridge through which he felt connected to a larger cosmos.

A Theosophical astrologer: Alan Leo

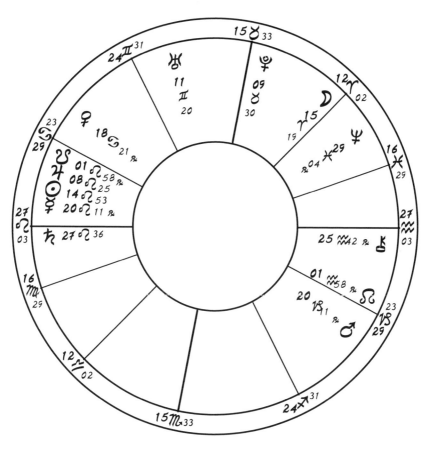

Alan Leo
7 August 1860, 5.49 am, London
Placidus cusps

Here is another great astrologer of modern times. To him we owe the fact that astrology is alive and well and rescued from the dustbin of medieval superstitions to which it had been relegated by the Enlightenment. Although both men were fiery, there are some very clear differences between this chart and Rudhyar's. Those of you familiar with Alan Leo's work will know that his world-view encompasses a much sterner, more Saturnian vision.

For a long time Alan Leo's work was the only astrological literature available. When I began studying there wasn't much else on offer. But it was not a bad place to begin, and his work is still well worth reading, even though we may now find his world-view and morality somewhat antiquated. Leo was a Theosophist, and it is through the Theosophical Society that astrology came back into public awareness in Britain early in the 20th century. Inevitably, it was an astrology that was very much circumscribed by Theosophy's highly structured spiritual overview. Looking at Saturn placed exactly on the Ascendant in 27° Leo, opposite Chiron in 25° Aquarius at the Descendant, with the Moon in the 9th in Aries trine a 12th house Sun-Jupiter conjunction in Leo, we might understand why spiritual and moral law was so important in this man's astrology. When one reads his work, the element of moral certitude comes through in an extremely powerful and sometimes unpleasant way. He was a devoted subscriber to the "higher and lower" school of astrology.

We don't get this hierarchical outlook in Rudhyar's work. Rudhyar seems to have had a profound awareness that there are many different varieties of human being, and his morality takes the form of encouraging consciousness rather than in judging behaviour. With Alan Leo there is only one right path. There are those who have the self-discipline to continue on the path, and those who fail because their lower natures have got the better of them. Yet despite this stern Saturnian tone, and a liberal dose of Jupiterian self-righteousness, his thoroughness and depth are remarkable, and the clarity of his thinking is sometimes quite breathtaking. Also, unlike Rudhyar, he is a *useful* astrologer. We can immediately apply his theories and interpretations. We owe him an enormous amount. I would still recommend his work to any astrological student.

Audience: The Moon in the 9th also suggests that he was a great packager and disseminator of astrology.

Liz: Yes, he was a great salesman, and it is interesting to look at the Moon's trine to Sun-Jupiter-Mercury in this context. Leo was responsible for the first astrological journal in this country, as well as for a great number of books. Fire is very powerful in this chart, as it is in

Rudhyar's. But the chaotic, visionary, intuitive qualities of fire are tightly reined in here by the Saturn-Chiron opposition. There is another very interesting thing we might think about. He was not, of course, christened Alan Leo. The cosmos is not usually so obliging. He was born William Frederick Alan, but he chose to call himself by his Sun-sign. In doing this he set a fashion, and so we have works by people like C. Aquarius Libra on our bookshelves. We could say that the Sun-Jupiter conjunction in Leo suggests an inclination to self-mythologising, and he amused himself by broadcasting his astrological makeup to all and sundry. But it is deeper than mere Jupiterian theatre. What kind of conflict does the Saturn-Chiron opposition reflect?

Audience: It's a conflict between wanting to belong, and wanting to be special and different. I think most of him wanted to be special. But I keep thinking of when you have a tooth abscess, and you keep rubbing it with your tongue, even though it makes it hurt more.

Liz: That is an astute if unlovely analogy. Uranus is in the 10th and Chiron is at the Descendant. Both houses are concerned with the public. Leo may have carried a deep sense of social ostracism. He was a Promethean spirit carrying stolen fire, an act for which he knew he was going to suffer through isolation. Perhaps something in him felt he *should* suffer – it is the fate of the spiritually evolved. Choosing to call himself Alan Leo is a brave, flamboyant statement of identity in the face of collective ostracism. It is, in its way, heroic. Chiron in Aquarius at the Descendant suggests that he felt like an outsider long before he got involved with astrology. I don't know anything about the family background, but this Chiron placement implies that this is a theme running through more than one generation. He needed to feel special, and he accepted the inevitable consequences of his ferocious individuality. But I believe it must have gone on hurting. This may have something to do with his spiritual elitism.

Audience: His flamboyance really ensured that the collective punished him. I was thinking about what you were saying earlier. The sense of guilt and shame makes some astrologers try to appear ultra-respectable and scientific. But it makes others court their own punishment through becoming a kind of caricature.

Liz: Leo wasn't a caricature in that sense. He didn't go around like la Zingara, wearing robes embroidered with stars. But he made an inarguable statement to the public. And he attracted a Promethean punishment as a result, which on some level he wanted, needed, and expected. He would have been lost without it. Stuart, what if you decided that you weren't going to work at your advertising agency under your own name any more, but that in future you were going to be known as Stuart Aquarius?

Audience: I would probably have great trouble with my managing director!

Audience: Aquarians don't do that sort of thing anyway. They are more likely to call themselves Stuart Everybody.

Liz: C. Aquarius Libra did it, which is even more outrageous – the personal name has disappeared altogether. However, I am not sure whether the Aquarius part was his Sun, Ascendant or Moon. The C. stands for Cancer, by the way, not Charles or Cecil.

Leo's astrology, like Rudhyar's, is a grand cosmic vision by which the collective can evolve and become more conscious. Both are Sun-Jupiter astrologers. The language is different, but Leo belongs to the pre-psychological age and he used the terminology appropriate for the time. Both also have strong Chiron placements, but Rudhyar's is connected with the Sun, whereas in Leo's chart it does not aspect either of the luminaries. One senses that he was a lonely and wounded man, but did not have much time for those who did not espouse his world-view. His wound seems to have made him a spiritual elitist. It is as though he is saying, "I belong to a very special, spiritually superior group of people, so it doesn't matter if you lot don't want me." His nomenclature is a last-ditch battle in the face of overwhelming odds, rather like Leonidas and his Spartans at Thermopylae. It is a statement of specialness.

Audience: There is tremendous arrogance in this chart.

Liz: I see it more as a battle between feelings of specialness and feelings of deep inferiority. The former compensates for the latter, and the latter is projected in the form of Chiron at the Descendant. I don't think he was consciously arrogant, but spiritual elitism as a compensation for isolation and alienation comes through very powerfully. Alan Leo seems to view astrology as a means of fostering spiritual evolution. He is very preoccupied with the lower nature and the spiritual strength to rise above it. One needs to have learned enough from one's past incarnations to transcend the darker side of the chart. One uses one's Sun-Neptune to transcend one's Venus in Scorpio. There is a good deal of the Orphic in Leo, perhaps linked with the strongly tenanted 12th house.

Many astrologers today adopt this perspective. They perceive the horoscope as a battleground between the higher and lower aspects of one's nature. The struggle between spiritual aspiration and the pull of the instincts is part of the heritage of the last two millennia. It isn't just Alan Leo's issue. With his strong, fiery 12th house, he carried a powerful psychological and spiritual inheritance from the past, and gave voice to it as a kind of mouthpiece. You used the word "arrogance". It is the spiritual certainty of the preacher. There is a potential for this in all of us.

Audience: Yes, I can see that. I have seven planets in Leo.

Liz: At least you don't call yourself Claire Leo.

Audience: I'm thinking about it.

Astrology as the enemy: Pope John Paul II

It might be useful to look next at the horoscope of someone who is not an astrologer, but who is well known to be virulently opposed to astrology. I will withhold the name for a moment, although many of you will probably recognise the chart. Let's examine it in the same way we did those of Alan Leo and Dane Rudhyar. What archetypal background fuels this individual's world-view?

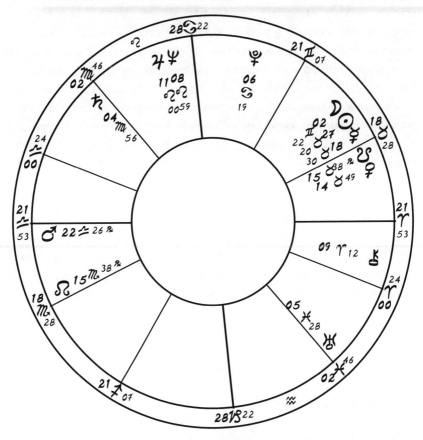

Pope John Paul II
18 May 1920, 5.00 pm, Wadowice Poland
Placidus cusps

Audience: This looks like the chart of the Vatican.

Liz: No, it is a person – someone who perceives astrology as the enemy, and who has considerable influence over the thinking of a large number of people.

Audience: Patrick Moore.

Liz: No, it's not Patrick Moore. It's the Pope.[6] I do realise that sometimes it isn't easy to choose between them. I have put this chart up, not to attack him, but to try to explore why his world-view is so vehemently opposed to astrology. After all, if I had told you this was an astrologer, you would have found all kinds of reasons in the chart to explain it – Pluto in the 9th trine Uranus, Uranus aspecting both luminaries in the 8th, and so on. We can learn a lot about ourselves and our own issues by understanding his, because there may not be as much difference as you might think. When we harbour a vehement hatred of something, it is usually because we have that thing within us, and are very frightened of it. What is this man frightened of?

Audience: He is afraid of the irrational.

Liz: I would hardly call Catholicism rational – or Christianity in general, for that matter. Are immaculate conception and resurrection after death rational? There is an opposition here between Saturn in the 11th in Virgo and Uranus in the 5th in Pisces. The new Moon in Taurus is square to both. There is a terrific conflict within this man, and the focal point is the 8th house, the house of mysteries and of the hidden forces underpinning worldly life.

Audience: He is afraid of the destruction of his Church at the hands of Uranian forces. And he knows it is going to happen.

Liz: Saturn and Uranus at war reflect a battle between the past and the future. Tradition battles with innovation, and structure with chaos. There is a fear of destruction and disintegration coming from Uranian forces, because Uranus is more likely to be projected than Saturn. Saturn is more congenial to a Sun-Moon conjunction in Taurus; they are friends, despite the squares. This Pope has a deep commitment to the continuity of the traditions of the Church, and unlike John XXIII, he

---

[6]The chart given for Pope John Paul II in Hans-Hinrich Taeger's *Internationales Horoskope Lexikon* is set for 12.00 pm GMT, but Taeger classes this chart as "Group 4" – questionable data. The above birth time is from Lois M. Rodden's *Data News* No. 66 (August 1997), quoting the Pope himself.

does not believe in modernisation. This Saturn-Uranus conflict is characteristic of all religions. It is an archetypal conflict. The world is changing; do we adapt the religion to fit the changes, or do we attempt to control or contain the forces of change by insisting on adherence to what has worked for centuries? It is important for us to understand not only what the Pope is projecting on us, but also what we are projecting on him.

Audience: Astrology doesn't just threaten his sense of personal stability, it threatens his whole ethos. Astrology is associated with Uranus.

Liz: Yet his commitment to his spiritual world-view is as great as any astrologer's commitment to his or her world-view. It is simply a different world-view, and a different cosmic authority. You probably all know that in a recent Vatican encyclical, astrology and psychoanalysis were named as grievous sins. Any person who consults an astrologer or an analyst is flouting the religious authority of the Church. You are clearly all in a lot of trouble. I'm in even worse trouble, since I practise both. But we need to look more deeply at why these two fields – astrology and psychoanalysis – are so threatening. It is not just Uranus which we must consider.

Audience: Is it the Chiron-Jupiter-Neptune configuration? But, you know, what you said before – that it could be the chart of an astrologer – makes sense. Pluto in the 9th is so often involved in esoteric studies, and the Chiron-Jupiter-Neptune could make him very interested in things like alternative healing.

Liz: Faith healing, which could probably be seen as "alternative", is an acceptable tradition within the Church. Let's try to get a sense of the archetypal background before we pinpoint chart configurations. The Pope harbours a very great fear of something. He would not feel the need to severely condemn something which he did not deem to be a threat. One of the aspects of his fear may be a terror of the disorder that comes when there is no recognisable, clearly defined spiritual authority. This disorder is, of course, something he fears within himself, since

Uranus is in the 5th, but he also grew up in a world where the authority of communism crushed the spiritual life of the people, and his 8th house emphasis makes him acutely aware of the collective undercurrents in the world around him. I believe this is, in part, an issue of authority. One of you said earlier that our authority as astrologers is derived from the body of knowledge we have inherited through empiric observation and practise over the centuries. Whatever the source, empiric or intuitive, we claim an authority which permits us to interpret the signature of the heavens – which, in older language, means interpreting the will of God.

The Pope, like other heads of religious institutions, also believes he is in a position to interpret the will of God. He too plays the role of *pontifex maximus*. He is claiming the same thing we are. But the problem arises from the different authorities which give us the right to make this claim. The Pope relies on a traditional body of teaching. We would say that it is not built on empiric evidence, but rather, on dogma, which requires an act of faith rather than an act of observation and deduction. This has always been the parting of the ways between religion and science. I have some question about the degree to which astrological symbolism rests only on empiric observation; it seems to me there is also a good deal of intuitive vision involved. But the two are not mutually exclusive, and intuitive vision is not the same as an act of faith. What we are really facing is two different interpretations of reality. At the moment I am playing devil's advocate. Why are we certain we are right and he is wrong?

Audience: He lacks consciousness.

Liz: Are you certain of that? Or is it that he is conscious of different things?

Audience: Astrology recognises the value of the individual. Church doctrines do not take any notice at all of the individual's nature and needs. We could look at someone's chart and say, "This person might be happier without children." Church doctrine says everyone must reproduce as often as is biologically possible.

Liz: Once again, you are articulating a different world-view. Western astrology, as you rightly point out, is individual-centred, and has been since the Greco-Roman period. The individual's spiritual journey, or, put in other terminology, his or her psychological journey or process of "individuation", is unique and needs to be understood and honoured as such. All the great religious institutions require the individual to be subsumed in the greater whole. Orthodox religion is concerned with the collective, not the individual. Because we place the highest value on the individual as the vessel for godhead, we make an automatic assumption that this man lacks consciousness and doesn't know what he is talking about. Yet his consciousness of and sense of responsibility to the collective are very great. We believe the individual should not be made to suffer in order to fit a set of collective religious precepts which seem to us nonsensical. But the world's Catholic population, which is much larger than the world's astrological population, will trust him rather than any one of us.

Audience: He looks more trustworthy.

Liz: Thank you.

Audience: I am looking at it from the feeling point of view, and the feeling many people get in analytic work is of being cast into chaos. In therapy you might spend a long time feeling very confused, and no one can tell you what to do. A psychological chart reading has the same effect. Church dogma is nice and stable. It's been built up through the ages. It's easy to know what to do. When you are in troubled waters, do you want somebody to tell you, "Everything is okay, we can give you absolute answers!" or do you want somebody to say, "Well, it could mean this or it could mean that!"? It feels safer to rely on a traditional religious body. I think that is why most people do. Thinking for yourself can be scary.

Liz: So the God from whom the Pope takes his authority is a good parent, who provides comfort and simple, reliable answers. You are describing a lunar-Saturnian God, or rather, a lunar-Saturnian institution, which refers to itself as Mother Church – father and mother rolled into one. It was not always so. In the days of early Christianity, before a Church had formed, it was the Christians who were the outsiders, the persecuted mystics and visionaries. It is only in the context of the Church as an institution that the Pope's authority is a safe authority. It is also a tangible authority, with a great deal of money and political power behind it. There is the building, there are the symbolic objects, there is the altar, and there is the priest conducting his mass, consistent wherever we go in the world. There is the Vatican, enormously wealthy and comprising an independent state. What have astrologers got? A tatty little bit of paper covered in funny squiggles that no one can understand.

Audience: And we can't prove it works, either.

Liz: Well, neither can the Pope. What we may fail to appreciate is that he is totally committed to his world-view. I don't think this man is a hypocrite; I think he believes deeply in his Church. Mars is rising in his chart; he is a crusader. There have been Popes whom one might have reason to suspect are primarily in it for the power. This one, although he clearly enjoys having political clout, seems to be deeply dedicated to what he promulgates, and he is prepared to fight for it. His sincerity is not in question. But his world-view is antithetical to the world-view that most of us here espouse. Apparently some of you have tried to believe in this kind of religious structure, and have gone away disappointed and disillusioned. There appears to be an irreconcilable conflict, although it seems some individuals are able to live with both sides.

Audience: I feel the conflict is irreconcilable. I wouldn't attempt to solve it. It requires theological gymnastics of a kind I am not interested in.

Liz: Intellectually, perhaps you are right, but on the emotional and intuitive level it may be possible to find ground in the middle. During the Renaissance, as we have seen, there was far less conflict. Certain Popes were themselves astrologers, or availed themselves of the services of astrologers, and astrologers like Marsilio Ficino considered themselves devout Catholics. Today this is apparently not the case, at least not with this Pope, unless he is a shameless liar, which I doubt. I think this Renaissance flexibility was not so much a display of theological gymnastics as a spiritual inclusiveness which allowed more than one symbol of the truth. Some individuals need to make the effort to reconcile the conflict, because they feel that both the Church and astrology have value. I have had several clients over the years who were Catholic priests, monks or nuns, who had found a way to live with both world-views. No one can tell you how to solve this kind of conflict – it is a very individual and personal thing.

Audience: No one has a monopoly on the truth, even if the Church thinks it does.

Liz: No, and we don't have a monopoly over the truth either. We have a world-view that we assume is valid. We are convinced that the cosmos that we perceive is the real one, and this papal lot have got it wrong, or have only a bit of the truth. We have no basis for this assumption other than our individual experience of our own charts and those of our clients – and individual experience is fraught with subjective perception. We cannot proclaim to have the truth in any absolute sense. We have one which works for us, but we have no way of knowing how it might fit together with other truths. And within astrology itself there are many philosophical perspectives. If we insist that we have the only truth, we will always polarise with individuals like the Pope, who also claim to have the only truth. And because there are many more people who follow a collective form of religion than there are people who pursue an individual path, we will always feel persecuted by the collective if we maintain this stance.

Audience: There is a difference. We aren't expecting people to adhere to our idea of how they should be.

Liz: Aren't we?

Audience: *I'm* not. Most astrologers aren't. We don't get that sort of believe-it-or-you-are-damned stuff in CPA seminars, or in most astrology groups in this country. Astrology has a much more universal viewpoint.

Audience: Really? Try reading the *Astrological Association Journal,* or the *Astrological Lodge Journal.* Some astrologers can be just as dogmatic.

Liz: Perhaps it is a question of degree. There is an effort at tolerance and mutual respect amongst most astrologers, at least most of the time, and such tolerance is not often available within the body of organised religions. I take your point – you are not posing as a collective authority. You are presenting yourself as an individual authority whose morality is personal. Nevertheless you will present your personal morality to the client. You can't avoid it. Nor can the client avoid unconsciously projecting a much greater spiritual authority onto you.

Audience: That's true, but I think it's different. I make it clear to the client that my suggestions are mine, not the infallible word of the Church. Astrologers are not part of a group which is trying to create rules.

Liz: Not in the main, no, although as someone has just pointed out, the astrological community occasionally produces its own would-be Popes who know what the "right" astrology is. But even if you go to great pains to tell the client that your perspective is subjective, there is an archetypal projection which the client will bring to the session, which makes him or her see the chart as an objective message from God. We have come round full circle, and are back where we started – with the role of the priest, which we carry whether we wish to or not.

As you say, we are not trying to create rules. Yet look at what we become, just *because* we are not trying to create rules. We are condemned by a Papal encyclical. We insist that no one has the authority to dictate to others what they should believe in, or what they should become as individuals. This is the voice of Prometheus, the thief who stole fire, and this is what the Pope fears. And we also have a mini-Pope inside us, a Saturnian superego that says, "The collective knows what the truth is." Even if on a conscious level we talk about moral and spiritual truths being multifaceted, do we really believe it? And are they as relative as we think? If we really believed it, why do we feel guilty and ashamed about what we do? When we get a client whose morality is different from ours – sexually, emotionally, financially – what do we do with that client?

Audience: I try to respect his or her perception of morality. I try not to impose mine.

Audience: But what if the client is coming to you hoping to find moral guidance? A lot do.

Audience: Then hopefully you can try to see what would be appropriate for that particular chart.

Liz: You make it sound so simple. Neutrality is an ideal toward which we aspire. Do we truly achieve it? No, I didn't expect any of you would think so. But at least we can be conscious of the fact that we can never be wholly neutral.

Audience: Isn't there gross self-deception in this chart? Mercury is square Neptune. To me that would mean gross self-deception.

Liz: Forgive me for saying this, but if you saw that Mercury-Neptune aspect in, say, Rudhyar's chart, you would undoubtedly have something much more positive to say about it. You would probably mention his fine intuition, his imaginative gifts, and his attunement to the spiritual realm. "Gross self-deception" sounds rather absolute. I am not a friend of the Pope, but I cannot help hearing an example of exactly what I have been talking about – the tendency to polarise and project. Venus is square to Neptune in this chart, and Mercury just slips into the square, but the new Moon is square Saturn and Uranus, not Neptune. I would understand the Venus-Mercury square Neptune as impossibly idealistic, especially about his messianic role in the world, since Neptune is with Jupiter in the 10th. But the dominant configuration in this chart is the T-cross. When we looked at Rudhyar's chart there was also a T-cross, involving Sun, Chiron, and Jupiter, and we talked about the conflict between his Chironian awareness of the inevitability of human suffering and his Jupiterian vision of freedom from suffering.

Here is a similar kind of dynamic – order versus chaos, traditional structure versus a new, visionary world. The Sun square both ends means he feels personally involved – he has a sense of mission, of needing to turn this conflict into a message to others. Of course the nature of the Pope's beliefs will align with his chart, and as he is a double Taurus he will side with Saturn against Uranus. If he were fiery or airy, he might do the opposite. The nature of the planetary conflict is as important as how he has attempted to resolve it. Those people who have a similar kind of conflict, and are also aligned with Saturn, may feel that there is great truth in the Pope's views. Those who have a similar conflict but are aligned with Uranus will feel the Saturnian world of orthodox religion is the enemy and the oppressor.

Audience: Saturn-Uranus is the only opposition in the chart, which makes it even stronger.

Liz: Yes, there is profound irony in the fact that the Pope is really a gift to astrologers, because he lives his chart so totally.

What happens in an astrological session

Transference and counter-transference

Now we should move on and begin to look at what happens in an astrological session. First we can explore the extremely important issue of transference and counter-transference. These are clinical terms that describe the mutual projections which take place in the psychotherapeutic situation. They also apply to the meeting between astrologer and client. The client comes to the astrologer already carrying his or her own unconscious agenda. The astrologer is carrying his or her own unconscious agenda as well, and the two agendas are going to intersect at a certain point. The client will project certain things onto the astrologer and the astrologer will project certain things onto the client – either independently or in response to the projections coming from the other person. This energy exchange usually takes place below the threshold of consciousness. The psychotherapist is trained to recognise transference and counter-transference and work constructively with them, but the astrologer who has not trained psychotherapeutically has no such advantage.

Since Freud's time, enormous emphasis has been placed on transference-counter-transference phenomena in therapy, because the interpretation of the interaction between analyst and patient helps to reveal the unconscious issues at work in the patient. Many astrologers don't acknowledge, let alone work with, this important dimension of interchange with the client. This is partly because, in non-psychological schools of astrology, the unconscious is simply not a reality. It is an abstract concept for which there is no proof. Even if the psyche is recognised as real, the astrologer may say, "There is no ongoing relationship in an astrological session. This isn't the same as therapy. I'm reading a horoscope, and it is objective."

Such astrologers really believe, if a client arrives with a fraught question like whether he or she should leave a difficult marriage for a lover, that they will not impose any of their own unconscious complexes on the client. They are simply going to read what it says in the chart. They may see a configuration like Saturn rising, with Venus opposition a 5th house Mars. They may forget, at that moment, the ancient pain and anger involved in their own parents' divorce. They may say to the client, "Yes, I can see that there is a lot of loose passion flying around, but you really need to learn to discipline these emotions. Stick with the commitment you have made, because otherwise you will damage your children irrevocably. I'm not projecting, I'm only interpreting what it says here." It's a bit like saying, "There is gross self-deception in the Pope's chart because he has Mercury square Neptune."

Audience: All right, I take it back.

Liz: No, don't take it back. Just be conscious of it. You may well be right. But that isn't the point. When we interpret a client's chart, we need to take into account not only the archetypal issues which I spoke about earlier, but also the issues in our own charts with which we have not dealt fully. Things of which we are unconscious, or don't handle very well, have a way of creeping into the astrological session, especially if the client triggers them, or if they are being triggered at the time by transits or progressions in one's own chart.

Parental projections

Projections between astrologer and client have a great range. Among the most powerful are the parental images both people carry. I will tell you a story to illustrate this. Many years ago, before I had begun my analytic training and before I understood what transference and counter-transference really involved, I had an astrological client. This lady taught me a hard lesson about how the unconscious can invade an astrological session. From the moment that she rang the doorbell, I didn't like her. There was something about the way she leaned on the bell for several seconds which irritated me. When she came in the door I liked her even less, because she had a sort of moist-eyed, downtrodden, professional victim's look. When she began talking about her pain, and about how everyone treated her badly and how miserable she was, I found I could not feel sympathetic. All that kept going through my mind was, "I do wish you would stop whining."

Usually I empathise fairly readily with a client's unhappiness. But I couldn't experience any sympathy for this woman. She was genuinely distressed, but she presented it in a way that I found hard to handle. As she went on, I kept trying to be constructive. I gave her positive suggestions about how to start putting her life in order. I was encouraging about her abilities. But every time I suggested something, she gave what is known in psychological circles as the "Yes, but..." response. "Yes, I'm sure you're right, but I couldn't do that because I don't have enough money." Or, "Yes, I could try that, but I don't think I have the talent." Or, "Yes, that is a good idea, but I don't think I could manage it."

Everything I offered was flattened in this way. I was being made to feel useless and ineffectual, although at the time I did not recognise that this is a characteristic counter-transference response to someone who himself or herself feels useless and ineffectual and is attempting to feel better by unconsciously making others feel worse. She cried continuously throughout the session. Everything that was said by either of us brought tears to her eyes. The fact that she hadn't bothered to bring her own Kleenex annoyed me even more. After about an hour and a half of this I finally snapped. I said, "I'm getting very bored listening to you whine. Do whatever you like with your life. But do stop moaning and making everyone else responsible for your misery. Grow up." She looked at me in horror and said, "You sound just like my mother!" And I looked back at her stonily and said, "And you sound just like mine."

From that experience I learned a good deal about transference and counter-transference, and I also learned that this occurs in the astrological session no less than in the therapeutic session.

Audience: What happened in the end?

Liz: She got up, tears streaming from her eyes, and said, "I'm going to throw myself under a bus!" I said in a bored voice, "Don't do it in front of my flat, please. I don't like messy gutters." Then she stormed out. I did hear later from a mutual acquaintance that she did not, in the end, throw herself under a bus. In fact she managed very well. I may have had a hefty counter-transference, but I was quite right in sensing something tough, aggressive, and highly manipulative under all that bleeding.

Two sets of parents are always present in our astrological sessions, although they may not necessarily intrude, or intrude destructively. In my story they clearly did. When we react to clients with dislike, or with an inability to respond to what they are trying to say, it may simply be that their charts are incompatible with ours. They live in a world with which we cannot connect. We must then make a special effort to enter the client's reality and experience some empathy for it. But it may also be that our complexes are triggered by the client, and his or her complexes are triggered by us. We will all meet our parents during the course of our work, and the less consciousness we have about our parental issues, the more certain we are to attract clients who are carrying this energy for us. And they will invariably choose an astrologer who carries their parental issues as well.

Thus we are not only Prometheus, Orpheus, or Moira for the client; we are also their Mum or Dad, and they may be ours too. The way we respond to the client's situation is going to be coloured not only by our parental complexes, but also by the intensity and quality of the parental projections that we feel coming from the client.

Complexes at work in the astrological session

Transference and counter-transference do not merely mean the astrologer and the client perceive parental qualities in each other. Projections carry energy and produce effects, and create relationship patterns in an active way. When we have an unresolved complex that is hurting, we will try to get other people to respond to us according to the energy of that complex. If, for example, we have had a mother who was unsympathetic and didn't want to be bothered with a lonely child, we may go through life unconsciously pushing other people into acting out that cold, rejecting parent. We keep trying to heal the wound but we don't know how to begin, so we recreate the original situation in the hope that someone else will give us the love and acceptance which we do not know how to give ourselves. And we may try to make ourselves feel better by putting another person in the situation we ourselves are in, so that we can experience relief from the constant hurt and anxiety. In this way we may precipitate the rejection we fear so much, without recognising that we ourselves are rejecting the other person from the outset.

The client who has unresolved issues of this kind may unconsciously try to push the astrologer into acting out the rejecting parent with whom he or she has experienced the original conflict. But that client may also, simultaneously, try to make the astrologer feel like the undervalued child. A person like my client, with Moon opposition Saturn, who is suffering from deep feelings of inferiority and an assumption that others will refuse their warmth and support, may want the astrologer to carry the hurt Moon, so that the client can get to be

Saturn for a change. Whatever we say, such a client doesn't want to hear it. We are put down and made to feel useless and ineffectual. Then we display our annoyance, and the client feels rejected. Or the client may display an uncomfortable dependency, ringing up at all hours for advice and prognostications, because he or she is seeking an unconditionally loving mother who will always be available. Naturally the astrologer grows irritated and asks the client to stop ringing, whereupon the client is plunged into the same experience of rejection that he or she felt in childhood.

Our responses as astrologers may be genuinely our own, but they may also be governed by the complex that the client is projecting. And the same applies the other way. If I sit facing my clients with an unresolved mother-complex, and expect all my clients to be mature, self-contained, and willing to immediately and energetically act on what I am saying regardless of their individual natures and past experience, then of course I will make any needy and dependent client feel denigrated, and in desperation he or she will begin to present me with the helplessness of the unwanted child. Such clients will resist the self-discipline I am demanding of them, and will start acting out precisely what I do not wish them to become.

The narcissistic wound of the helper

A book which should be essential reading for anyone involved in counselling, astrological or otherwise, is Alice Miller's *The Drama of the Gifted Child*.[7] One of things Miller suggests is that the helper is secretly motivated, in large part if not entirely, by a narcissistic wound. For those of you who are unfamiliar with the term, in Miller's view we begin our training as helpers at around two days old. There is usually a deeply painful issue around the relationship with the mother – we have been called upon, from a very young age, to mother our mothers.

When that happens, we are deprived of the right to be a child, and we dare not express dependency on the mother because she is too dependent herself. "Narcissistic wound" means that we are injured by

---

[7] Alice Miller, *The Drama of the Gifted Child*, Faber and Faber, London, 1983.

being deprived of the mirroring every child needs from the mother in order to begin to form a defined individuality. Instead we are expected to mirror the mother's needs from the very beginning – usually because she is depressed, unhappy, or childlike herself, and sees her child as a potential redeemer. Not all children are so sensitive to the mother's unconscious psyche, but the child who is especially gifted at responding to others' feelings will suffer most. The helper thus grows up trained to help from birth. It is not a vocation that one chooses rationally, out of idealism or humanitarian concern. It is something for which one has been groomed in infancy. The primal relationship teaches us that we must give constant support, empathy, and understanding if we wish to receive any sort of love at all. We dare not fail this needy parent, for if we do, and she dies, then we die too.

With this background of a primal relationship wound, we can do two things. We can become either the victim or the one who helps victims. We can be the one who suffers because of a lack of nourishment, or we can be the one who provides nourishment. Both responses reflect the same archetypal core. If one has been unmothered, there are two ways of dealing with it. Either we remain children looking for a mother, or we become a mother looking for children. Either way, we are attempting to connect with the archetypal source of life in order to be healed. I am not suggesting that either way is "neurotic" or "wrong". Both ways may achieve deep and permanent healing. But both ways may also go badly awry. It is wise to be conscious of the nature of the wound, and if we have elected to be the helper, it is wise to be aware of our secret identity with the unnourished patient.

The kinds of wounds connected with father come a bit later. They may be equally important in personality formation, but they are not so primal, and they are not usually reflected by the Moon in the birth chart. The nature of our cross-projections in therapeutic and astrological work often involves this most fundamental and earliest of wounds. What does lack of mothering mean, if we put it in a deeper context? What happens to us when we must mother our mothers, and receive no mothering ourselves? I don't mean this on the physical level, but psychologically.

Audience: Mother is a container.

Liz: And what does this container provide? Psychologically, what is the most fundamental thing mother gives us?

Audience: A feeling of security.

Liz: Yes, she tells us that it is right and safe for us to be alive. We are wanted and protected. A good enough mother, to use Winnicott's phrase, will let us know that we are wanted and protected because we are what we are. We do not have to work to earn that love and protection. We do not have to try to become someone else. We are permitted to take safety and love for granted, without anxiety. Thus we learn to love ourselves and trust life. Many people suffer from the wound of being told, subtly if not overtly, that they must behave in a certain way if they are to merit love and security. They learn to despise themselves and fear life.

So if our clients seek a mother in the astrologer, what are they really seeking? They want confirmation that it is right that they are alive, that they are welcome in life as the people they truly are, and not just as prospective redeemers of their mothers. The astrological chart provides a way of communicating that to the client. Much of what we do for the client has nothing to do with the specific configurations we are looking at, but rather, with the fact that the chart, and ultimately God or the gods through the patterns of the chart, affirm the right of that person to be what he or she is. In this sense the astrologer acts as intermediary for the cosmos, affirming the individual's identity regardless of the parental expectations imposed on it. A chart reading can be a revelation of unconditional cosmic acceptance. This can be profoundly and unexpectedly healing on a permanent basis, although an astrological session may only last for a short time.

When we offer this unspoken but powerful affirmation to the client, we are aligning ourselves with those female deities that stand behind astrology as much as the solar and Uranian ones do. I believe it is extremely important to look at the issue of why do we do this work. Why do we want to help people? And if it is because we have been wounded, in what way? What is the most basic wound you can think of?

Audience: Being told I have no right to exist.

Liz: Yes, that is the bottom line. We have to constantly work to earn the right, or have to become somebody else to merit the right. We must have validation to believe that we possess the right. But in ourselves, we do not believe we have the right to exist. That is the most powerful wound that can be inflicted by any parent on any child, and that is the primal wound that we seek to heal. If Miller is correct, and I believe she is, it is also the wound which has drawn us into astrology, because we have sought confirmation of the right to exist in the planetary patterns. This bit of paper covered in funny squiggles says, "You have the right to be alive as what you are." This very profound theme enters every chart session. It is there regardless of the level of pathology or health of both astrologer and client. It is not a pathological issue; it is archetypal. Mythology is full of tales about children being rejected or nearly murdered by their parents, and these stories tell us that the issue of believing one has no right to exist is one of the most fundamental human wounds.

Audience: Would you try systematically to avoid transference or projection? And if it does become part of the dynamic of the consultation, to what extent can it be controlled? What basic guidelines would you suggest when the astrologer realises it is happening, to bring it into a creative or useful context?

Liz: I don't believe it is possible to avoid it. It is a natural psychological phenomenon. Transference and counter-transference – or cross-projections, if you prefer the term – are an inevitable by-product of what we do, because we are invoking the unconscious psyche when we work with astrology. Its symbols are archetypal and affect both us and our clients very powerfully. It is extremely naive to believe that one can stop it happening.

Consciousness of what is happening can allow us to work with the projections constructively. For example, if the client is making you feel useless and ineffectual, and you recognise the nature of your counter-transference, you can also recognise how deeply useless and ineffectual the client feels inside, and can begin to address that problem – indirectly if not overtly. If the client is projecting a divine figure onto you, you can recognise both the spiritual basis for this and also the maternal basis, and can respond without getting caught up in thinking you are really able to give ultimate answers or unconditional loving. And if you recognise that you are projecting your parents on the client, this can help you to understand your own parental relationships better, as well as allowing you to empathise more fully with the client. I can't give you guidelines in a nice neat list. It is something one learns from both one's own therapy and from a good therapeutic training.

Audience: Can you say something about what happens if the energy involved in projection is taken back?

Liz: If projections are owned, we are much freer as individuals, because we are not compulsively driven to act and react to other people according to the dictates of our complexes. This also applies to our work. We can see the client more clearly, and read the chart more clearly as well. But I doubt that it is possible to withdraw all projections, and it may be that we need these projections in an astrological session – at least to some extent – for anything dynamic to happen. Projection is the fuel which motivates relationship. If there were no projections between us and our clients, there would be no energy in the contact, and no avenue for creative insight or healing. Projections create a bond, albeit sometimes an uncomfortable one. The ego does not choose to project unconscious components; the unconscious projects itself, because something is ready to be integrated into life. Projection is a natural psychological dynamic. The moment it happens in a session, there is energy and vitality in the exchange. But we need to learn to work with that energy, rather than being unconsciously controlled by it.

Synastry between astrologer and client

Now I would like to briefly mention the synastry between ourselves and our clients. The importance of noting important synastry contacts should be obvious, and it ought to be an automatic part of the preparation for a session, whether we do the exercise on paper or just keep it in mind during the session. Sometimes a composite chart is useful, if the synastry looks particularly fraught.

If there are strong planetary contacts between my chart and the client's – easy or difficult – then I know that each of us is going to have a powerful reaction to the other. If the planets invoked in my chart are planets with which I have a problem – either through lack of awareness or because they are involved in stressful configurations – then I need to be especially conscious during the session, because my complexes will be triggered. An understanding of the astrological interaction can help enormously in monitoring our responses to the client, as well as understanding the client's responses to us.

Consciousness of transference and counter-transference requires a great deal of honesty. It is something we have to work at. It doesn't come automatically, and it is sometimes quite painful. Synastry is an astrological technique which can facilitate this process. It is not a substitute for one's own therapeutic experience, but it can help to turn that experience into a useful tool in astrological work. Recognising powerful cross-aspects with a client can help us to be aware of our unconscious feelings toward that client, and his or hers toward us. Feelings are often expressed in covert ways. A client may refuse to look one in the eye, or picks his or her nose when one is trying to say something profound. Or he or she accidentally spills coffee over the carpet, or forgets to pay at the end of the session.

I once did a chart for a woman who insisted on bringing her dog into the session. Although I prefer cats, I generally have no problem with dogs, and I am happy to have them in the consulting-room if they are reasonably well-behaved. But this dog seemed to be carrying all the unexpressed aggression of my very passive, victimised client. It barked throughout the session. It peed on the carpet. It chewed the chair leg. My client casually said that Fifi always behaved like that – "So sorry, I hope you don't mind too much, but the poor thing simply can't be left alone in the car." I wondered whether she had any friends left. Had this lady been in any sort of contact with her very difficult natal Mars, no doubt Fifi would have been delightful. As it was, Fifi was faithfully acting out my client's unconscious, and was perfectly vile. Fortunately, I was able to convey this to her without killing the dog, and it was quite a revelation.

Such things are a means of unconscious communication, and they can trigger one's own unconscious complexes. How do we react to this kind of situation? Do we get blindly angry? Or can we read the secret language? My Mercury opposition a client's Saturn tells me that this client may feel intellectually intimidated; that could be why he or she is engaged in concentrated nose-picking. My Saturn conjunct a client's Pluto tells me that I may mistrust this client and fear his or her power to hurt me. My Venus conjunct a client's Sun tells me that I will probably like this client, and will feel instinctive empathy for him or her. The client with Neptune opposition my Sun may come in and say, "I've read all your books, and I think you are absolutely wonderful, and I have been waiting two years to see you, and I know you are going to be able to solve all my problems." Because the client's Neptune is involved, I know that whatever I say, it will never meet such impossible expectations. I must be prepared for the client to communicate a feeling of disappointment at the end of the session, and I need to be careful not to take this as an indication that I have failed.

Although it may be politically incorrect, it is wise to bear in mind that the sex of the astrologer will invoke specific projections from the client. Although you may be a fully liberated female astrologer with an angular Mars-Uranus and twenty planets in air and fire, who has much more affinity with Apollo than with Moira, the client will still see you as Moira, because your femaleness, however much you might try to disguise it, will invoke the archetypal Great Mother, not to mention the client's personal mother. If you are a sensitive and intuitive male astrologer with twenty planets in water and an angular Neptune, the client will still see you as Apollo, and expect cool, clear, rational answers. Your maleness will invoke the archetypal celestial father, not to mention the client's personal father. And if a client also has Oedipal issues, he or she may invoke your own Oedipal issues, and I leave the possible scenarios to your imagination.

An understanding of astrologer-client synastry is also important because we cannot like all our clients or relate to them with the same level of empathy. Many of the most effective astrological sessions emerge from a temperamental incompatibility with the client, which, if we are sufficiently conscious, can impel us to work hard to understand what somebody else's reality is all about. We all have favourite signs and aspects, as well as those that we dislike. "Oh, marvellous," we say, "my next client is a double Sagittarian. I love doing charts for Sagittarians. They're such fun." Or, "Oh God, not another Cancer. They're so evasive." Or, "I can't bear Sun-Pluto people, they're so manipulative." We all have highly subjective astrological preferences. Such likes and dislikes may reflect simple synastry incompatibility, but they may also involve shadow projection. We may actively dislike some clients because undeveloped or unloved bits of our own charts are being triggered by the client.

Try to imagine what it might be like if Dane Rudhyar gave an astrological session to the Pope. Rudhyar was a visionary, a fire sign with a fire sign Ascendant and a strong Sun-Jupiter. Along comes a new Moon in earth with Saturn rising in an earth sign. Rudhyar would not have responded to this earthy mentality easily. He may have been intellectually flexible enough to enter the world of a double Taurean. But not every astrologer has this gift. So we have to make a conscious effort to recognise our prejudices, and try especially hard with a client whose element balance emphasises areas where we are not very well adapted.

How many of you would see yourselves as aligned with the psychological or spiritual side of astrology? All of you have your hands up. Yet you may get a client who doesn't want to hear about archetypes and psychology and spiritual evolution. He or she is after practical advice – what is a good time to sell the house? We can say, "Well, yes, I realise you want to know when to sell your house, but what is really important is *why* you want to sell it. Let's look at the inner meaning." And the client looks back at us blankly and says, "Yes, fine, but what is a good time to sell my house?"

We may need to extend our skills and find out what aspects indicate a good time to sell a house. The mundane world is of primary value to many people. It is important to know that it is of value, even if we are not very good at working with it – as astrologers or as individuals. And if we don't wish to work with it, then we can ask the client why he or she wants the appointment before we even book it, and we can say, "I'm sorry, but this isn't my area of expertise. Let me give you the number of an astrologer who specialises in mundane matters." This is vastly preferable to saying, "Your material concerns are not important. I'm going to tell you what I think is important, and selling houses is not as important as your spiritual evolution." If the astrologer is unconcerned with the material world, fair enough – we all have areas where we are poorly adapted or simply disinterested. But the client should not be made to suffer for our lack.

Audience: We might attract clients like that because we have an unconscious need to make contact with that world.

Liz: As one of you mentioned earlier, we generally attract people who are attuned to what we have to offer. But you are right – we sometimes get clients who embody all the difficult or undeveloped bits in ourselves. We may attract them even if we claim we don't want them, because we unconsciously need them. The more we try to avoid a particular issue, the more frequently we will encounter the issue in our clients, and this gives us a chance to understand something about a level of reality that we have been undervaluing or denying. Such synchronicities can be very creative. However, it is unwise to attempt to convert the client in order to avoid facing ourselves. We can learn an enormous amount from clients who are not very interested in the particular kind of astrology we practise.

Audience: I am interested in the idea that somebody can be aware of their unconscious responses to another person in a close relationship. If you have two people who are aware of their responses, they wouldn't respond in the same way any more.

Liz: Being conscious of your responses doesn't necessarily stop you from responding. It may, however, stop you from acting out your responses in a destructive way, and you may understand the other person much more deeply because you understand yourself better. The great disappointment of this work, for many people, is that it doesn't cure us of being human. One may, like Woody Allen, have chalked up forty years of analysis, not to mention forty years of chart interpretation, and one may know how to monitor one's responses with a microscopic eye. But one will still react to the client who pushes one's mother-complex button. It doesn't prevent the energy from creating a dynamic interaction. But it may allow a bit more choice, in terms of whether one acts things out blindly or turns the responses into a productive interchange.

If two people are aware of what is happening, they have a chance to talk more deeply about what is going on, with greater honesty. A lot can come out of that, but it isn't going to prevent projections from occurring. Nothing that we do as astrologers or therapists is going to exempt us from going through the same human experiences as those who are not involved in this work. Our emotions are not going to magically disappear. Our thoughts are not going to suddenly be free of personal opinion. Our world-view is not going to suddenly become objective; it will still be our own. But the more awareness we have, the less we cheat. Also, the less likely we are to bludgeon the other person, overtly or covertly, into becoming what we need them to be. Likewise, we are less likely to unconsciously try to become what they want us to be. Consciousness of our responses creates a different kind of relationship exchange, which may not necessarily be easier, but will probably be a lot freer and more tolerant. However, this costs a lot, because we no longer possess the luxury of blindly acting something out and then saying, "It's *your* fault."

First encounters with astrology

Before I begin to put up charts from the group, I would like to talk a bit about the transits and progressions that were at work in our charts when we first took up astrology. What was going on? These planetary movements may give us insight into what astrology really means to us. Such movements have a long-term meaning; they are not just transitory. When we begin something under a particular planetary configuration, it carries the qualities of that configuration. In other words, the chart for the moment you discovered astrology is not only a picture of the transits occurring in your chart – it is also the birth chart for your involvement with astrology. And that birth chart interacts with your birth chart, reflecting how your pursuit of astrology affects you. Unfortunately, most people do not note the time for such an event, because usually only astrologers recognise the importance of the moment, and at that moment one has not yet become an astrologer. So we may need to be satisfied with exploring the transits.

For example, if one encounters astrology in a great revelatory burst when Uranus transits over the natal Sun, the whole course of one's study will be infected by a sense of excitement and revelation. Twenty years later, the Uranian vision which first awakened a sense of individual purpose will still be operative, and therefore the archetypal background of one's particular world-view as an astrologer will be coloured by the Promethean quality of that configuration. We may think we took up astrology for one reason, but our charts may tell us that we took it up for another. It is very useful to explore this, because it reveals a great deal about what archetypal pattern came alive at that moment. Have any of you checked what was happening at the time you commenced studying astrology? What did you find?

Audience: Saturn was opposing my Saturn and transiting over the MC when I began studying. Well, it was when I came to England. I was involved in astrology before that, but not seriously. When I first started getting interested, I was in the middle of my Saturn return.

Liz: That is a lot of Saturn. It is not what we might expect, although during the Renaissance Saturn was in fact perceived as the planet of philosophy and wisdom. How do you understand this Saturn emphasis?

Audience: I think it has to do with commitment, and with a feeling of finding my life's work.

Audience: I have got a square between Saturn and Neptune. Transiting Saturn was on Neptune at the time, square natal Saturn. I needed to find something to contain my Neptune. Astrology has given me that ever since.

Audience: Can I mention a laundrette in Bath? I was in that laundrette in 1974, at the age of twenty-six. I was a Marxist existentialist, plotting the overthrow of the British state every second Thursday at the seat of the local Communist party. I ran into this wee guy, and I only realised many years later that my progressed Sun was right on the asteroid Urania in the 1st house, and transiting Neptune, appropriately for a laundrette, was on my IC. He dragged me back to his house for a cup of tea, announced he was an astrologer, and drew up my chart. I thought, "This is a load of rubbish, but I don't have anything better to do for the next hour." He predicted that in my early thirties I would start to study astrology. I thought, "This is crazy!" But it really disturbed me. Then transiting Uranus hit my IC, progressed Sun squared my Uranus, and when I was thirty-two I started to learn astrology, right on cue.

Liz: Uranus and Urania seem to have been in league together to ensnare you. It seems the asteroid carries something of the inspirational qualities of the Muse of *astrologia*. It is also interesting that the IC seems to keep coming up – the place of one's roots. It is a kind of homecoming, a connection with the source.

Audience: I have Scorpio at the IC, and for me Uranus was like a lightning bolt that revealed the depths. It worked its way deep down in me, showing me things I didn't know I had, and making me aware of levels I didn't know existed. I still feel that way, every time I learn something new.

Charts from the group

Example chart 1

Liz: I wish we had more time to spend on this issue. But I would like to make time to put up a chart which someone from the group has given me. The question we have just been exploring – why does one become an astrologer? – will undoubtedly be relevant as we look at individual charts, as well as the kinds of issues that a particular astrologer is likely to encounter in his or her practice. Are you working as an astrologer, Nicola?

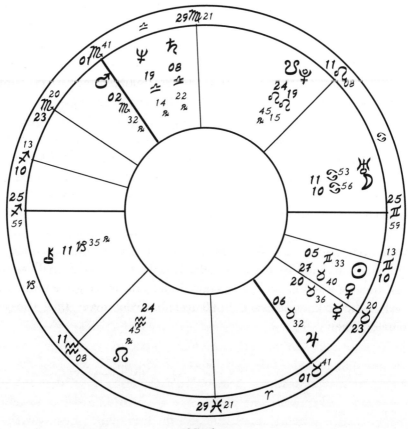

Nicola
Chart data withheld for reasons of confidentiality

Nicola: Yes. I wanted to discuss the Uranus-Chiron-Saturn T-cross. I am interested in what you have been saying about why we become astrologers. I think the T-cross is connected with that in some way, especially with the 9th house so emphasised.

Liz: This T-cross involves other planets as well. Chiron is in 11° Capricorn in the 1st, opposition a Moon-Uranus conjunction in 10° and 11° Cancer in the 7th, and all three are square Saturn in 8° Libra and Neptune in 19° Libra, both in the 9th. The involvement of the 9th house suggests that this configuration is indeed relevant to your work and your world-view. Out of interest, do you know what was happening in the chart when you got involved in astrology?

Nicola: It was in 1974. Transiting Pluto was conjunct my Saturn.

Liz: Yes, Pluto was sitting on natal Saturn, and transiting Saturn, which was square Pluto in the heavens, was sitting on the natal Moon-Uranus conjunction. Both transits were setting off the T-cross very powerfully. Transiting Uranus was in the last decanate of Libra then, moving back and forth over the MC. And transiting Chiron, which was opposition Uranus in the heavens, was at the IC. This is an enormous amount of transit activity occurring during the course of a single year, and part of it involves the most difficult configuration in the birth chart. What I said earlier may be applicable here – often we go into astrology because of our own wounds. What is the nature of the wound described by this configuration?

Audience: I always have problems working out where to start when so many planets are involved in a configuration.

Liz: Try to work out who is friends with whom. Whenever we see a configuration, regardless of how many planets are involved, we need to work out where the affinities lie between the planets, rather than trying to take each aspect piecemeal. Chiron has many Saturnian qualities, and it is in Saturn's sign. So Chiron and Saturn, despite the square, are not going to feel antipathy in the same way that the Moon, which is in its own sign, is going to feel antipathy toward both of them. Saturn and Chiron can get on, forming a tough, realistic, defensive, us-against-the-world kind of alliance. Uranus can get on with both of them, despite the fact that it is in the Moon's sign. Uranus co-rules Aquarius along with Saturn, and there can be affinity between them; and Chiron has some Uranian qualities, as it is a mediator between Saturn and Uranus. What Uranus brings to the alliance is detachment, intellectual breadth of vision, and a tendency to dissociate if life gets too difficult. This is a valuable planetary alliance for an astrologer, because it reflects depth of thought, objectivity, realism, and the ability to apply a broader picture to others' difficulties.

The planet in the configuration which is marginalised, and which will probably hurt the most, is the Moon. Neptune is also marginalised, but it is not a personal planet. It contributes its primal longing and vulnerability to the Moon's emotional state. We can see how the other planets will periodically gang up on the Moon, and we can begin to get a feeling of what the configuration might describe. The Moon in Cancer in the 7th needs close emotional contact with other people, but it may not be heard over the noise that the other planets make. It is an isolated Moon. Only Neptune is its friend, and Neptune just keeps whispering, "Let's go home."

This situation is exacerbated by the Sun in Gemini in the 5th, which is detached and intellectually inclined, and wishes to express itself through some creative medium – but without getting its hands wet. Great strength and tenacity are reflected by Saturn square Chiron, by Uranus square Saturn, by Uranus opposite Chiron, and by the Sun trine Saturn. These are very sturdy aspects, giving powers of endurance as well as the ability to disconnect and walk away. They help you to stand alone, to detach, and to move through life without getting bogged down by emotional needs – your own or others'. Sagittarius on the Ascendant adds its own fierce independence to the combination. But the Moon-Neptune, which is probably projected a good deal of the time, sits in the basement and cries, "I'm lonely! No one wants me! And I daren't ask, because everyone will think I am too clingy, like my mother. Therefore I have to be strong, independent, and detached." Underneath, this Moon has suffered a good deal.

Then, in 1974, transiting Saturn came along and conjuncted the Moon. It looks as if relationship issues were pretty fraught at that time – perhaps a time of loneliness and disappointment, following a loss or breakup of some kind.

Nicola: Yes.

Saturn in the 9th: the need for universal laws

Liz: At the same time, Pluto moved onto Saturn in the 9th. This natal placement sometimes describes a particularly narrow religious background. One way or another, there is often disappointment with the family religious attitudes, because one is seeking a solid, reliable spiritual overview which will never let one down. What is the religious background of your family?

Nicola: My parents are officially Church of England. But my father used to be in the Far East, and more or less turned to Buddhism.

Liz: So were you were not given a strong moral or religious upbringing?

Nicola: I don't feel it was. It was all rather vague and nebulous. I sometimes think it wasn't moral or religious enough.

Liz: Sometimes the absence of something early in life can be as hurtful to Saturn as too rigid or restrictive a display of it. Saturn in the 9th reflects a powerful need for clear, unambiguous truths, and it is usually dissatisfied with whatever formulae are offered by the family background. There is something within you that needs to find some kind of reliable law at work in life, so that you can understand why things happen to you. Transiting Pluto going over Saturn would awaken that craving for finding a universal structure which explains how things work. At the same time, great personal unhappiness seems to be suggested, by both transiting Saturn on the Moon and transiting

Pluto square the Moon. This might provide the impetus to completely tear down and rebuild your world-view.

Nicola: It was actually when a very bad, destructive marriage came to an end. I had to find out why I had got into it. I wanted sensible, clear answers that would explain what happened to me.

Liz: The nature of the god we seek – and perhaps also find – is largely coloured by what is in our 9th house. We look for universal truths which can give meaning to our more painful experiences. We emerge from the burning-ground of the 8th house, with its shattering revelation of the unknown depths, and seek meaning in our suffering through the god-image reflected in the 9th. We want an overview which can restore our faith in life's goodness. Saturn in the 9th wants a very particular kind of overview – a law or set of laws which, if we obey them, will ensure that we do not suffer any more. And if we do, then clearly we have consciously or unconsciously disobeyed the law, and merit our punishment.

You were going through the fire and wanted to know why. The 9th house is the place where we ask why, and any planet in the 9th describes what we come to perceive as the answer. We ask the question, and a god appears who bears the face of whatever is placed in the 9th. If there are no planets in the 9th, the question is not usually asked with such urgency. Here there are two planets in the 9th, so the question is urgent. If the chart contained only oppositions between 1st and 7th house planets, there would be a difficult relationship pattern. But the involvement of the 9th house turns these difficulties into a philosophical and spiritual quest. Because Saturn is exalted in Libra, it has a good chance of finding a balanced perspective, because the universal law which Saturn in Libra perceives is a fair law. Ethics and fairness would probably be extremely important in your work. The client may carry your suffering Moon-Neptune, and you will make the effort to communicate the essential fairness and clarity of the cosmos.

Neptune in the 9th: redemption from personal pain

Although it conjuncts the MC and therefore also has bearing on the 10th house and the relationship with the mother, Neptune is in the 9th. As I said earlier, Neptune is sympathetic toward the Moon; it is the only friend the Moon has got. So the philosophical question which finds an answer in universal law also contains a personal question: "If I can understand the law, and live my life by it, will I be loved? Or will I still have to be lonely? Will I be able to stop the pain? Will I understand my mother's pain as well?" There is not only a quest for truth – there is also a longing for redemption, arising out of a very personal sense of unhappiness. This could be a valuable quality to bring to astrological work, because it gives you compassion for others' loneliness and an antidote to Saturn's sometimes rigorous moral expectations. In some ways astrology is a means by which you counteract the ongoing sadness and disappointment of the Moon-Neptune. Do you feel you have found some resolution of the things that propelled you into astrology?

Nicola: Yes, definitely. But I have only been looking at the psychological side for three years. I have found out so much more about myself and my relationship with my mother. These issues have been equally important, or more important perhaps, than the spiritual side of astrology, which I studied first. Sometimes I think I did it the wrong way round.

Liz: No, it was probably the right way for you. The Moon is likely to be the last planet in this configuration to emerge into consciousness.

Audience: Sagittarius is rising, so the big picture has to come first.

Liz: Yes, it is a Jupiter-ruled chart. Jupiter is sextile Moon-Uranus and trine Chiron, so it offers the big picture to help alleviate the Moon's stress. It may also be connected with your father, Nicola. He seems to have found a philosophy of nonattachment more satisfying than the Christian ethos. It is interesting that the Buddha himself was said to be born under Taurus. Although Jupiter is quincunx Saturn, they are both in Venus-ruled signs, and do not really quarrel; the laws of the cosmos are benign as well as fair. This chart is a powerful illustration of how personal conflict and pain can generate the need to ask larger questions. The question, "Why am I miserable in a bad marriage?" becomes, "Why do human beings suffer? What laws have we violated? How can we find peace?" You have invoked Cronos the Lawgiver to bring you out of the darkness, and have made something highly creative and useful out of a personal wound. Are you aware of attracting a particular kind of client in your work, or are there particular issues that you have trouble dealing with?

Nicola: Yes. The clients I attract always seem to have relationship problems. I don't actually have trouble with this, although I am learning more about myself through it. The clients I have trouble with are usually people whom I can't connect with. I want to give my ideas, my view of the cosmos, as you say, so I do find it difficult to connect with people who don't really think things through, but who are very emotional about what they want.

Liz: It sounds as though the people who give you trouble are people who are in some way an embodiment of your Moon-Neptune. Can you see any relationship between the Moon-Neptune's emotionality and your relationship with your mother?

Nicola: Yes. I had to mother my mother. I did feel that I was not allowed to be emotional when I was a child. My father is quite strict about matters of conscience. He is an intellectual. But he also had love affairs. I suppose he is a very Jupiter-like figure in that way as well. My mother was a woman totally out of her time. She was very Uranian in some ways; I think she had a couple of young men as lovers. But she was also Neptunian. She could get quite hysterical, and I had to pacify her. I must admit that when she died, I didn't feel alone. I actually felt better, which is a horrible thing to say.

Liz: There is a lot of pain and conflict associated with her in the chart. Despite what you call her Uranian side, she probably wasn't a clear thinker. Perhaps the areas where you find it hard to work with clients are also the ones you found most difficult in her, and perhaps also the ones you find most difficult in yourself.

Chiron in Capricorn: mistrust in authority

Now, what about Chiron in Capricorn? Many of you will have it placed here – it doesn't move that fast in this part of the zodiac. How do you understand it?

Audience: I think it has something to do with not knowing your proper place. You don't know where you belong. You don't "fit".

Audience: I think this configuration represents what Nicola said about not being allowed to be herself. It is in the 1st house, so there is a wound around becoming an individual. Chiron is opposition the Moon in Cancer, and square Saturn. I am a Capricorn with a Cancer Ascendant, and my perception of Capricorn is that it is about the formation of the individual. My perception of Cancer is that it is about the child and dependence. In the middle of this opposition in Nicola's chart there is Saturn taking responsibility for all of it. It takes responsibility for a bad marriage, and tries to find a balance between individuality and dependency.

Liz: Yes, that is a very astute way of reading Saturn at the peg of the T-cross. It takes responsibility for everything, so living by the law becomes doubly important. What about Chiron in Capricorn? As a Sun in Capricorn, presumably you know your place in the scheme of things. Can you imagine what it might feel like not to trust any authority or structure?

Audience: I want to say that I don't trust authority either, but that is not really true. I only mistrust authority in the world. I trust the authority of astrology. I also trust some people who have real authority. I suppose my work gives me a sense of my "right" place.

Liz: Chiron in Capricorn is connected with a wound inflicted unfairly by life, in the sphere of authority. Often it reflects the early discovery that authority is hypocritical and false. There is sometimes a tremendous disillusionment with the father, and with father-surrogates. Nicola, you said your father was very strict in matters of conscience, yet he went off to have love affairs. There may be great disillusionment around marriage as an institution and codes of behaviour as a means of hiding other things. All one's natural, instinctive faith in authority goes down the plughole, because authority is demonstrated to be false.

I think this is one of the things that people with Chiron in Capricorn must deal with. Many have had an early experience of wounding in the sphere of their trust in the natural hierarchy. We need to believe in some kind of authority to which we can answer, and which we believe will guide us in life. Children seek authority in their parents, even if they also kick against it. But with Chiron in Capricorn, the early models turn out to be untrustworthy. It becomes impossible to believe in any rules at all, and yet without rules one has no code for living. Moral issues become confusing, and your parents' marriage seems to have been an example of this – saying one thing and doing another, under the guise of something collectively acceptable. This may have left you with a great deal of uncertainty, and it may have undermined your trust in your own authority. All this seems to be part of the meaning of Chiron in Capricorn in the 1st house.

Nicola: What you are saying is something I recognise. There were three generations of my family caught in the dilemma of who was really in control. In the course of three generations we have split between those who are the realists and apparently run the show, and those who are emotional and needy and have no authority at all. But the realists like my father also couldn't control their impulses. He had no authority over his personal life. And he couldn't control my mother when she got emotional. I had to calm her down. I don't know much about my grandfather. I do know that he was another Jupiterian, and had lots of fun, apart from the war. I expect my grandmother didn't have any more fun than my mother did.

Liz: Perhaps it is Chiron in the 1st square Saturn in the 9th, both harassing the Moon, which perceive life and relationships as an issue of who has authority and who doesn't. Your lunar, emotional clients look to you to provide them with structure and authority. I don't doubt that you can offer it, in a far more creative way than your father dealt with your mother. To some extent this T-cross will always cause tension and conflict. But it allows you to work with people who suffer from a similar conflict, and discover some healing for yourself through your work.

Nicola: It is true that I try to give my clients containment and structure. I was always able to do this for my mother. It is ironic, because I seem to treat my own feelings much more harshly.

Audience: If we have a certain conflict, we are going to see it in our clients. It is not necessary that these clients have exactly the same problems as we do, but that is what we will see. It is also not completely true to say that that it is just our projection. It is a meeting of two realities, and both people can benefit.

Liz: No client will ever have exactly the same problems as we do. But the archetypal themes may be similar, and that can create great empathy. And we may discover resolutions which we couldn't think of for ourselves, but which we suddenly find we are offering a client. Nicola experiences a great conflict between her emotional, needy side and her strong, independent, authoritative side. She is torn between her mother and her father, because she has something of both of them within her, and she is trying to find a way to balance this polarity creatively – something her parents could not do in their marriage. The perception of relationship as a struggle in which someone dominates and someone submits makes it hard for her to live the whole of herself. But when a client comes who enacts the bruised Moon in Cancer, she finds a way to offer the client qualities which are both rational and compassionate. At those moments she has redeemed her parents' failed marriage, and experienced integration within herself.

As you say, we can perceive our own conflicts everywhere, and carry one message which we flog to death because all we can see is our own pain. This usually happens when our dilemmas are not fully conscious – we project them onto others because we have not got to the bottom of the issue. Yet our projections on our clients can connect us with something that we find difficult to face in ourselves. If we can become aware of this, we can gain a great deal, and be very helpful to the client as well. We often end up playing a role for our clients which makes us use something in our charts that we have great trouble living. They need this thing from us and we are forced to come up with it, and in doing so we discover we have got it.

Nicola, the clients who come to you show you that you can express Chiron and Saturn in very positive ways, because you are able to listen to their feelings and offer them structure and grounding. You become their authority, but without stifling them as your father evidently did you. Your clients are really giving you back a piece of yourself, or a way of integrating conflicting pieces of yourself. This often happens in a very powerful way in astrological work, and when it does it is a kind of grace, because it is deeply healing – even if the feeling does not last. One way of reading Chiron in the 1st opposition Moon in the 7th is that one's own healing comes through one's encounters with others. You will learn a lot from the clients who are most like you – and most like your mother – because you feel you must give them grounding rather than suppression of their feelings, and that is what you are trying to learn to do for yourself. Thank you for letting us discuss your chart.

Interlude: Alfred Adler and the will to power

Before we look at another chart from the group, I would like to briefly put up the chart of a psychoanalyst, now dead, who is well-known for his particular psychological perspective. You may occupy yourselves for a few moments with guessing his identity. This chart demonstrates nicely that the psychological perspective one adopts is the one which describes one's own psyche. Like astrologers, psychologists draw from an archetypal background, and this is often clear in the importance they give to particular dimensions of human character and behaviour.

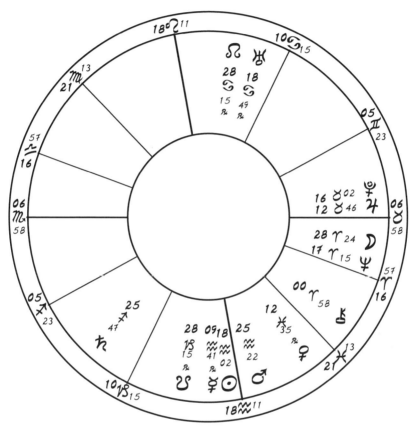

Alfred Adler
7 February 1870, 12.15 am, Vienna
Placidus cusps

We can see Freud's preoccupation with the compulsive nature of the *id* reflected in his Scorpio Ascendant with Pluto conjunct Venus at the Descendant – a symbol of his own compulsive passions. We can see his Promethean vision of psychoanalysis as a universal system in his Sun-Uranus-Mercury conjunction, which made him identify closely, if unconsciously, with the great Titan of myth. We can also see Jung's vision of the collective psyche, and his own rampant Promethean inclinations, in his Uranus-ruled Ascendant. His spiritual leanings reflect his 9th house Jupiter and his close Sun-Neptune square. And the term "individuation" could only have been invented by a person with the Sun in Leo. There are many schools of psychology, and while we may be flexible enough to recognise truths in all of them, we will inevitably feel most aligned with one or another according to our own natures. And, of course, we will feel our precepts are confirmed over and over again by our clients, who will usually come to us because they are also aligned with this same pattern. What world-view propelled this man to become a psychoanalyst and formulate a particular psychological vision?

Audience: Power.

Liz: What particular configurations are you looking at?

Audience: Sun conjunct Mars, and Pluto conjunct Jupiter square the Sun. Is this the chart of Assagioli?

Liz: Why Assagioli? He did write a book called *The Act of Will*, but his psychology is much gentler and focused on discovering the Self as the centre of the psyche. It is the integration of the personality with the Self that concerned him. You have mentioned Sun-Mars and Jupiter-Pluto in this chart, and you are right about power. There are other placements which support this. Mars and Pluto rule the Ascendant, and both make strong aspects to the Sun. The Moon is in Aries, a Mars-ruled sign, and it is sextile Mars. Chiron is in Aries in the 5th house, square to Saturn. Try to get into this man's world-view. What was his psychological vision?

Audience: He is full of aggression. He would see aggression in everyone else.

Liz: Yes, issues of will, power, and aggression do tend to scream out at us from this chart. Who could it be but Alfred Adler? Adler postulated the will to power as the dominant human motivation. He was originally a disciple of Freud, but he focused on one particular dimension of the *id* and developed it into a complete psychological model. He coined the term "inferiority complex", which in his framework is both the cause and the result of aggressive behaviour. Because Adler came out of Freud's school, he recognised and worked with the unconscious. But his perception of the dominant drive in the psyche was, of course, coloured by his own psyche. As an Aquarian, it would be natural for him to take his perceptions and embed them in a framework of ideas.

Because this is a Martial chart, Adler was inevitably attuned to those individuals suffering with problems in expressing will, power, and aggression. Chiron in Aries in the 5th may also have contributed to his preoccupation with feelings of inferiority. As is the case with all creative individuals, what Adler created in the outer world reflected his effort to resolve the conflicts of his inner world. Anyone who is not orientated along these lines would not find his psychology congenial. In Jung's chart, for example, power and aggression are not the chief issues. His world-view and perception of others, as well as the psychological edifice he created, are dominated by his Sun-Neptune square. That is why clinical psychologists see him as a mystic – he *was* a mystic. Adler's psychological edifice is dominated by his Sun-Mars conjunction. There is a certain inevitability about his falling into conflict, not only with Freud but with everyone else as well, and pursuing his own independent path.

Adler's work, although not as well-known as Freud's or Jung's, is sound and insightful within its own sphere. He formulated a very elegant psychology based on the particular archetypal background with which he was personally aligned. Why did he choose to pursue psychology rather than medicine, or some other sphere in which he could battle against illness and misery? After all, Saturn trine the Moon in the 6th suggests a need to offer some practical service to others, and Saturn semi-square Mercury reflects a pragmatic turn of mind. And psychologists need a great deal of patience, which is in rather short supply in this Mars-dominated chart.

We might look at configurations like Mercury in the 3rd in Aquarius square Jupiter-Pluto in the 7th, combined with a Scorpio Ascendant, and conclude that his deep and inquiring mind, and his awareness of the hidden levels of life, led him to seek understanding of what motivated human beings. We might look at the Sun in Aquarius in the 4th, and conclude that he was driven by a quest for universal roots. But without hindsight, we cannot be certain of the form his work might take. His profession in a specific sense is not clearly marked. The myths which fueled him are more obvious.

Another chart from the group

Example chart 2

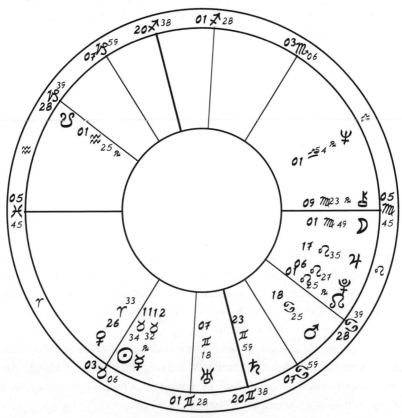

Michael
Chart data withheld for reasons of confidentiality

After that little interlude, here is a second chart from the group. Are you an astrologer?

Michael: Yes.

Liz: What did you want us to focus on?

Michael: I am concerned about progressed Saturn coming up to square Neptune and going into Cancer. I feel that when this aspect is exact, it may make a big difference to my work.
Liz: The Saturn-Neptune square is a very slow applying aspect. You have been living with it since your birth, although Saturn's shift from air to water may have deep repercussions on the emotional level. Could I ask you first what was happening in the chart when you got involved with astrology?

Michael: I had a Jupiter return at that time. That's all I can remember. It was in the late 1970's.

Liz: Jupiter was in mid-Leo in the summer of 1979. At that time there were a number of other interesting things going on. Perhaps we should look at this first, because the auspices under which we enter astrology seem to make an important statement about what motivates our work and world-view later.

Sun square Pluto and the crusade against fate

During that summer Chiron made a station retrograde in 13° Taurus, very close to your Sun-Mercury conjunction. Uranus had finished opposing Sun-Mercury the previous year, but it was still within orb, and it made a station direct in 16° Scorpio a month before Chiron's station. So this transiting opposition of Chiron and Uranus in the heavens had been triggering the natal Sun for some time. As the Sun is square Pluto in the birth chart, this natal square was being strongly activated, although your encounter with astrology appears to have occurred at the tail-end of the Uranus transit. It was the result of a long process of inner change and awakening of the natal Sun-Pluto.

An earthy Sun in an earthy house, square Pluto in another earthy house, suggests that being of service, being useful, is a very important part of what drives you in life. "Drive" is the operative word, because Sun-Pluto people, especially in fixed signs, do not do things by halves – it is total commitment or nothing at all. The battleground of Sun-Pluto must be transformed into skills and resources which can make a useful, tangible contribution to life. But behind the service is the archetypal dragon-fight. What are you crusading against?

Michael: I suppose I am crusading against pain and ignorance. I do feel I can help people in becoming more responsible for their lives, and seeing that they have more choices. I see so many people who don't know how to get themselves out of their messes. They passively endure blind suffering because they can't see where they are going.

Liz: So you are a crusader against Moira, against the passive acceptance of fate. You are aligning yourself with solar light and pitting your will and consciousness against the inertia and regressiveness of the Great Mother. That is one of the themes of your archetypal background, and the transits of Chiron and Uranus called it into being as a vocation. What you call blind suffering – the pain people live with because they are unconsciously repeating their ancestors' patterns – belongs to Pluto's world. These blind, instinctual compulsions are usually imaged in myth as one of the variations of the Great Mother. The Furies are symbols of the ancestral compulsions that torment people. Apollo is the god who breaks family curses. What about your own family curse?

Michael: Castrated males.

Liz: I don't need to inquire any further, do I? You have put it very succinctly.

Saturn square Neptune

Audience: Saturn in this chart falls on the Sun-Pluto midpoint. So there is a need for a strong Saturnian structure whereby a practical sense of self is established, firmly rooted in the here and now.

Liz: Yes, Saturn on this midpoint underlines the earthy emphasis of the chart. It is right at the IC, so it is in some way connected with the father. Perhaps what your father failed to achieve in terms of self-sufficiency and autonomy is now your responsibility. But Saturn is square Neptune, and the anxiety of that square makes the Sun-Pluto square more urgent. In the summer of 1979 transiting Saturn was in Virgo, and was moving across your Moon, Descendant, and Chiron. During the subsequent year or two it transited over Neptune and squared its own place. I don't want to probe too much into personal issues, but this suggests that you went through some hurt or disappointment in a relationship which in some way echoed your father's plight – the "castrated male" – and this might have provided the emotional impetus to seek answers in astrology.

Pisces is rising in your chart, and Neptune is your ruler, but it is in the 7th, and I would expect your allegiance to be more with Saturn – although there is a great conflict between them. Neptune may be projected onto others, and could contribute to a feeling that the world is full of suffering people. I am thinking this not only because you are an earth sign, but also because Saturnian qualities are what you hoped for from your father. It is what you need as the basis, the foundation of your life. As someone has just pointed out, its place on the Sun-Pluto midpoint emphasises its importance. Perhaps it isn't what your father turned out to be, or at least not on a deeper level, but Saturn the lawgiver is the father you really wanted. A castrated father would be a terrible disappointment, because it is the antithesis of this. But the suffering, passive victims you see around you are also your own Neptune.

Michael: I don't see them as blind or passive.

Liz: They are the words you yourself used earlier. How then do you see them?

Michael: I see an aspiration for spiritual growth. That is the sort of client I attract. People who are into personal growth seek me out.

Liz: You put it another way a few minutes ago. But never mind. That must have been Mercury-Pluto speaking, and now we are hearing Mercury-Jupiter. Who are the castrated males you referred to? Your father?

Audience: Yes, my father, although in outer life he was pretty powerful – he was a policeman.

Liz: So Saturn the lawgiver could only give laws at work, not at home.

Michael: My mother ruled in the home, and my father and my mother sometimes both symbolised my Saturn. My own experience of Saturn as a strong container was that the container was hollow. It couldn't keep out the chaotic undercurrents. Then I tried to find the container elsewhere, through religion. For a while I felt protected by being instructed in the Church.

Liz: So for you Saturn is a container for chaos.

Michael: A container for the imagination.

Liz: You keep telling me two quite different things. First you describe something quite starkly, with passion, and then you edit it immediately afterward and turn it into something much more polite. Are you aware of this?

Audience: He is castrating what he says.

Michael: I have got Saturn in Gemini. I try to be careful about what I say.

Liz: But Neptune and Pluto keep slipping out anyway. You seem to be very clear and positive about what you perceive in your clients, and what purpose astrology serves for you. Your clients are people on the path of growth, who are seeking spiritual realisation. Astrology provides a structure which can contain the imagination and the intuition, and give a language to ineffable experiences which otherwise would be very difficult to grasp or communicate. But you have also told us a good deal more. You started by saying very passionately that what you are crusading against is the blind instinctual compulsions that drive people into states of suffering about which they have no understanding. You can't have it both ways, Michael. The blind suffering victims and the enlightened people on the spiritual path are the same people.

Michael: They may be further down the path.
Liz: I wonder whether your personal issues and the rationale of your vocation are being very carefully kept separate?

Michael: I do feel that suffering is part of the cross we all bear on this planet. It is all part of the process of incarnating. I feel very strongly that I can't put a lot of energy into helping people who don't want to be helped.

Liz: Go on.

Michael: There isn't anything I can really do for people who don't want to be helped. But when people want to be helped, when their awareness has been switched on by some inner experience, they are ready to be told that they have the option to choose again. This can empower people. Astrology can empower them even more so. Rather than try to solve the plight of those who don't want help, it is much more practical to help people who want some assistance. It is a pragmatic process of going from the enormity of the human condition, which I am quite powerless to do anything about, to the hopeful achievement of some progress in a small number of people.

Liz: Now both sides of you are speaking together – at least for the moment. Thank you. You asked initially about the closing of the Saturn-Neptune square. I wonder whether the division that I keep hearing when you speak is connected with this square, and whether its slow progression toward exact aspect reflects a sharpening and potential resolution of the division. For you there seems to be a vast sea of human beings flailing about in their unhappy condition, amongst whom is your father, and his father, and his father's father, going right back through the male line. The blind suffering which afflicts them is so huge that there is not a lot of point in trying to struggle with it. Therefore your energies and talents are better utilised working with those who have at least recognised that there is a condition from which they are trying to free themselves. Yet there seems something tense and highly controlled about this sharp division. And on which side do you yourself belong?

Michael: I don't ignore the knowledge of my father's and grandfather's pain. I have looked at my father's chart to see how the synastry operates, and how his wound feeds on my wound. But you are right about what you said earlier – I feel I must be what they could not be, and find an inner strength they couldn't find. Does that mean I belong on their side, trying to become stronger through helping other people?

Liz: Something like that, yes. But I would see that as a positive and creative way of dealing with the difficulty. I am pushing you a bit because it might be important for you to know where your real identification lies. You have developed Saturn to a high degree, trying to find its inner strength rather than its outer form. Your father had only the outer form of the policeman, but no strength inside – yet he must have wanted to express Saturn, or he wouldn't have become a policeman. You have inherited respect for the law from him, but it is the inner law which matters most to you. Your earthiness, and the semisquares between Saturn and the Sun and Saturn and Pluto, give you better access to that inner core of strength that Saturn represents.

But Neptune is your chart ruler, and what has happened to it? Is it only these clients on the spiritual path? An important part of you is Neptunian. It is not only attuned to the world of the spirit. It is also lost and blind, weak and vulnerable, like all other human victims. It isn't castrated; it simply hasn't formed yet. It is a dreamer and a romantic. It wants human love and companionship of a particularly intense kind. If you overlook this dimension of Neptune behind the spiritual aspirations of your clients, and if you overlook it in yourself, then the spiritual path becomes a substitute for ordinary human hunger and loneliness. Then this applying square may make you painfully aware of that hunger, possibly through your personal life. The time when a progressed or transiting square is exact is a time when it is most important to hold both sides together, rather than rejecting one side and identifying with the other.

Michael: I feel my transition may be toward leaving astrology behind to become a monk.

Liz: Somehow I am not surprised. It is certainly one option. But would you say that this is a way of holding both sides together? I am a little worried that it might reflect a running away.

Michael: From what?

Liz: From Neptune, odd though it may sound. And perhaps even more from Pluto. The monastic life is not necessarily Neptunian, contrary to the lay person's perceptions. It can be profoundly Saturnian. It is highly structured and hierarchical, and even authoritarian. Great restraint and control are required.

Saturn square Neptune is concerned with working with the emotional, imaginal and spiritual dimensions of life in a practical way. These planets are inimical to each other, but when they are in aspect they must work together. This can't happen if there is an attempt to suppress Neptune. It seems that you are a person of very strong convictions and great passion. It is clear that you are deeply committed to what you do. I don't know whether the monastic life would be appropriate. The only thing I can comment on, in terms of the closing of the square, is that you may not fully understand what Neptune represents within you. Consequently you may not realise what Neptune represents in your clients, or what motivates you to retreat from the outer world. I am also thinking of Venus square Mars and Venus square Pluto. We have not discussed these aspects, but they could have bearing on what you may be trying to avoid.

In this chart there is an enormously powerful need to control. I associate this with both Sun-Pluto and a strong Saturn. This quality can be extremely positive, but it is also potentially very destructive, especially if it leads to excessive self-control. It is you rather than others who are likely to suffer from too much rigorous self-restraint. Saturn and Neptune could work together, but in thinking of retreat into a monastery, it sounds as though you are trying to come up with a final solution rather than a means of harmonising the square.

Whatever else you might have got from this discussion, please think again about what Neptune might mean for you. I am also thinking about Chiron conjunct the Moon, which puts the Moon under great pressure and constraint. There is also a Moon-Uranus square, which is inclined to repudiate the instinctual realm if it proves too difficult. The Moon is under quite a lot of pressure in the chart, and both Moon and Neptune concern me because they reflect the hungry and needy side of you. And the Moon is at the Descendant. Rather than sacrificing the possibility of an intimate relationship, a path to healing may lie in direct personal involvements in which you are neither the one who submits nor the one who is in control.

Audience: In a way the monastic life is a castration.

Liz: It could be seen that way. It depends on the reasons why people choose it. It can also be the opposite; it can require great courage and commitment. I would be reluctant to make such a judgment in Michael's case, because he does not lack courage.

Audience: When Michael said something about the cross carried by all souls incarnating on this planet, I thought this was a really beautiful way of describing his experience of Neptune square Saturn at the IC.

Liz: Reconciling the duality of spirit and matter is one of Saturn-Neptune's chief concerns. This planetary combination is extremely relevant for anyone involved in astrological work. How many of you have got it? A lot of you have put your hands up. I don't think that is coincidental, given the theme of the seminar. The urgent need to reconcile the eternal with the mortal tends to gnaw at people with

Saturn-Neptune. That dichotomy is ever-present for a person with these planets in aspect, and astrology is a very powerful means by which one can achieve at least a little of that reconciliation.

But it is a very tricky means, because we tend to side with one or the other. And whichever one we are siding with, we are usually unconsciously aligned with the other one. The moment one thinks one is getting closest to Neptune through asceticism, one discovers one is on a Saturnian path. The moment one believes one is totally committed to practical service, one is dissolving in Neptune's waters, identified with a messianic source. Saturn-Neptune can be enormously creative, but it seems to work best when involved in human life, rather than removing itself from life. Removal from life is what many Saturn-Neptune people try to do, especially with the square, opposition, and conjunction, because life hurts so much. The divide between incarnation and eternity may sometimes seem insurmountable, and one wants to retreat from the suffering.

Splitting is not a wise way to deal with Saturn-Neptune. There is a middle ground where one can identify with human suffering, yet at the same time encourage individual responsibility. It is a very rich aspect, but it takes a lot of work to handle. You will probably have to find new ways of reconciling it when it comes exact, Michael. You might not have any option.

Audience: Sometimes Saturn is connected with the shadow-side. And with Sun square Pluto, I wonder whether there are things to do with control and domination which haven't come out yet.

Liz: Perhaps. Michael, do you know Goethe's *Faust?* No? Then I am assigning it to you as your homework. Goethe had Sun square Pluto, and the figures he created – Faust and Mephistopheles – embody in an extraordinary way the relationship between these two planets. Faust must experience both the transcendent and the depths of darkness. I think that you would have a lot of resonance with this poem, and might get certain insights into the struggle that Sun-Pluto represents. Thank you for allowing us to discuss your chart.

The astrologer and money troubles

Now I would like to look at the general issue of money in relation to the astrologer. It is obvious that many astrologers have a problem about asking for and receiving money, as well as establishing the amount of money they should charge. Many of you are nodding vigorously. From this response it is clear that this area is relevant to everything we have been exploring.

There seems to be a lot of guilt amongst astrological practitioners about feeling one deserves the money one receives for a chart consultation. The fee may be far too low, and may be wildly inappropriate if one views it in relation to the amount of labour involved, the amount of time and energy invested in the client, and the amount of training and money spent on training that has gone into the expertise one is applying. We may well ask, "Why do we have this problem?"

Sometimes difficulties with money are related to a lack of self-value, and there may be configurations in the individual chart which suggest personal issues. Such configurations may reflect a Neptunian dilemma – for example, Neptune in the 2nd house making hard aspects to other planets. Sometimes a dominant Neptune alone is enough, because the Neptunian temperament often feels uncomfortable in the material world and there may be a deep longing to abjure it and go home. This is the path of Orpheus, who turns his back on worldly satisfaction in the hope of spiritual reward. Although this may be an individual dilemma, it has an archetypal background.

We may also find placements such as Chiron or Saturn in the 2nd, 6th, or 10th house. These may reflect a wound to the individual's sense of self-worth, or an issue around the parents and their worldly expectations. We may also find a lack of earth in the chart. This can suggest a deep discomfort and awkwardness around the material world, and a sense of inferiority around competence. The reasons some astrologers give for their inability to make a living through their work are often extraordinary. They say things like, "One should not charge for spiritual guidance." But that is not what one is being paid for. One is being paid for the skills that one applies in interpreting and communicating the spiritual dimension of the horoscope. Psychotherapists also suffer from this difficulty. They don't feel right about receiving money for the love, compassion, and acceptance they give to the client. But that is not what *they* are being paid for. They are being paid for their skills in working with the client's problem. The love is free.

We don't seem to be able to distinguish between what we give from the heart and the spirit, and the long training and carefully honed skills which we put to work in the service of the client. Why not? We must go back to the archetypal background. Prometheus is a thief, and a thief has no right to charge for the thing he or she has stolen. As astrologers, unless we are highly Mercurial, we may carry a sense that we should not have this knowledge to begin with. How dare we ask people to pay us for it?

We may also be affected by an archetypal fear of punishment. I have heard quite a lot about this from astrologers – they feel they can give practical advice to other people about how to make more money, but they dare not apply their knowledge to their own financial situation. I know people in the financial astrology world who happily and confidently give advice to businesses and businessmen, but who are terrified of applying this to their own lives because they fear something terrible will happen. They will be punished for any selfish gain. The fear of punishment may be a very powerful issue. We believe there is something wrong in asking for something oneself. We can give, but we are not entitled to receive. One of you expressed this sentiment earlier, when you said that we should put others' needs before our own.

I have talked quite a bit about the archetypal background to this problem. But there is also a deeply personal dimension, and we are back to Alice Miller's description of the narcissistic wound. One dare not charge one's mother for the love one gives her, especially when she has made it clear that she will not survive without it. I think the issues of the parental complex, the early wound, and the training of the helper from infancy tell us a lot about why we may fear asking for something in return for our efforts. How can one send a bill to one's mother for redeeming her? Of course one can't – first of all because the guilt would be intolerable, and secondly because she might turn nasty. She might withhold her love in the future.

A powerful unconscious need to be loved by our clients, who stand in for the parent we desperately wanted to redeem in childhood, can make us fear that we will alienate them and lose their love and acceptance if we ask them for payment. Any of you who have particular problems around money might do well to consider this dimension. The narcissistic wound may also be expressed subtly. We may name a reasonable fee to the client and then forget to ask him or her for the fee at the end of the session. We may burden ourselves with so much work that there is no time left to enjoy the rewards of our efforts. We may unconsciously sabotage ourselves by setting up situations of failure in the external world, just when we are trying to ground ourselves professionally. One way or another, we may ensure that we punish ourselves if we ask for recompense from our caretaker. And equally, there are also clients who resent paying the astrologer because of the same complex – why should one have to pay mother for her love and understanding?

Audience: This really resonates with me. I get so many clients who are unclear about what I do, and they think I am psychic. Then I start getting worried that I'm not giving them what they expect. I feel I should be psychic, or totally understanding, or whatever they want me to be.

Liz: I am sure you can see how the early relationship between mother and child involves such psychic expectations. The narcissistic wound that Miller talks about is one which is inflicted unconsciously and covertly. Mother expects to be mirrored, and this message passes unconsciously, and the child flails about in confusion and anxiety trying to read the cues. That is what you are describing.

Audience: I got so anxious once that I went on and on telling a client what I couldn't do, and in the end she said, "Well, what *can* you do?"

Liz: What we are really offering in a chart consultation is very difficult to define, even without considering the childhood issues that underpin our wish to be helpers. We can claim that we are giving practical advice or psychological insights. But so many subtle things occur during an astrological session that we cannot hope to articulate these to the client. We have trouble identifying them ourselves. It is worth thinking as clearly as possible about what you *are* giving rather than what you *can't* give, especially because of the unconscious background of the narcissistic wound.

The nature of the unconscious contract between the redemptive child and the needy mother is vague and unspoken. It isn't clear what is wanted, except that it seems to be nothing less than everything. How can a young child know what he or she should be giving? What, after all, is redemption? When this surfaces in adulthood, one is plagued with the vague sense that one must be everything for everyone, and this generates great confusion and anxiety – especially when we are totally unaware of the deeper roots of the expectation. Reflecting on what we really do offer, rather than on what we don't or on what we imagine others want from us, can be a very useful exercise for all of us.

Audience: I always give interested people a leaflet, which contains all the information I want them to have about what kind of approach I take, what sort of issues I work with, and so on.

Liz: We can all learn from that – it is an extremely practical, clear, and professional way of conducting your work. Putting it into writing in that way probably helps you to avoid losing contact with the real core of what you do.

Audience: Yes, it gives me a structure. But I spent years struggling with the issue of charging reasonable fees – I felt I shouldn't be doing it because I wasn't worth that much. I have had to learn the hard way.

Liz: Being unclear about one's worth seems to afflict a great many people in this profession, for all the reasons we have been exploring. Any self-employed professional has to face the issue of defining his or her value in material terms. There are always general market guidelines, and one can ask other consultants. We can do that too. But then, somehow, we lose our confidence. All the deeper psychological conflicts begin knocking at the door. Employment spares us having to define our value, because somebody else has defined it for us. As long as we fulfil the job description and do what is required, we deserve the salary. When we are self-employed we must name our own value. Astrologers do have a community to whom they can turn for advice. Yet when we get sound advice, our inner issues may make it difficult to act upon.

Audience: Even if you are self-employed, it is easier to put a value on something tangible, like a hand-built kitchen or a design for somebody's garden. But during an astrological consultation there isn't anything concrete to evaluate. What you give is invisible. Maybe you plant a seed, and six months or ten years later it will flourish or find its place in that person's life. It's very hard to place a value on that.

Liz: Yes, you are quite right – the nature of what we offer is not material, and also may not reveal its true worth for a long time. But that is not a sufficient explanation for the dilemmas astrologers have with money. Any kind of consultancy work deals in intangibles. If you give advice to a company director on how to manage funds over a five-year period, that is also intangible and plants a seed which only matures with time. Yet the financial consultant has no problem about asking for £300 an hour for those intangibles. Certainly it is harder to set a value on what is unseen. But we are dealing with archetypal patterns and images in our work, which makes things much more complicated. We are not dealing merely with market forces. We are dealing with human souls, whether we wish to or not.

The priest is in an even worse position. Your local Anglican vicar is unlikely to own the house he (or more recently, she) lives in. He receives a minimal stipend for the work he does, and on this very thin recompense he is supposed to support his family while he does his parish work. He is not valued very much by his own parent body, and in addition his conscience tells him that he dare not ask for more because he is supposed to be a mediator between his parishioners and God. Any effort to improve his material situation is viewed as greed. We also get caught in this dilemma. We might learn a lesson from the Renaissance bishops and cardinals, who had no such qualms.

Audience: If I am not charging anything, and a friend comes around and says, "Oh, will you do my chart?" then I will be confident. But if I expect money in return, then I lose my confidence.

Liz: Money, like all the other important things in life, is archetypal. Once again I would suggest that you look beneath the surface for the deeper issues, on both the family complex level and the archetypal level, because what you are doing is hurting you. You are devaluing yourself and losing touch with the nourishment your work could give you, and it will not help the client either.

Audience: If people walk away satisfied, I feel okay. But every time, there is this terrible anxiety.

Liz: If you are so preoccupied with pleasing your clients, you may be gearing what you say to what you sense they want to hear, rather than what you are really able to give them.

Audience: That woman whose story you told earlier – did she pay you?

Liz: Oh, yes, she paid me. I had, after all, spent a full session with her, and had prepared the horoscope correctly, and had done my best to read it constructively and insightfully. I only let rip at the end, and why should that cancel out the rest of the work? She was not paying me to like her; she was paying me for my astrological skills. All of it went on tape as well. She handed me the cheque as she was on her way out the door, before looking for a bus to step under. Why should she not have paid me? And why should I not have accepted payment? She didn't stop payment on the cheque either, which is interesting. Although the session ended in an unpleasant fashion, she had still got something positive from it, although I would have been the last person to whom she would have admitted it.

　　Financial issues amongst astrologers may be social as well as archetypal. The class system in Britain is still very powerful and pervasive. Although I am British, I was not raised here. I did not absorb the class ethos in childhood, and I can't think in those terms. For me, individuals are what they make of themselves. Whether their parents were poor is important psychologically, but irrelevant in terms of their potential and value. Those of you who come from other parts of Europe probably can't think in class terms either. Those of you who grew up in Britain know how cruelly imprisoning the class system can be – even though, in theory, it is breaking down. An astrologer from a working-class background may struggle with asking for a reasonable fee because there is deep guilt about earning more than one's parents and moving beyond one's class. But usually, if such social issues are causing conflict, they will be connected with archetypal issues as well. And it is possible that no resolution of the former can be achieved without exploring the latter.

The problem of power

The final issue I want to mention is power, although we have been looking at in various forms on and off throughout the day. There is a useful little book which I would recommend, called *Power in the Helping Professions* by Adolf Guggenbuhl-Craig.[8] He explores the shadow-side of the helper in a very honest and direct way. The astrologer is particularly vulnerable to unconscious power-problems. This is in part because he or she is so often unanalysed and has no experience of the unconscious psyche, yet encounters the unconscious psyche in every astrological consultation, however mundane the discussion. Working as an astrologer invokes the archetypal role of the priest, the intermediary for the gods. When one plays such a role, one can easily begin to believe that one is partaking of the godhead in a way that those whom one counsels do not. And the greater one's secret insecurities, the more tempting such an inflation becomes.

The issue of power is an ongoing dilemma which is always with us. None of us is exempt from its dangers, and the better and more successful we are at what we do, the more we are endangered. If we are

[8]Adolf Guggenbuhl-Craig, *Power in the Helping Professions*, Spring Publications, Zürich, 1976.

not very good at our work, people will tell us quickly enough, so our inflation tends to get shot down fairly soon. But if we are really connecting and able to give something important and valuable to the client, the sense of inflation can grow in the dark like a mushroom. It feeds on all the personal hurts and feelings of inferiority that we carry from early life. Alfred Adler was quite right, although his focus may have been somewhat narrow. There is a power-drive in all of us, because we all have Mars and Pluto in the birth chart.

There is something in every human being which wants to be king or queen of the dung-heap, the best and most important person around. The extent of this drive may vary from one individual to another, but it is a universal human attribute. To the extent that we were brought up feeling unimportant, undervalued, neglected, rejected, overlooked, or made to feel second-best, there will be a nice accumulation of anger and pain on which unconscious inflation feeds. Inflation is the process of identifying with an archetype, in order to find a value and potency that one cannot find in one's human personality. Power is the underbelly of altruism. This is one of the chief reasons why I am so strongly in favour of some kind of psychotherapy for anyone involved in the helping professions.

At the risk of incurring the wrath of many people, I would even include teachers under the category of "helping professions". Teachers must deal with children's psyches as well as their minds, and they so often make a mess of it because they are offering politics rather than education. Self-knowledge of a deep and honest kind is relevant for all professions in which human beings have power over others, because someone has come to us asking us to give them an answer which they cannot find themselves. To the extent that we are ignorant of where our secret wounds lie, we will carry inflation of a big or little kind. Unconscious inflation is a normal hazard of this work. It is not limited to special pathological situations. We are all are prone to it because of the primal wound of the helper. The less we know about our hidden feelings of inferiority and powerlessness, the more our inflation grows, and the less responsibly we will deal with our clients.

As a result of unconscious inflation, we can get into power-battles with clients. We become determined to make the client see it *our* way, because we have access to the Truth. But the abuse of power in astrological work can be much subtler. It can also appear through encouraging dependency in the client. Many people like to come back to astrologers. They go away and digest the session, and they want to come back again for an update a year or two later, or they want to come for several sessions. The therapist, of course, sees the client on a regular basis for an extended period of time. In therapeutic work the opportunities for unconsciously encouraging dependency are rife. But the astrologer is not exempt. The unconscious need for power may make us want to keep other people infantile, so that we can feel strong and needed. We may also try to keep our partners, children and friends dependent on us through our astrological insights, because then we feel we have a currency with which we can buy other people's love.

Inflation may be very hard to recognise. We may begin to believe we can solve other people's problems, and then we go where we have not been invited and start telling our friends what is going on in their charts when they haven't asked us. Or if they do ask, we might not recognise when it might be more appropriate to say, "I'd love to do your chart, but you are my best friend, and maybe it would be better if you went to see my colleague. I don't feel right about playing this role with you when we have a different kind of relationship." And the client, as we have seen, will often project numinous qualities on the astrologer. He or she will come looking for redemption, for wisdom, for clarity. Redemption is unlikely, but we may be able to give our clients some clarity and a bit of wisdom, to the best of our abilities. This puts us in the driver's seat, and gives us power. That is inevitable, but if we identify with the power, we can get into bad trouble. And we will not have any friends left – only acolytes.

The more unconscious the narcissistic wound, the more the empty places in one's soul fill up with a drive for power. This is why we need to know what our wounds are. We may also have to heal them in ways other than through astrology – despite the healing our clients might experience through our work. We may heal our wounds, or at least come to terms with them, through certain relationships – particularly the relationship with one's therapist. But if we rely on astrology to heal our wounds, we may entirely overlook the problem of unconscious inflation.

Although we may get involved with astrology hoping that it will heal our wounds, in fact it is often the wrong tool for dealing with the kind of hurt that propelled us into it in the first place. Astrology gives us something profoundly important – understanding and a cosmic context for our wounds – but in itself it will not heal the wound, because the wound was not inflicted by astrology. It was inflicted by relationship. That is where all our hurts begin, and we only can heal our hurts through the channel by which we first experienced the hurt. It is homeopathic, if you like – only the same poison, taken in a different form, can heal the wound that a specific poison originally inflicted. Or, as Mephistopheles says to Faust, we can only get the devil out through the door by which he first entered.

Audience: Is there anything basically wrong with doing charts for friends?

Liz: I am not sure whether "right" and "wrong" are relevant. It is the consequences which need to be considered. Much of the joy of friendship lies in the psychic equality between friends. A great deal depends on how deeply you go into the chart. You may wind up knowing far more about the person than he or she knows about you, and this may make your friend very uncomfortable. In a friendship where there is a great deal of honesty and a minimal amount of projection, doing a friend's chart can be very helpful. It can also be helpful between two astrologers, because they are evenly matched. But many friendships contain boundaries which should not be breached. Things need to be left unspoken. There is no place for discussing the disturbing issues that an astrological reading can bring up. And archetypal projections will inevitably begin to creep in, spoiling the ease of exchange and creating psychic inequality. Then you will have gained a client, but you may have lost a friend. You must ask yourself which is more important. It may be wiser to refer your friend to a colleague, and take your colleague's friends as clients.

Audience: I have been having difficulty with something all day. You have said that we are priests, yet you have also talked about the danger of identifying with what the client projects on us. You said the client mustn't project something archetypal.

Liz: I didn't say the client *mustn't*. I said the client *does*. I also said it is not a good idea to identify with the projection.

Audience: I hear all you have said, but with my Saturn square Neptune the two things seem completely irreconcilable. If we are priests, then we are entitled to that projection. If we must not carry the projection, how can we be priests? It amazes me that for you there doesn't seem to be a contradiction. I understand that I am splitting Saturn and Neptune. But could you please help me put them together again? Our knowledge connects us with the cosmos. Yet at the same time we cannot identify with the power this gives us. I cannot see how we can avoid this.

Liz: I understand your confusion. I cannot give you a solution – only a personal response. Although I have said that we are priests, I do not mean this in any personal sense. In choosing to work as astrologers, we are playing a role, consciously or unconsciously, which the priest has always occupied. It is an archetypal role, rather than who we are as individuals. Perhaps we have found ourselves in this role unwillingly, yet at the same time we get meaning and fulfillment from playing it. But we do not have to identify with it. The operative word is *identification.* The theatre is always a useful analogy. If I am an actor and I am playing Ophelia in a production of *Hamlet,* I can say, "I am Ophelia this season. That is the role I am playing in the drama." If I am any sort of decent actor, I will pour my heart and soul into that part, and play it as fully and deeply as I can. I will draw on every acting technique I have ever learned, as well as my own emotional experience. But when the curtain comes down and I go home, I don't have to go on thinking I am Ophelia and drown myself in the bath. I am merely an actor playing an archetypal role, one of the great roles in the history of theatre. I didn't write the script, and can take no credit for it. I can honour both the role and the playwright. I can attend to the director's wishes and respect my fellow actors, and enjoy the fame and money I earn. I can be warmed and inspired by good reviews and the audience's positive response to me. But Ophelia is a role, a character in a play. She is not who I am. That is why Saturn and Neptune can be reconciled through the arts. And astrology is no less an art than theatre. If we can understand that Saturn is the vessel for Neptune, then we can begin to make sense of the aspect. But such understanding means that Saturn has to relinquish a little of his Luciferian pride and accept being a vessel and a craftsman, rather than a creator-god.

No one has coerced me to become an astrologer. I choose to do this work, and therefore I must take the consequences. Like it or not, I wind up acting as an intermediary between the client and the archetypal patterns at work in the client's life. I am inserting myself between the client and the archetypal realm, or, put another way, between the client and the cosmos. I do my best to make sense of what the chart patterns describe, in the hope that the client will be able to use the information constructively. That means that I am playing the role of a priest. But I do not have to identify with the archetype of the priest. Archetypes don't make transference-counter-transference messes like the one I described earlier. Nor does the archetype go home and say to her partner, "That was a really heavy seminar. There was a woman in the group who kept going on about her Saturn-Neptune square. I'm starving, let's go out for a meal."

There are two effective antidotes to inflation. One is consciousness of why we might secretly need to borrow power from the archetypal realm. What are we attempting to compensate for? That is why I spent a lot of time today talking about the narcissistic wound. The other antidote is a sense of humour. If we choose to play the role of priests, we need to do it well. But we can also laugh at ourselves. We too sometimes need a priest, because we cannot always make sense of our own charts or our own lives. If we identify with an archetype for power, we will wind up selling our souls. But it would be equally unhealthy to avoid a role which gives our lives, and the lives of at least some of our clients, a glimpse of meaning and purpose. We can hold the middle ground if we remember our ordinary humanity and retain our sense of humour. It is possible that we sometimes take ourselves too seriously, and our work not seriously enough.

That takes us to the end of the seminar. Thank you all for coming today.

About the CPA

Director: Liz Greene, Ph. D., D. F. Astrol. S., Dip. Analyt. Psych.

The Centre for Psychological Astrology provides a unique workshop and professional training programme, designed to foster the cross fertilisation of the fields of astrology and depth, humanistic, and transpersonal psychology. The main aims and objectives of the CPA professional training course are:

- To provide students with a solid and broad base of knowledge within the realms of both traditional astrological symbolism and psychological theory and technique, so that the astrological chart can be sensitively understood and interpreted in the light of modern psychological thought.
- To make available to students psychologically qualified case supervision, along with background seminars in counselling skills and techniques which would raise the standard and effectiveness of astrological consultation. It should be noted that no formal training as a counsellor or therapist is provided by the course.
- To encourage investigation and research into the links between astrology, psychological models, and therapeutic techniques, thereby contributing to and advancing the existing body of astrological and psychological knowledge.

History

The CPA began unofficially in 1980 as a sporadic series of courses and seminars offered by Liz Greene and Howard Sasportas, covering all aspects of astrology from beginners' courses to more advanced one-day seminars. In 1981 additional courses and seminars by other tutors were interspersed with those of Liz and Howard to increase the variety of material offered to students, and Juliet Sharman-Burke and Warren Kenton began contributing their expertise in Tarot and Kabbalah. It then seemed appropriate to take what was previously a random collection of astrology courses and put them under a single umbrella, so in 1982 the "prototype" of the CPA – the Centre for Transpersonal Astrology – was born.

In 1983 the name was changed to the Centre for Psychological Astrology, because a wide variety of psychological approaches was incorporated into the seminars, ranging from transpersonal psychology to the work of Jung, Freud and Klein. In response to repeated requests from students, the Diploma Course was eventually created, with additional tutors joining the staff. The CPA continued to develop and consolidate its programme despite the unfortunate death of Howard in 1992, when Charles Harvey became co-director with Liz Greene. Finally, in February 2000, Charles Harvey tragically died of cancer, leaving Liz Greene as sole director. In the new Millennium, the CPA continues to develop along both familiar and innovative lines, always maintaining the high standards reflected in the fine work of its former co-directors.

Qualifications

Fulfillment of the seminar and supervision requirements of the In-Depth Professional Training Course entitles the student to a Certificate in Psychological Astrology. Upon successfully presenting a reading-in paper, the student is entitled to the CPA's Diploma in Psychological Astrology, with permission to use the letters, D. Psych. Astrol. The successful graduate will be able to apply the principles and techniques learned during the course to his or her professional activities, either as a consultant astrologer or as a useful adjunct to other forms of counselling or healing. Career prospects are good, as there is an ever-increasing demand for the services of capable psychologically orientated astrologers. The CPA's Diploma is not offered as a replacement for the Diploma of the Faculty of Astrological Studies or any other basic astrological training course. Students are encouraged to learn their basic astrology as thoroughly as possible, through the Faculty or some other reputable source, before undertaking the In-Depth Professional Training Course. The CPA offers introductory and intermediate courses in psychological astrology, which run on weekday evenings.

THE CPA DIPLOMA DOES NOT CONSTITUTE A FORMAL COUNSELLING OR PSYCHOTHERAPEUTIC TRAINING. Students wishing to work as counsellors or therapists should complete a further training course focusing on these skills. There are many excellent courses and schools of various persuasions available in the United Kingdom and abroad.

Individual Therapy

In order to complete the In-Depth Professional Training, the CPA asks that all students, for a minimum of one year of study, be involved in a recognised form of depth psychotherapy with a qualified therapist or analyst of his or her choice. The fee for the CPA training does not include the cost of this therapy, which must be borne by the student himself or herself. The basis for this requirement is that we believe no responsible counsellor of any persuasion can hope to deal sensitively and wisely with another person's psyche, without some experience of his or her own. Although it is the student's responsibility to arrange for this therapy, the CPA can refer students to various psychotherapeutic organisations if required.

Criteria for Admission

The following guidelines for admission to the In-Depth Professional Training Programme are applied:

- A sound basic knowledge of the meaning of the signs, planets, houses, aspects, transits and progressions, equal to Certificate Level of the Faculty of Astrological Studies Course. The CPA's own introductory and intermediate courses will also take the student to the required level of knowledge.
- Being able and willing to work on one's own individual development, as reflected by the requirement of individual therapy during the programme. Although a minimum of one year is required, it is hoped that the student will fully recognise the purpose and value of such inner work, and choose to continue for a longer period.
- Adequate educational background and communication skills will be looked for in applicants, as well as empathy, integrity, and a sense of responsibility.

Enrolment Procedure

Please write to the Centre for Psychological Astrology, BCM Box 1815, London WC1N 3XX, for fees, further information, and an application form. Please include an SAE and International Postage Coupon if writing from abroad. The CPA may also be contacted on Tel/Fax +44 20 8749 2330, or at www.cpalondon.com.

PLEASE NOTE:
- The CPA does not offer a correspondence course.
- The course does not qualify overseas students for a student visa.
- The course is for EU and Swiss residents only, although exceptions may sometimes be made.

About the CPA Press

The seminars in this volume are two of a series of seminars transcribed and edited for publication by the CPA Press. Although some material has been altered, for purposes of clarity or the protection of the privacy of students who offered personal information during the seminars, the transcriptions are meant to faithfully reproduce not only the astrological and psychological material discussed at the seminars, but also the atmosphere of the group setting.

Since the CPA's inception, many people, including astrology students living abroad, have repeatedly requested transcriptions of the seminars. In the autumn of 1995, Liz Greene, Charles Harvey and Juliet Sharman-Burke decided to launch the CPA Press, in order to make available to the astrological community material which would otherwise be limited solely to seminar participants, and might never be included by the individual tutors in their own future written works. Because of the structure of the CPA programme, most seminars are "one-off" presentations which are not likely to be repeated, and much careful research and important astrological investigation would otherwise be lost. The volumes in the CPA Seminar Series are meant for serious astrological students who wish to develop a greater knowledge of the links between astrology and psychology, in order to understand both the horoscope and the human being at a deeper and more insightful level.

The hardback volumes in the series are not available in most bookshops, but can be ordered directly from the CPA or purchased from Midheaven Bookshop, 396 Caledonian Road, London N1, Tel. +44 20 7607 4133, Fax +44 20 7700 6717, www.midheavenbooks.com. Paperback volumes may be ordered from Midheaven Bookshop, www.midheavenbooks.com, or from The Wessex Astrologer, PO Box 2751, Bournemouth BH6 3ZJ, Tel/Fax +44 1202 424695, www.wessexastrologer.com.

Hardback volumes available in the CPA Seminar Series:

The Family Inheritance by Juliet Sharman-Burke

Venus and Jupiter: Bridging the Ideal and the Real by Erin Sullivan

Water and Fire by Darby Costello

Where In the World? Astro*Carto*Graphy and Relocation Charts by Erin Sullivan

Planetary Threads: Patterns of Relating Among Family and Friends by Lynn Bell

Earth and Air by Darby Costello

Astrology, History and Apocalypse by Nicholas Campion

Paperback volumes available in the CPA Seminar Series:

The Horoscope in Manifestation: Psychology and Prediction by Liz Greene

Apollo's Chariot: The Meaning of the Astrological Sun by Liz Greene

The Mars Quartet: Four Seminars on the Astrology of the Red Planet by Lynn Bell, Darby Costello, Liz Greene and Melanie Reinhart

Saturn, Chiron and the Centaurs: To the Edge and Beyond by Melanie Reinhart

Anima Mundi: The Astrology of the Individual and the Collective by Charles Harvey

Barriers and Boundaries: The Horoscope and the Defences of the Personality by Liz Greene
Direction and Destiny in the Horoscope by Howard Sasportas

The Astrologer, the Counsellor and the Priest by Liz Greene and Juliet Sharman-Burke

The Astrological Moon by Darby Costello

The Dark of the Soul: Psychopathology in the Horoscope by Liz Greene

Incarnation: The Four Angles and the Moon's Nodes by Melanie Reinhart

The Art of Stealing Fire: Uranus in the Horoscope by Liz Greene

Relationships and How to Survive Them by Liz Greene

When Chimpanzees Dream Astrology: The Four Quadrants of the Horoscope by Alexander Graf von Schlieffen

Mapping the Psyche: An Introduction to Psychological Astrology, Vol. 1 by Clare Martin

The Outer Planets and Their Cycles by Liz Greene

The CPA Master Class Studyshop Series

Due to the numerous requests from students for live recordings of CPA seminars, selected seminars given by CPA tutors are now available as Studyshops – classic audio workshops supported with articles, images and background information, all contained on one CD. Each Studyshop contains around four and a half hours of lectures via MP3 files which play in a computer's CD or DVD drive, and are designed to play on Windows (Windows 98 or later) and any Mac or Unix platform. The CPA Master Class Studyshops are published by Astro Logos Ltd. in conjunction with the CPA Press. The following Studyshops are currently available:

The Soul in Mundane Astrology by Charles Harvey
Karmic Astrology by Howard Sasportas
Astrology, Myths and Fairy Tales by Liz Greene
Neptune by Liz Greene

The following Studyshops are currently available in the Astro Logos Master Class Series:

Delineation: Unfolding the Story Within a Chart by Darrelyn Gunzburg
The Practice of Relationship Astrology by Bernadette Brady
Predictive Astrology by Bernadette Brady
Build Your Own Astrolabe by Bernadette Brady
Fixed Stars Volume 1: Sky Myths, Star Phases by Bernadette Brady

Information on the purchase of Studyshops can be obtained on line at www.AstroLogos.co.uk or by mail order from Astro Logos Ltd., PO Box 168, Fishponds, Bristol BS16 5ZX, United Kingdom.